Decision at Tom's Brook

*George Custer, Thomas Rosser,
and the Joy of the Fight*

William J. Miller

SB

Savas Beatie

California

Library of Congress Cataloging-in-Publication Data

Names: Miller, William J., 1959- author.
Title: Decision at Tom's Brook: George Custer, Thomas Rosser, and the Joy of the Fight / by William J. Miller.
Description: First edition. | El Dorado Hills, California: Savas Beatie, 2016. | Includes bibliographical references and index.
Identifiers: LCCN 2016017908| ISBN 9781611213089 (hardcover: alk. paper) | ISBN 9781940669656 (ebk.)
Subjects: LCSH: Tom's Brook, Battle of, Va., 1864. | Custer, George A. (George Armstrong), 1839-1876. | Rosser, Thomas Lafayette, 1836-1910.
Classification: LCC E477.33 .M55 2016 | DDC 973.7/37--dc23
LC record available at https://lccn.loc.gov/2016017908

First edition, first printing

SB

Published by
Savas Beatie LLC
989 Governor Drive, Suite 102
El Dorado Hills, CA 95762

Phone: 916-941-6896
(web) www.savasbeatie.com
(E-mail) sales@savasbeatie.com

Savas Beatie titles are available at special discounts for bulk purchases in the United States by corporations, institutions, and other organizations. For more details, please contact Savas Beatie, P.O. Box 4527, El Dorado Hills, CA 95762, or you may e-mail us at sales@savasbeatie.com, or visit our website at www.savasbeatie.com for additional information.

Proudly published, printed, and warehoused in the United States of America.

To my father,
William A. Miller,

with gratitude and respect for his life-long devotion to his family,
to his country and to the rule of law.

Table of Contents

Table of Contents (continued)

Maps and photos have been placed throughout the book
for the convenience of the reader.

"Come, Let us Die Like Men"

A warrior spirit pulsed through many of the men of the Civil War generation. For them, war was an opportunity to embrace danger, scorn fear and earn a reputation as a man to be respected. Lieutenant George W. Patten, 2nd U.S. Infantry, a soldier-poet, not only possessed this spirit himself but tried to spread it and explain it to others so they might understand what motivated men like him. A West Point graduate who served for 35 years in uniform and through three wars, Patten lost his left hand while charging the enemy heights in the Battle of Cerro Gordo, Mexico, in 1847.

"COME, LET US DIE LIKE MEN"

Roll out the banner on the air,
And draw your swords of flame.
The gathering squadrons fast prepare
To take the field of fame:
In serried ranks, your columns dun
Close up along the glen;
If we must die ere set of sun,
Come, let us die like men.

We seek the foe from night till morn,
A foe we do not see.
Go, roll the drum and wind the horn,
And tell him here are we.
In idle strength we wait the prey
That lurks by marsh and fen;
But should he strike our lines to-day,
Come, let us die like men.

'Tis not to right a kinsman's wrongs,
With bristling arms we come,
Our sisters sing their household songs
Far in a peaceful home.
We battle for a stranger's hall,
The savage in his den,
If in such struggle we must fall,
Come, let us die like men.

Remember, boys, that Mercy's dower
Is life to him who yields,
Remember that the hand of power
Is strongest when it shields:
Keep honor, like your sabres, bright,
Shame coward fear — and then
If we must perish in the fight —
Oh, we will die like men!

— George W. Patten, Fort Moniac,
Florida, Dec. 16th, 1838

Preface

The Cavalrymen
and the Joy of Battle

In June 1873 in camp on the Heart River in the still-wild Dakota Territory, Lt. Col. George Armstrong Custer, 7th U. S. Cavalry, heard a call from outside his tent. Custer replied immediately: "Hallow, old fellow! I haven't heard that voice in thirteen years, but I know it. Come in and welcome." The visitor was Thomas Lafayette Rosser, with whom Custer had last spoken in the spring of 1861 at the U.S. Military Academy. They had been close friends in those waning days of peace before the Civil War, but Rosser had quit just weeks before graduation and took his military education to his native South and to the Confederate States army. Custer had remained at West Point to be graduated at the bottom of his class in June 1861, and he proceeded to fight for the Union. During the war, they had both fought in the Virginia theater, and exchanged notes or left word for each other here or there, but had seen each other only across battlefields and at a distance. Now, with the war behind them and Rosser spearheading the Northern Pacific Railroad's construction through the Territory, the two men rekindled their friendship, and Rosser became a regular visitor to Custer's army camp.

"We talk over our West Point times and discuss the battles of the war," Custer wrote to his wife. "I stretch the buffalo-robe under the fly of the tent, and there in the moonlight he and I, lying at full length, listen to each other's accounts of battles in which both had borne a part. It seemed like the time when we were cadets together, huddled on one blanket and discussing dreams of the future."[1]

They had been on the same battlefield often—at Buckland Mills in October 1863, at Todd's Tavern in May 1864 and at Trevilian Station in June 1864, where Rosser had enjoyed the pleasure of defeating troops led by his friend Custer. On October 9, 1864, however, they had squared off for the first time face-to-face. They saw each other plainly a few hundred yards apart. They were separated by a small stream called Tom's Brook, and each man commanded a division of cavalry. Before the shooting commenced, the flamboyant Custer, in view of all of the assembled troops, made a show of publically bowing to his old friend, and Rosser returned the tribute. The unusual greeting reminded some present of the rites between gladiators of classical times. Though Custer and Rosser did not intend that the morning's combat would be a mortal encounter between the two of them in which one or the other would die, each likely understood that this would be a day they would both long remember.

The engagement at Tom's Brook was not, by the standard of Civil War battles, either bloody or of enormous strategic significance. The fates of nations did not, on October 9, 1864, hang in the balance on the banks of a creek winding through rural Shenandoah County. In military terms, Tom's Brook cost the Confederates soldiers, arms and materiel that they could not afford to lose, but the war was nearing its end. Precisely six months later, to the day, Gen. Robert E. Lee would surrender his Confederate army at Appomattox Court House and end the war in Virginia. Nevertheless, Confederate cavalrymen recognized the defeat at Tom's Brook as a humiliating catastrophe. The Southerners knew that the disaster did not amount to any great strategic importance, but that knowledge did not soothe the deep bruise to their collective ego. While a Northerner crowed, "Never has there been a more complete victory," Southerners expressed feelings of mortification, embarrassment, shame and disgrace. Nor was the toll solely emotional. For about two hours, men were shot, stabbed, sabered, concussed, bled dry, terrified and otherwise physically or psychologically abused. Some died on the field; others lost limbs or gained permanent handicaps. Many went off to debility or death in prisoner of war camps or

1 Elizabeth B. Custer, *"Boots and Saddles": Or, Life in Dakota with General Custer* (New York, 1885), 91, 275.

hospitals. Still others doubtless bore internal scars of many kinds for many years. As with any battle, the resulting morass of misery spread far beyond the battlefield and endured for decades. Widows, orphans, children, siblings, mothers, fathers all knew suffering because of a few decisions made at Tom's Brook.

Thomas Rosser, who made many of those important decisions, was especially sensitive to the sting of embarrassment. No other major participant wrote as much in self-exoneration as did he. Nine years after the fight he could stretch on a buffalo blanket and privately chaff good naturedly with Custer about what had happened that day, but the sting remained, and years later he would publically seek vindication. Until that October day in Virginia, the careers of Rosser and Custer had followed similar trajectories. Both had served in uniform the entire war and had grown from junior rank into positions of great responsibility. Both were respected by peers and held the trust of superiors. Each was a controversial and polarizing figure with many detractors—to some Custer was "vainglorious"[2] and Rosser was a "peacock"[3]—yet both were well on the road toward achieving the dreams of martial glory they had nurtured and shared at West Point. At Tom's Brook, however, fate forced the two friends into a face-to-face confrontation in which each would strive to achieve success at the expense of the other. And there the twin trajectories would diverge. The fame and career of one would continue to rise toward still unknown heights, while the renown and legacy of the other would begin to fall away toward an apex less lofty.

Custer and Rosser had succeeded so well on the battlefield because they loved being there. They possessed the crucial trait of the warrior—they enjoyed the fight. Men in many cultures through centuries have discovered that the experience of facing fear while vanquishing foes and uniting in a brotherhood of shared danger can be intoxicating. In Anglo-Saxon Britain they called it "Battle-Joy." In Norse mythology warriors spent the afterlife in Valhalla, fighting battles by day and boasting with brother warriors by night. In their memoirs of war in the 21st century, U.S. Navy SEALs Chris Kyle

2   James D. Ferguson, "Memoranda of the Itinerary and operations of Major General Fitz. Lee's Cavalry Division of the Army of Northern Virginia, from May 4th to October 15th 1864, Inclusive." Jedediah Hotchkiss Papers, Library of Congress, microfilm reel 49, frame 399.

3   Notebook, Robert Thruston Papers, 1860-1866, Special Collections, University of Virginia, Charlottesville, VA.

and Marcus Luttrell describe the irresistible pull that combat exerted on them and their brothers in arms. The poet Homer tells us that Greek warriors believed their ability to immerse themselves, body and soul, in the fight and to find joy in battle was a gift from the gods. Custer and Rosser had that gift. Soldiers who followed them into action noted their intensity and buoyancy and their desire to achieve something glorious. This love of the fight was even more indispensable for a cavalry commander, for leading cavalry in combat required a high degree of boldness. True cavalry leaders like Rosser and Custer did not stand hat in hand before Fortune and cross their fingers. Cavalrymen of their stamp possessed a philosophical outlook that allowed them to reject fate and to place absolute confidence in their own abilities to make their own luck—to impose their own will on circumstances and to enjoy doing so. The French called it "élan"—a vigorous, fearless, determined, overwhelming energy and verve founded on self-confidence. It was the supreme idea behind a cavalry charge.

On October 9, 1864, the two embodiments of the spirit of élan came together on the open fields above Tom's Brook. Custer was fortunate in that a superior had made the important decisions for him and had ordered him to attack Rosser's cavalry. Rosser, however, was alone, far from any officer willing and able to assert control, and he had to make decisions for himself. His decisions, more than those of any other participant, led to the fight at Tom's Brook and to the results. It was a battle that need not have been fought, not at that time and place, and likely would not have been fought if Custer and Rosser—two men almost addicted to the joy of the fight—had not been in command.

Elan, or "dash" as Americans called it, like nitroglycerine, is a volatile and unstable substance that can lead to disaster if mishandled. Too much aggressiveness, too much decisiveness, too much self-confidence will turn a daring hero full of dash into a fool who dared too much. In the vernacular of the day, a man who did not temper his dash with at least a modicum of judgment was dismissed as having "more dash than discretion." Such men were prone to rashness, and the line between admirable dash and behavior that was rash was thin and easily—very easily—crossed. This was the essential dilemma and peril faced by the cavalry commander. At Tom's Brook, both Custer and Rosser were true to the spirt of élan, as they always were, but on that day one capitalized upon every advantage that fate gave him while the other so eagerly sought to impose his will on unfavorable circumstances that he willingly courted disaster and found it.

Acknowledgments

To the many people who have shared their time and knowledge and offered support in the 17 years since I first began investigating Tom's Brook, I extend my gratitude, especially: John Coski, Horace J. Mewborn, Richard L. Armstrong, Richard N. Griffin, Marshall Krolick, Keith S. Bohannon, Eric Campbell, John D. Crim, Janet Wagniere, Vicky Newell, Kathryn Shively Meier, Kinzie W. Stanley, and Richard B. Kleese. I thank the following librarians and archivists: Penny White and all the staff at Albert and Shirley Small Special Collections Library at the University of Virginia; Anne Sheridan of the Cincinnati Museum Library; Kayla Payne, Melissa Davidson and all the reference and desk staff at the Staunton Public Library; Amber Paranick, Library of Congress; Jill M. D'Andrea, National Archives; Karen Whetzel and Barbara Feichtinger of the New Market Library, and Alicia Mauldin-Ware of the U.S.M.A. Archives.

I especially acknowledge the invaluable assistance of Garland Hudgins, Robert K. Krick and Gary W. Gallagher during the research phase of the project and of Robert F. O'Neill, J. Jeffrey Cox and Robert E. L. Krick, who read and commented upon the manuscript.

To my wife, Susan, who lived with astonishing serenity for too long with the embryo of this book and even more patiently with its irascible author, I again profess my gratitude for everything she does and is.

Dramatis Personae
in the Story of Tom's Brook,
in Order of Rank

SERVING THE UNION CAUSE

Lieutenant General Ulysses Simpson Grant

After directing victorious campaigns in the western theater, he comes to the east, where Federal armies have often met defeat. President Lincoln promotes him to general in chief of all the armies of the United States, and through the spring and summer of 1864 the new commander pushes to the doorstep of the Confederate capital at Richmond and lays siege to its sister city, Petersburg. A realist committed to winning the war, he demonstrates his intention to use death and suffering as instruments of victory. He seeks to weaken the Confederate army by denying it the essentials of life and orders that Virginia's Shenandoah Valley, a region of great agricultural bounty, be made into "a desert."

Major General Philip Henry Sheridan

The 33-year-old career soldier is raw energy, impatience and unrelenting aggression in human form. In him Grant sees a ruthlessness that will help win the war and gives him command of the Army of the Shenandoah and its 40,000 men. His orders are to destroy the enemy and its resources.

Brigadier General Alfred Thomas Archimedes Torbert

Valued for his competence and reliability, he cannot match Sheridan's fire and resolve, but few can. Sheridan trusts him to lead his most important weapon, the cavalry. He commands three divisions—a total of nearly 9,000 cavalrymen and artillerymen, just under one quarter of Sheridan's force.

Brigadier General Wesley Merritt

A 30-year-old West Pointer and a thorough soldier who will spend his life in the army, he compiles a record of excellence as a cavalry commander and rises quickly in rank, responsibility and the esteem of his superiors. He is of the type to be found all walks of life whose exceptional abilities are known mainly by those nearest him and whose fate it is to be overshadowed by colleagues of lesser modesty. He leads one of the cavalry divisions under Torbert, some 3,000 men.

Brigadier General George Armstrong Custer

A prodigy of leadership ability, he so loves amusing himself and others that he nearly frolics himself out of West Point. In war, however, he finds his calling. He loves the battlefield and all of its challenges and emotions. Though his ostentatious style causes some to dismiss him as frivolous, his daring and ability in action win him the devotion of his troops. His already abundant self-confidence grows with every passing engagement. He has recently been promoted to command a cavalry division of about 3,000 men, and though his immediate superior is Torbert, he often deals directly with Sheridan, who loves him like a brother.

Colonel William Wells

One of Vermont's leading soldiers, his heroics at Gettysburg bring him acclaim and, later, a Medal of Honor. He commands a brigade of more than 1,000 men in Custer's division.

Colonel Alexander Cummings McWhorter Pennington, Jr.

A close friend of Custer from their West Point days, he has served without fanfare as a much respected junior artillery officer. In October, he is literally raised overnight to command the 3rd New Jersey Cavalry and then to command of a brigade of roughly 1,500 men in Custer's division. His first test comes at Tom's Brook.

Colonel Thomas Casimer Devin

He is at 41 much older than most of the men who surround him, and his careers as a housepainter and owner of a paint company in New York City have done little to prepare him to lead men in war. Nevertheless, he is competent, respected, reliable and rises through merit from captain to command of a brigade of roughly 1,000 men in Merritt's division.

Colonel Charles Russell Lowell

Valedictorian of his class in 1854 at Harvard and a businessman afterward, he lives uncomfortably with tuberculosis. While commanding the 2nd Massachusetts Cavalry, Lowell establishes a reputation throughout the cavalry for his fearlessness. Sheridan honors his courage and intelligence and gives him command of a brigade in Merritt's division.

Colonel James Harvey Kidd

A former scholar at the University of Michigan, he rises steadily from captain to colonel in the 6th Michigan Cavalry. At Tom's Brook, he commands Custer's old "Michigan Brigade," roughly 1,000 men, in Merritt's division.

SERVING THE CONFEDERATE CAUSE

General Robert Edward Lee

A Virginian and the commander of the South's most important army, his courtly demeanor masks a mixture of soldierly gifts rare in American history. Shrewd, cunning, an able administrator and a peerless reader of men, he is also aggressive and bold to the point of recklessness. He leads the Confederate Army of Northern Virginia to astonishing success against great odds for more than two years but knows the Confederacy has lost its best chances for victory. As the odds against him increase, he must take larger risks.

Lieutenant General Jubal Anderson Early

A product of West Point and a veteran of the Mexican War, he leaves his Virginia law practice to join the Confederacy. His experience and ability as a general leads him to high rank among Confederate commanders. His firmness in his loyalties, however, make him equally firm in his biases. Caustic in manner and impatient with those of lesser dedication, he alienates many of his subordinates, yet Lee so trusts him that he gives him an army of more than 15,000 precious troops and the difficult mission of defeating Phillip Sheridan in the Shenandoah Valley.

Major General James Ewell Brown "Jeb" Stuart

By early October 1864, he is nearly five months in his grave, but his influence and status as one of the Confederacy's leading soldiers lives. As Lee's chief of cavalry, he exerted the strongest formative influence on Confederate cavalry in Virginia, both by establishing high expectations and promoting those who could exceed those expectations.

Major General Lunsford Lindsay Lomax

A West Pointer and son of a soldier, he learns his trade campaigning against the Cheyenne in the West. Though boyish in appearance, he has the respect of many and the trust of Robert E. Lee and Jubal Early. He commands a troubled division of cavalry in Early's army and leads a mere 800 men at Tom's Brook.

Brigadier General Bradley Tyler Johnson

A 36-year-old lawyer from Maryland with degrees from Princeton and Harvard, he has struggled to become a leader of soldiers. He succeeds well enough to rise to general and to command a brigade in L. L. Lomax's division of cavalry. At Tom's Brook he commands fewer than 350 men.

Brigadier General Thomas Lafayette Rosser

One of Custer's companions at West Point, he resigns on the cusp of graduation to serve the Confederacy. Twenty-seven years old, forceful, impetuous, resolute and physically durable, he is considered by superiors an ideal cavalry commander in the field, but his brash manner often gives offense. In his pride, he frequently feels himself wronged and clashes with those who do not acknowledge his superiority. At Tom's Brook he shoulders a larger responsibility than ever before—he commands a cavalry division for the first time—three brigades amounting to some 1,400 men.

Colonel Thomas Taylor Munford

A graduate of the Virginia Military Institute, he is much valued by his superiors for his steadiness and reliability, but he lacks the inspiration and dash that would carry him to higher command in the cavalry corps. At age 33 he is the senior cavalry colonel in the Army of Northern Virginia, and he will rise no higher. He leads a brigade of 500 officers and troopers in Rosser's division.

Lieutenant Colonel Richard Henry Dulany

A horse breeder from an old and prominent family in northern Virginia, he is 44 years old, hard of hearing and entirely adequate as the commander of the 7th Virginia Cavalry. He bears the scars of three wounds, and with the elevation of Rosser to division command, Dulany temporarily leads the "Laurel Brigade" of roughly 600 men in Rosser's division.

Colonel Richard Welby Carter

A cousin to R. H. Dulany, he is likewise of Old Virginia stock. As commander of the 1st Virginia Cavalry, he has only recently returned to his regiment after being wounded and spending months in a Northern prison. His performance at Tom's Brook brings him humiliation and shame.

Colonel William Henry Fitzhugh Payne

An attorney by training and a man of considerable learning, he possesses uncommon gifts as a soldier. A bullet nearly kills him early in the war, and he spends months in hospitals and in Northern prisons, yet he returns always to the battlefield. A devout patriot, he professes to love the exhilaration of combat and eagerly leads men toward the enemy. He commands a brigade of 300 men in Rosser's division.

Lieutenant Colonel Mottram Dulany Ball

Twenty-nine years old, twice wounded and lacking robust health, he will at Tom's Brook again face the enemy with his 11th Virginia Cavalry and will again fall wounded.

Lieutenant Colonel William P. Thompson

A 27-year-old lawyer from western Virginia, he is intelligent, energetic and destined to amass vast wealth in the decades to come. Though only lieutenant colonel of the 19th Virginia Cavalry, wounds to his superiors leave him in command of a brigade of some 500 men in Lomax's division at Tom's Brook.

Major James Breathed

A fervent believer in Southern independence, he is a trained physician who delights in spilling the blood of the enemy. Without any military experience at the beginning of the war, he fights so ferociously that his superiors must promote him. At age 26, he commands a battalion of three artillery batteries.

Captain James Walton Thomson

After leaving the Virginia Military Institute to fight, he earns renown as a marvel of reckless fearlessness. Well respected and but 20 years old, he commands a battery of artillery, but at Tom's Brook will fight with just two guns, those of Lt. John W. Carter.

Lieutenant John Wright "Tuck" Carter

Another member of the fraternity of fearlessness in Breathed's Battalion, Carter is 19 years old and charged with the command of two pieces of artillery in Capt. J. W. Thomson's battery.

Lieutenant John R. McNulty

With all his senior officers absent, this Marylander is fated to command a decrepit battery of six cannon, not all of which are operable. At Tom's Brook he is tested as sternly as any man on the field.

CHAPTER ONE

Devastation in the Shenandoah

"If the War is to Last Another Year . . ."

By March 1864 the war was almost three years old. For much of that time, the most successful army north, south, east, or west, had been Gen. Robert E. Lee's Confederate Army of Northern Virginia. On battlefields across Virginia and Maryland, Lee's army had regularly flogged its principal opponent, the Army of the Potomac. Abraham Lincoln, president of the United States, almost despairing, knew that if he were to win reelection in the coming November and see the Union restored, the Federal armies would have to defeat Lee. Lincoln's long search for the man to direct the Union's military efforts and win victories in Virginia ended on March 9, 1864, when he promoted Maj. Gen. Ulysses S. Grant to lieutenant general and named him general in chief of all the Federal armies. From the time of his appointment Grant stressed unity and cooperation among the Union's armies, and he brought a single-minded relentlessness to the drive for victory. To emphasize the importance of victory in the Eastern Theater, Grant decided to direct the war from his headquarters in the field in Virginia.

Grant's goal in Virginia was simple: Destroy Lee's army as a fighting force. To accomplish this goal, he planned to apply unremitting pressure on Lee's army and on all of the resources of the Confederate government and the Southern people. By using his larger army to threaten Richmond, Virginia, the Confederacy's capital, Grant would force Lee to defend it with his smaller force. The necessity of protecting Richmond would, Grant hoped, deprive Lee of one of his great assets—his inventive aggressiveness.

The confident and capable Gen. U. S. Grant, shown here in June 1864 at Cold Harbor, Virginia, made control of the Shenandoah Valley an essential part of his plans. *LOC*

Throughout the war Lee had displayed a bold and creative military mind and a willingness to accept risks. Grant believed constant pressure would chain Lee and his army to the defenses of Richmond and rob him of the freedom to use his army offensively. This strategy would instead give Grant the freedom to maneuver and to attack the weak points in Lee's static defenses. To a large degree Grant would be able to choose where and on what terms he wished to fight, while Lee would only be able to react to circumstances rather than create them. In other words, Grant intended to seize the initiative and never let it slip away.

Throughout the spring and summer of 1864, Grant launched attacks that bought him closer to Richmond and sapped the strength of Lee's army. In his effort to weaken the Confederate army however he could, Grant increasingly ordered attacks against Lee's supply lines. In the hope of cutting off food, medicine, equipment, and other necessities of war, Grant's focus changed to the city of Petersburg, a transportation hub 21 miles south of Richmond. He also sent troops against the railroads west of Richmond that connected the capital to the rest of the Confederacy. Federal columns focused on the Virginia Central Railroad at Staunton and Trevilian Station. Though Lee's cavalry foiled the Federal cavalry movement aimed at Trevilian, Federals reached Staunton, destroyed machinery and warehouses there, and moved on toward an even more important logistical target: The railroad nexus at Lynchburg, Virginia. The intersection of three railroads—the Orange and Alexandria, the Virginia and Tennessee, and the Southside Railroad—made Lynchburg one of the key military points in Virginia. Desperate to preserve his vital logistical links, Lee detached the Second Corps of his army, about one-quarter of his entire strength, that June and sent it to Lynchburg by rail and forced marches under Lt. Gen. Jubal A. Early. The corps arrived at Lynchburg in time to drive off the Federal raiders.

The increasing Federal activity in western and central Virginia made plain to all what Lee already understood: While Richmond could be threatened from the north, east, and south, the key to the city might well lie to the west. The decision of the Confederate government to move its capital to Richmond in the spring of 1861 ensured that the armies would fiercely contest control of the 96 miles of Virginia Piedmont between Richmond and the U.S. capital at Washington. Confederate strategists had soon recognized the advantages offered by Virginia's Shenandoah Valley just west of the Piedmont region.

The Valley stretched 140 miles from Lexington northward to Harpers Ferry. While the Valley lay 90 miles west of Richmond, it lay only 55 miles west of Washington, a fluke of geography that gave the Confederates the advantage of a secluded path behind the mountains to a point close to, and even north of, the U.S. capital. Two years earlier, when an enormous Federal army under Maj. Gen. George B. McClellan had threatened Richmond from the east, Lee found that an active and aggressive Confederate force operating in the Shenandoah could be an important component in the defense of his

Gen. Robert E. Lee, whose greatest battles in 1864 were logistical. *LOC*

capital city. In that spring of 1862, Maj. Gen. Thomas J. "Stonewall" Jackson dazzled observers and befuddled opponents by marching his small army more than 600 miles and fighting six battles in less than three months, four of them on the tactical offensive. Jackson's performance aided Lee's defense of his capital in two ways. First, it had forced President Lincoln and

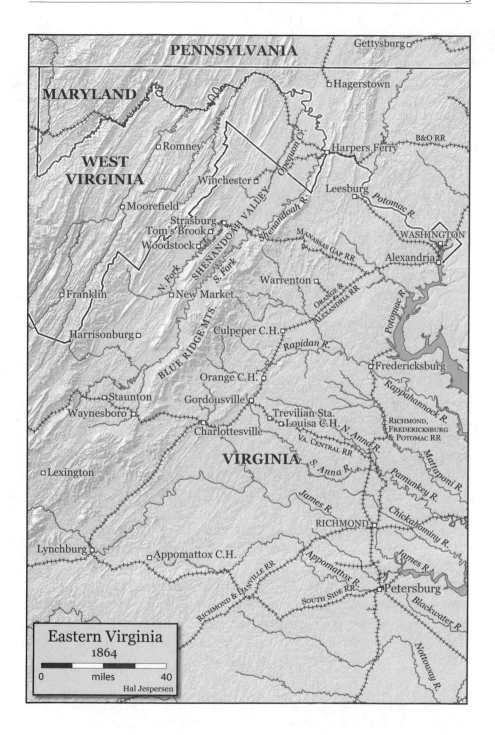

PENNSYLVANIA

Gettysburg

MARYLAND

Hagerstown

B&O RR

WEST VIRGINIA

Romney

Harpers Ferry

Winchester

Leesburg

Potomac R.

Moorefield

Strasburg
Tom's Brook
Woodstock

SHENANDOAH VALLEY

Shenandoah R.

MANASSAS GAP RR

WASHINGTON

Alexandria

N. Fork

S. Fork

Warrenton

Franklin

New Market

ORANGE & ALEXANDRIA RR

Potomac R.

Harrisonburg

BLUE RIDGE MTS.

Culpeper C.H.

Rapidan R.

Fredericksburg

Orange C.H.

Rappahannock R.

Staunton

Gordonsville

Waynesboro

Trevilian Sta.
Louisa C.H.

RICHMOND, FREDERICKSBURG & POTOMAC RR

Charlottesville

VA. CENTRAL RR

N. Anna R.

VIRGINIA

S. Anna R.

Mattaponi R.

Pamunkey R.

Lexington

James R.

Chickahominy R.

RICHMOND

Lynchburg

Appomattox C.H.

Appomattox R.

James R.

RICHMOND & DANVILLE RR

SOUTH SIDE RR

Petersburg

Blackwater R.

Nottoway R.

Eastern Virginia
1864

0   miles   40

Hal Jespersen

his advisors to divert reinforcements that otherwise would have gone to the Federal army moving on Richmond. Second, Jackson's active operations had created fear in the White House. The president's counselors had worried that Jackson might threaten Washington and began to think defensively rather than offensively. By June 1864 Jackson was dead, but Lee believed the same strategy might again relieve pressure on the defenders of Richmond. He sent another active and aggressive commander to the Shenandoah with a force just large enough to divert the Federal focus on Richmond. After General Early's troops drove off the Federals threatening Lynchburg, Lee directed Early to move into the Valley and operate against Federal targets there.

Lee had chosen the right man for the job. Jubal Early was by temperament one of the more impatient and aggressive leaders in the Confederate service. A graduate of West Point in 1837, the Virginian had served in Florida against the Seminoles and in the Mexican War. For most of the two decades before the secession crisis, however, Early had practiced law and dabbled in Virginia politics. Though he had opposed secession, he immediately joined the Confederate army and served competently at every grade from colonel to corps commander. Early was, above all, a patriot, intensely loyal to the cause and to R. E. Lee. He served at his assigned post without absences, except for a brief period when wounded. During the slow weeks of inactivity in February 1864, Early asked Lee if he could have leave to travel home briefly, adding, "I wish you, however, to understand that I am willing to do any service that you think I can do with benefit to the country. . . . I think all private considerations should give way to the public interests in these times."[1]

Early was forty-seven years old but looked older. A lifelong bachelor who was sometimes too fond of drink, Early had a good many rough edges and could be difficult to work for. "Early had a reputation of being somewhat rude at times," wrote one man who had served in his staff. "He was stricken while in Mexico with that dread disease, inflammatory rheumatism. He got over the rheumatism, but he never got over the inflammatory part of it, and that is what gave him his reputation." Early had many detractors, but Lee

---

1   U.S. War Department, *The War of the Rebellion: A Compilation of the Official Records of the Union and Confederate Armies*, 128 vols. (Washington, DC, 1880-1901), Series 1, vol. 33, pt. 1, 166 (hereafter cited as *OR*; all references are to Series 1).

Gen. Jubal A. Early, irascible, profane, and difficult to please, was also aggressive, intensely loyal, and one of Robert E. Lee's most trusted generals in 1864. *LOC*

valued his loyalty and commitment, his ability to work independently, and, perhaps most of all, his aggressiveness. Whether it was a match of intellect in a courtroom, a public battle of wits in the press, or a contest of wills on a battlefield, Early never shied away from a scrap and was always eager to get at the enemy.[2]

In following Lee's orders, Early wasted no time before moving northward through the Shenandoah Valley. In the first week of July, "Old Jube," as the soldiers called him, led his army across the Potomac River into Maryland. After defeating a small Federal force on July 9 at the Monocacy River near Frederick, Early pushed southeastward and two days later stood on the outskirts of Washington itself. General Grant detached two divisions of infantry to ensure the safety of the capital, but Early had already decided the fortifications around the city were too formidable for him to breach with his relatively small force. Instead, he turned his men westward and marched away from Washington with the intention of returning to Virginia. Before re-crossing the Potomac, Early sent a force of cavalry into Pennsylvania with orders to occupy Chambersburg and demand a ransom. Federal troops in the Valley had recently destroyed the homes of prominent citizens, and Early sought retribution. Under orders from Early, Brig. Gen. John McCausland demanded the people of Chambersburg pay $100,000 in gold or $500,000 in greenbacks. When they could not pay the ransom, McCausland ordered the town burned, an act that would further accelerate the cycle of brutality in the war's fourth summer.[3] Early's forays into Maryland and Pennsylvania had served Lee's purpose: Grant had yet another distraction from his efforts at Petersburg.

Although Early' efforts were indeed a distraction, Grant also viewed the situation in the Shenandoah Valley as an opportunity to advance his goal of grinding down and eventually destroying Lee's army. Grant welcomed every opportunity to strike any portion of Lee's army no matter where, so Early's force operating in isolation almost 100 miles from Lee was an inviting target. Even more enticing to Grant was the nature of the Valley itself. He understood that the importance of the Shenandoah to the Confederacy went beyond its value as an isolated avenue of movement on the strategic flanks of Richmond and Washington.

---

2 "Daniel on Early," Unidentified newspaper clipping, Jedediah Hotchkiss Papers, Library of Congress, roll 58, frame 443.

3 Unidentified newspaper clipping, Jedediah Hotchkiss Papers, microfilm roll 58, frame 442.

The United States census of 1860 revealed that Virginia, which at that time included the future state of West Virginia, was one of the more fertile and productive areas on the continent. In the production of wheat, corn, rye, and oats, and in the cash value of farms, Virginia ranked among the leaders of all the states in the Union. Most of that production came on the expansive farms east of the Allegheny Mountains—in the Virginia counties that would join the Confederacy. The eight counties in the Shenandoah Valley included about 10 percent of the land area of Confederate Virginia and were home to about 10 percent of the state's population. However, according to the census figures, the Valley counties produced far more than 10 percent of the state's yields of important farm products. The counties of Augusta and Rockingham in the southern portion of the Valley were agricultural dynamos, each ranking among the top three counties in the state in the production of wheat, corn, wool, rye, hay, clover seed, and butter and cheese. More horses, milch cows, and hogs lived in Augusta and Rockingham counties in 1860 than in any other area of equal size in the state. The cash value of farms in Augusta totaled nearly $11,000,000, the most of any county in Virginia, and Rockingham was just behind at $9,700,000.[4] Travelers in the Valley looked upon mile after mile of rolling hayfields and flat, grain-covered bottomland with substantial brick farmhouses and full barns and grazing herds and mountain views and found it all so pleasing to the eye that even soldiers from the North declared it some of the finest and most picturesque country they had ever seen. A handful of large towns had grown up as market centers and, served by three railroads and excellent hard-surfaced turnpikes, the towns and their people thrived by selling the abundant produce of the region's acres. The Valley was the proverbial "land of plenty."

By 1864, three years of war had been hard on all of Virginia, but a Federal officer who campaigned in the Shenandoah Valley that year was struck by the region's fertility and resiliency. "Although army after army had swept up this garden of agricultural wealth on grand strategic missions," he wrote, "although huge granaries of golden grain, harvested and garnered by the ceaseless toil of the ever hopeful farmer, together with stacks of hay and forage, were the subjects of prior impressments by the contending armies . . . in short, after more than three years of systematic war and

---

4 Joseph C. G. Kennedy, *Agriculture of the United States in 1860; Compiled from the Original Returns of the Eighth Census* (Washington, DC, 1864), 154-65.

conscription by the Confederate authorities of all the resources necessary to support a desperate struggle, with monthly raids and annual campaigns upon this country, from Harpers Ferry to Staunton, with the most destructive and disastrous retreats—this valley was still overflowing with the necessary supplies of life."[5]

Grant understood the Shenandoah was a Confederate asset he must not ignore. It was this bounteous region of 4,000-odd square miles that he intended to transform into "a desert."[6] He directed that all food, forage, and livestock should be eaten, driven off or destroyed. He ordered that "nothing should be left to invite the enemy to return."[7] Grant wished the people of the Valley to understand that so long as an army could subsist in the Valley, Federal armies would return again and again. Because the Shenandoah remained the Confederacy's principal storehouse for feeding its army about Richmond, Grant believed Lee "would make a desperate struggle to maintain it."

Just as Lee recognized the value of a bold independent commander in the Valley, Grant reasoned that an aggressive general at the head of a strong Federal force could reap great advantages. First, every mile that such a commander advanced through the Valley would give the Federals possession of crops and livestock on which Lee relied. Second, Lee would not—could not—allow the loss of such a storehouse without fighting for it, which meant diverting part of his precious manpower from the defenses of Richmond and Petersburg.[8] Grant decided to weaken Lee by forcing him to fight in the Valley, so he sent to the Shenandoah the most energetic, demanding, and aggressive subordinate available: Maj. Gen. Philip H. Sheridan.

The diminutive Sheridan (he stood five feet, five inches tall) was, like Jubal Early, confrontational by nature, even to the point of pugnacity. As a cadet at the U.S. Military Academy, Sheridan had been disciplined for fighting and earned a reputation for not backing down from a confrontation.

---

5   Theodore W. Bean, "Sheridan in the Shenandoah," *Grand Army Scout and Soldiers' Mail* (Philadelphia), March 10, 1883, p. 1, col. 2.

6   *OR* 37, pt. 2, 329.

7   Ibid., 43, pt. 1, 698.

8   Ulysses S. Grant, *Personal Memoirs of U.S. Grant,* 2 vols. (New York, 1885-86), 2:316, 132, 319, 321.

The indefatigable Maj. Gen. Philip H. Sheridan proved himself the right man
for the job of "cleaning out" the Shenandoah Valley. *LOC*

Graduated from West Point in 1853, Sheridan served early in the war in the
infantry as a staff officer in the Western Theater. After being elevated to
general, Sheridan's aggressiveness at the Battle of Chattanooga in late 1863
earned Grant's admiration. When Grant later sought a relentless fighter to

As Sheridan's cavalry chief, the dandyish Brig. Gen. Alfred T. A. Torbert labored to meet his commander's high standards and succeeded. *LOC*

lead the cavalry in Virginia, he declared Sheridan "the very best man in the army" for the job, despite that Sheridan had almost no significant experience commanding the mounted arm.[9] Nevertheless, throughout the spring and early summer of 1864, Sheridan's performance as leader of the cavalry corps justified Grant's confidence and convinced the general in chief to create the Army of the Shenandoah and to promote the thirty-three-year-old Sheridan to command it. He assumed command in the Valley on August 7, 1864.[10]

As chief of cavalry for the Army of the Potomac, Sheridan had injected great energy into the mounted arm. When he took over command in the Valley, he determined that the cavalry would play a very large role in his operations. Grant agreed to the transfer of more than 8,000 cavalrymen to Sheridan's army, and gave him a free hand in organizing the troops and appointing their commanders, regardless of seniority. Sheridan immediately called for the services of Brig. Gen. Alfred T. A. Torbert, a cavalry commander with whom Sheridan had worked well.

Torbert hailed from Delaware and was remembered by his West Point classmates as a gentle young man with a ready sense of humor whose disposition was so open and innocent that they could not help but love him. He did not drink or swear and went to church by choice, but he put on no

9   Ibid., 331.

10   *OR* 43, pt. 1, 721.

moralistic airs. Those who knew him described Torbert as intelligent, competent, and dependable, and so Sheridan had found him to be. The two men had been at West Point together, and when Torbert arrived in the Valley on August 8, 1864, Sheridan at once appointed him chief of cavalry for the Army of the Shenandoah. Torbert was blessed with an abundance of good cavalry and good commanders, and his troops would be Sheridan's most effective weapon against Jubal Early.[11]

Even before appointing Sheridan to command in the Valley, Grant had been emphasizing to his subordinates the importance of denying food and supplies to the Confederate armies. If his goal was to destroy Lee's army as a fighting force, then starving Lee's soldiers and horses would move him toward that goal. Grant wanted his troops to "eat out Virginia clear and clean . . . so that crows flying over it for the balance of this season will have to carry their provender with them." After Sheridan took command, Grant issued specific orders for eliminating the Valley as a granary for Lee's army. "Give the enemy no rest," the commanding general wrote. "Do all the damage to railroads and crops you can. Carry off stock of all descriptions, and negroes, so as to prevent further planting. If the war is to last another year," Grant continued, "we want the Shenandoah Valley to remain a barren waste."[12]

Throughout August and deep into September, Early and Sheridan maneuvered their troops in the lower Valley like boxers in a ring. Early later wrote that his assignment was to "keep up a threatening attitude." By threatening Maryland and Pennsylvania and shutting down the Baltimore and Ohio Railroad and the Chesapeake and Ohio Canal, he would force the Federals to divert reinforcements from Grant's army to protect Washington.[13] Though elements of the armies skirmished frequently, neither commander found an opportunity to strike a heavy blow.

---

11 A.D. Slade, *A. T. A. Torbert: Southern Gentleman in Union Blue* (Dayton, OH, 1992), 18-19; *OR* 43, pt. 1, 421-22.

12 *OR* 37, pt. 2, 300-01; ibid., 43, pt. 1, 917.

13 Because the southern Shenandoah Valley is higher above sea level than the northern portion of the Valley, Virginians refer to the southern, or higher, region as the "upper Valley" and to the northern region as the "lower Valley"; Jubal A. Early, "Winchester, Fisher's Hill, and Cedar Creek," in Robert Underwood Johnson and Clarence Clough Buel, eds., *Battles and Leaders of the Civil War,* 4 vols (New York, NY, 1887-88), 4:522.

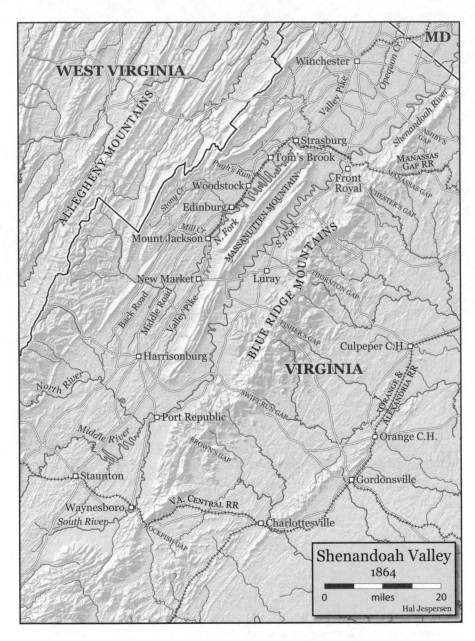

In the third week of September, however, Sheridan saw his chance. He thought Early's position on the Opequon Creek east of Winchester was vulnerable, and he devised a battle plan to strike the Confederates at dawn on September 19. Sheridan's 41,000 men soundly defeated Early's 15,500 Southerners there in what became known as the Third Battle of Winchester.

Though the infantry and artillery had battled since before dawn, it was Sheridan's cavalry that had arrived on Early's left flank at precisely the right moment and driven the Confederates from the field. Early withdrew his battered army to strong defensive positions at Fisher's Hill, 17 miles to the south near Strasburg. Sheridan attacked him there three days later and again routed Early. The defeated Confederates withdrew southward almost 70 miles to regroup near Waynesboro in Augusta County.[14]

In six weeks, Sheridan had done what Grant had sent him to the Shenandoah to do. He had forced Early to fight, defeated him soundly, and gained control of almost all of the Valley. The next move belonged to Robert E. Lee.

14 Scott C. Patchan, *The Last Battle of Winchester: Phil Sheridan, Jubal Early, and the Shenandoah Valley Campaign, August 7 - September 19, 1864* (El Dorado Hills, CA, 2013), 485.

CHAPTER TWO

Federal Cavalry Ascendant

"The Cause of All My Disasters."

The twin defeats at Winchester and Fisher's Hill in late September left Jubal Early's army in disarray and the general himself dispirited. He wrote to Lee to apologize for the reverses and protested that he was doing his best against vastly superior numbers. Lee replied with an encouraging letter expressing his confidence: "A kind Providence will yet overrule everything for our good." Lee firmly explained that he could give Early no more men because there were no more to give. "You must use the resources you have so as to gain success. The enemy must be defeated, and I rely upon you to do it. . . . We are obliged to fight against great odds."[1] Lee had no intention of abandoning the Valley.

General Sheridan considered his own mission in the Shenandoah Valley nearly accomplished. He had gained control of almost the entire Valley from Harpers Ferry to Staunton, and he believed that Jubal Early's Confederate army was no longer a serious threat. Sheridan turned his attention to the final details of his assignment—the execution of General Grant's plan to leave the region "a desert." On the night of September 28, Sheridan sent out orders to "Destroy all mills, all grain and forage . . . drive off or kill all stock, and otherwise carry out the instructions of Lieutenant-General Grant. . . . which

---

1   *OR* 43, pt. 2, 880-81.

Artist Alfred Waud's sketch suggests the buoyant spirits of General Sheridan's Federal army as it followed Jubal Early's defeated Confederate troops up the Shenandoah Valley. The men cheer for Sheridan (at left with his staff), who doffs his hat in response. *LOC*

means, leave the Valley a barren waste. In carrying out these instructions, no villages or private houses will be burned."[2]

Over the next 10 days, two brigadier generals would bear primary responsibility for carrying out Sheridan's orders for destruction: Wesley Merritt, commander of the First Cavalry division, and George Custer, who would lead the Third Cavalry division. In the final days of September and into the new month, the Federal cavalry would roam almost at will over the entire 25-mile width of the Valley from Brown's and Rockfish gaps in the Blue Ridge north to Luray and west to Bridgewater, burning mills, barns, and machine shops, and desolating the most fertile area of Virginia. After a single day, Custer reported that his troopers had destroyed nine mills filled with flour and wheat, about 100 barns stuffed to the rafters with hay and threshed wheat, many fields of cut and stacked hay and grain, and had

2   Ibid., 202.

Gen. Wesley Merritt's rise to high command was marked not by battlefield heroics but by energy, efficiency, and reliability. LOC

herded off 500 sheep and 200 cattle. Custer was careful to mention that "no dwelling houses were destroyed or interfered with."[3]

Wesley Merritt would go about fulfilling his mission in the same way he went about everything: systematically and thoroughly. He had been in command for only two months, but he had met the high expectations of his superiors. The New York-born and Illinois-bred Merritt seems to have been destined a soldier, though as a youth he had no inclination toward the military. As a teenager, he studied law in Salem, Illinois, and only joined the army as an afterthought. In 1855, his younger brother Edward received an appointment to West Point but declined it. Wesley decided to put aside his law books and go to the military academy with the appointment that had been his brother's.[4] Five years later he stood twenty-second of forty-one in the Class of 1860 and moved straight into the cavalry, where he served mostly as a staff officer until mid-1863. Although he had little command experience, Merritt was energetic, mature beyond his years and radiated an aura of sober reliability. His professionalism impressed those around him, but an officer who served under him praised him as well for his modesty and for his gentlemanly

---

3   Ibid., 202, 220.

4   Ibid., 158, 177, 218; *OR* 43, pt. 1, 421; Dumas Malone, ed. *Dictionary of American Biography* (New York, NY, 1928-1936) 12:572-74 (hereafter cited as DAB). The DAB biography suggests Merritt's birth date is sometimes given as 1836 rather than the correct date of 1834 because the army erroneously attached the birth year of younger brother Edward Merritt to the record of older brother, Wesley, after the latter accepted the appointment originally granted to the former.

demeanor. Merritt dedicated himself to doing things the right way without fanfare.[5]

The subdued and meticulous Merritt stood on the opposite end of the personality spectrum from his colleague Custer. Born in Ohio but raised mainly in Michigan, Custer was destined to become one of the great characters in the history of the U.S. Army. At West Point, he was by far the most popular cadet, even if he was possibly the worst student. During his cadet years Custer was the Great Tempter personified. Full of fun and caring little for consequences, "Fanny," as he was called, relentlessly sought diversion from his duties and thus became the master of ceremonies for those seeking relief from the unremitting cares of cadet life.[6] Whether it was breaking curfew and inviting fellow cadets to join him for some off-post drinking, killing an officer's hated crowing rooster and cooking it in the barracks, or inviting a young woman to a sleepover, Custer was ready for thrills even at the price of abysmal grades, mountains of demerits, and a case of gonorrhea. "My offences against law and order were not great in enormity," Custer later wrote, "but what they lacked in magnitude they made up in number."[7]

The officers in charge at the Academy sought to teach promising young men to accept responsibility, and heaped punishments upon those who were slow to grow up. A common punishment was to require wayward cadets to sacrifice their free time on Saturdays and perform extra tours of guard duty. By his own account, Custer devoted 66 Saturdays to punishment duty during his four years at West Point. His devotion to tom foolery, of course, heightened his appeal among fellow cadets, and his appeal was almost universal. The resolve of the brilliant and the industrious, such as Henry DuPont, Patrick O'Rorke, and Peter Michie, as well as the sluggish and the dull all fell in some manner before Custer's charms. "He had more fun," explained Michie, second in the Class of 1863, "gave his friends more

5   Association of Graduates, USMA. *Register of Graduates and Former Cadets of the United States Military Academy* (West Point, NY, 1990), 282-83; "General Wesley Merritt," *Journal of the Illinois State Historical Society* (1911), vol. 3, no. 4 , 131; James H. Kidd, *Personal Recollections of a Cavalryman with Custer's Michigan Brigade* (Ionia, MI, 1908), 151.

6   Frederick Whittaker, *A Complete Life of Gen. George A. Custer* (New York, NY, 1876), 33.

7   George A. Custer, "War Memoirs," *The Galaxy* (April 1876), vol. 21, no. 4, 454.

anxiety, walked more tours of extra guard, and came nearer being dismissed more often than any other cadet I have ever known." A close friend thought Custer "too clever for his own good. He is always connected with all the mischief that is going on and never studies any more than he can help." According to Custer, there were only two positions of distinction in a class—head and foot—and since he could not have the first he would have the latter. Custer did finish last in his class, and when he received his diploma from the superintendent at commencement exercises, he did so not with embarrassed relief but with ostentatious theatricality and a very low bow. Light hearted, generous, brash, romantic, joyous, and a devoted and loyal friend, Custer was also lazy and heedless beyond the point of recklessness. "And yet," wrote fellow cadet Morris Schaff, "how we all loved him."[8]

Just two months before his death in 1876, Custer published a short memoir of his years at West Point. He devoted two pages to recounting a small, but telling, incident that revealed him in an unfavorable light. It was July 1861, and within days Union and Confederate armies would clash at Bull Run in Virginia. The members of Custer's Class of 1861 had completed their course at the Academy, and the new graduates impatiently awaited the orders from Washington that would free them from the confines of their school, officially transform them from cadets to army officers, and symbolically convert them from boys to men.

This incident, the final contest between Custer and the authorities at West Point, arose at dusk on a day he had been designated officer of the guard. It was his duty to supervise the guards and ensure that good order and discipline reigned throughout the camp on his watch. Suddenly, sounds of disturbance roused him. He hurried to the scene where, at the center of a crowd of spectators, he found two cadets in an angry dispute. They began

---

8   Custer was treated for gonorrhea in August 1859. National Archives Record Group 94 (NARA RG94) Records of the Adjutant General's Office, 1762-1984, Series: Records relating to the U.S. Military Academy, Monthly Class Reports and Conduct Rolls, 1831-1866, box 3, Conduct Roll of the Cadets of the U.S. Military Academy for the month of August 1859; Jeffry D. Wert, *Custer: The Controversial Life of George Armstrong Custer* (New York, NY, 1996), 29-34; Peter S. Michie, "Reminiscences of Cadet and Army Service," in A. Noel Blakeman, ed., *Personal Recollections of the War of the Rebellion, Addresses Delivered Before the Commandery of the State of New York, Military Order of the Loyal Legion of the United States*, second series (New York, NY, 1897), 194; Tully McCrae, *Dear Belle: Letters From a Cadet & Officer to his Sweetheart, 1858-1865*, Catherine Crary, ed. (Middletown, CT, 1965), 42; Morris Schaff, *The Spirit of Old West Point, 1858-1862* (Boston, MA, 1912), 194.

swinging fists. Custer knew it was his duty to disperse the crowd, arrest the brawlers, and end the nonsense, but he hesitated. Instead of acting immediately, the twenty-one-year-old Custer watched while younger "more prudent" cadets tried to separate the combatants. When at last he reacted, it was not an impulse of intellect and maturity that moved him, and he sided not with the peacemakers but with the pugilists. "I pushed my way through the surrounding line of cadets," he admitted, "dashed back those who were interfering in the struggle, and called out loudly, 'Stand back, boys; let's have a fair fight.'"

Custer had seemed bent on career suicide since he had arrived at West Point in 1857, so the situation could not have surprised the two older officers who arrived on the scene and placed Custer under arrest. He knew that his actions were wrong and that he had no defense. He would soon face a court martial board, and he would plead guilty to all the charges. In retrospect, Custer never claimed the episode made him see the error of his ways, but his account of the affair shows that he clearly understood himself. He was not a cerebral creature. He was motivated by action, challenges, and the joys of physical contests. "The instincts of the boy," he rationalized, "prevailed over the obligation of the officer of the guard."[9]

War would temper, but not crush, the instincts of the boy. Once with the army in the field, Custer's rise was swift. Through enterprise, dash, and force of personality, he attracted the attention of a series of powerful generals including Philip Kearny, George McClellan, and Alfred Pleasanton, each of whom added him to his headquarters family. General James H. Wilson, who had been a cadet with Custer and who would later cross paths with him in the Shenandoah Valley, recalled a story from early in the war that demonstrated the essence of one of Custer's prime attributes—his "dash" or ability to recognize a key opportunity and to seize it. As Wilson told it, in 1862 when General McClellan's Army of the Potomac was advancing on Richmond through the swampy country along the Chickahominy River, McClellan was out personally reconnoitering. Among the "numerous staff of princes, counts, rich men, and distinguished regulars" who rode with the commanding general, Custer was merely a second lieutenant and trailed along at the tail of the column. McClellan paused, gazed at the river, and said, "I wish I knew how deep it is." As the horsemen with "Little Mac"

9 Custer, "War Memoirs," 455.

pondered and wondered and mused, Custer drove his spurs into his horse's flank and plunged into the river. After steering his mount to the distant bank and back again, Custer called out, "That's how deep it is, General," and returned to the rear of the column.[10]

Custer could not claim any great knowledge of the technical side of military success, but he had a genius for leadership. A fellow cavalryman thought Custer exuded vitality and vigor and with his six-foot, broad-shouldered, strong-legged frame he looked every bit like a cavalryman. He was recognized as "one of the best horsemen of his day."[11] Custer's most important gifts were not physical, but spiritual. He came to embody, for cavalry chief Gen. Alfred Pleasanton at least, the spirit most desirable in a cavalryman. Pleasanton wished to nurture and propagate that spirit, and so he did what was almost unthinkable. Late in June 1863, at Pleasanton's suggestion, Captain Custer, just two years and four days after being graduated last in his class, was promoted to brigadier general of cavalry. And at the same time, Pleasanton asked that Capt. Wesley Merritt also be made a general, as well as a third young staff officer, Capt. Elon Farnsworth. What Custer and Merritt lacked in command experience before becoming general officers, they made up for in energy and enterprise. They were charged with "giving life to the Cavalry Corps," and they succeeded.[12] No promotions of Federal junior officers were more astounding than those of the three "boy generals," and none had more far-reaching impact. Though Farnsworth would be killed at Gettysburg within a week of his promotion, Custer and Merritt would play important roles in the final 21 months of the conflict. In fact, within that span few Union officers would make greater contributions to shortening the war and ensuring a Union victory than Custer and Merritt.[13]

For all of Merritt's excellence as a cavalry leader, however, it was Custer who radiated that spirit Pleasanton hoped would infect the entire cavalry

---

10 James Harrison Wilson, *Under the Old Flag: Recollections of Military Operations in the War for the Union, the Spanish War, the Boxer Rebellion, etc.*, 2 vols. (New York, NY, 1912), 1:564-65.

11 Ibid., 565.

12 Philip Henry Sheridan, *Personal Memoirs of Philip Henry Sheridan*, Michael V. Sheridan, ed., 2 vols. (New York, NY, 1902), 1:474.

13 *OR* 27, pt. 3, 373.

corps. Pleasanton knew that military leadership began with the personal traits of the leader. "I have been a long time a soldier," he said in 1864, "and I do not know any people who have to be more of actors than military men who understand their profession."[14] To lead men, Pleasanton explained, to win their trust and their confidence, an officer had to be able to reach his men on a personal level. A man who put on airs and looked down on the men under his command could only with difficulty inspire loyalty or anything more that grudging obedience. To bring out the best in his command, an officer needed "the common touch"—the ability to get along with and be accepted by the common soldier. Pleasanton realized Custer had that gift. The appeal of Custer's buoyant, likable, companionable nature transcended the boundaries of class and education. Perhaps Custer was born with the common touch, or perhaps his stint as a staff officer to George McClellan permitted him to observe the masterly way in which "Little Mac" won over his troops with public shows of concern and comradeship. For the aristocratic McClellan, such displays were part genuine and part performance, as they likely were for the more plebian Custer, but both men could convincingly employ the common touch when it was most needed.

Custer added another dimension to his leadership that McClellan never could: a record of success in combat. McClellan certainly was not alone as a commander who was well liked by the rank and file but had not achieved great triumphs on the battlefield. Conversely, some commanders who did win battles, Stonewall Jackson, for one, never achieved an easy rapport with his troops. Because Jackson won battles, however, he gained the respect of his men, and upon the heels of that respect came an affection. During the Civil War, at least, if not after, Custer was the rare commander who was both personally liked and widely respected for his battlefield performance. "I know that the men do look to their officers, their leaders," General Pleasanton stated:

> I have frequently seen men, when under great excitement and trepidation, calmed
> down by a quiet, jocular, or encouraging remark from their commander, turning the
> whole tenor of their minds, so that the thing they looked upon before as dangerous
> they would go right into without hesitation. I have seen men when they have been

14 United States Congress, *Report of the Joint Committee on the Conduct of the War at the Second Session, Thirty-eighth Congress* (Washington, DC, 1865), 365.

Though just 24 years old, Gen. George A. Custer stood in the first rank
of battlefield commanders in 1864. *LOC*

hesitating or excited, and some gallant, dashing man would come up, and you would see the men brighten up at once. You could see an immediate change to a different state of feeling.[15]

Always game for contest of any kind, Custer was nothing if not a "gallant, dashing" man who brightened up those around him and whetted their appetite for the joy of the fight. "With Custer as a leader," boasted one Pennsylvanian, "we are all heroes and hankering for a fight."[16]

After his promotion, Custer made a name for himself by successfully leading a brigade of Michigan cavalry. He earned the affection of his Wolverines and recognition throughout the army, not least because he called attention to himself through his dress and his enthusiasm. Artilleryman George Perkins wrote to readers back home in Massachusetts that Custer was "a great favorite" who possessed not only "fire and courage," but also judgment. "In personal appearance," Perkins declared, Custer was "the very model of a dashing cavalry officer. His figure is slight and elegant,"

and he sits on his horse most gracefully. His costume is a dark red velvet cavalry jacket, with pants of a light drab. His long yellow hair flows out from beneath a broad brimmed hat, and streams in ringlets far behind him as he rides along at a swift canter. His features are strongly marked and pale. His voice is heavy yet musical. The members of his old brigade always cheer him always cheer him, and he always returns the compliment by waving his hat above his head. No wonder he is admired when to graces of person he adds excellence of mind. When he lifts his hat his fair complexion and hair, and finer contour of head give him the look of a young Apollo.[17]

Custer's dress and appearance reminded one staff officer at army headquarters of "a circus rider gone mad!" but the officer recognized that although Custer cut an amusing figure, he had a pleasing way of carrying off

15 Ibid., 365.

16 Theophilus F. Rodenbough, Henry C. Potter, and William P. Seal, *History of the 18th Regiment of Cavalry, Pennsylvania Volunteers* (New York, NY, 1909), 60.

17 George Perkins, *Three Years a Soldier: The Diary and Newspaper Correspondence of Private George Perkins, Sixth New York Independent Battery, 1861-1864,* Richard N. Griffin, ed. (Knoxville, TN, 2006), 300.

the absurdity of his costume with "a very merry blue eye, and a devil-may-care style."[18]

The buoyant persona that bubbled on Custer's surface could obscure, but not alter, the hard martial spirit that ran deep within him. He was a soldier through and through, made for the battlefield, and as such he looked at the world as a realist and as a believer in force. In September 1864, just weeks before the presidential election in which Lincoln was seeking a second term, Custer expressed his views about the war and the future of the country. Lincoln had vowed he would continue the war and press on to victory if re-elected. The opposing Democratic Party favored a negotiated peace if possible, and thus each voter in the North was either a "Union man" or a "peace man." Custer declared himself a "peace man," but did so by redefining the meaning of the term to accord with his beliefs that the war must continue:

> I am "Peace man," in favor of an "Armistice" and of sending "Peace Commissioners" . . . . The peace commissioners I am in favor of are those sent from the cannon's mouth. The only armistice I would yield to would be that forced by the points of our bayonets, whose objects would be to afford the opportunity for an unconditional recognition of the supremacy of the Federal Government. . . . To me it seems like madness to think of proposing an armistice, particularly at the present time, when success is everywhere attending our arms, and the rebel conspiracy is about to crumble to pieces.[19]

Covered as it was by the outlandish costume, the hard soldier at the core of Custer was generally misunderstood. Some wondered whether he was a merry cavalier or a foppish braggart, and which would be worse. The boyishness, the ostentation, and the air of carelessness struck some as unbecoming in a brigadier general. In October 1864, Custer had not yet reached his 25th birthday, yet in the previous 16 months he had enjoyed so much success and so completely won the support of his commanding officer, General Sheridan, that his triumphs put him in danger of defeat by hubris. He

18 George R. Agassiz, *Meade's Headquarters, 1863-1865: Letters of Colonel Theodore Lyman from the Wilderness to Appomattox* (Boston, MA, 1922), 17.

19 *The National Republican* (Washington, DC), October 31, 1864, p. 1, col. 6; Wert, *Custer*, 176.

would not be the first young man threatened by unbounded confidence in his own abilities. In August 1865, he would bungle an assignment in Louisiana by dispensing extremely harsh and illegal punishments. His men came to despise as him a tyrant, and he was officially censured. Two years later in Kansas Custer again abused his authority, and his men lost confidence in him. Desertion in his command skyrocketed. The army court martialed him, found him guilty of "conduct to the prejudice of good order and discipline," and furloughed him. He spent almost a year on probation before his benefactor Sheridan interceded to save him. Despite Custer's gifts as a combat leader, his personal shortcomings would bedevil him even after he put a general's stars on his shoulders.[20]

In the Valley in 1864, however, Custer was the right man in the right place. Circumstances there allowed the brightness of his gifts to obscure the unsightly flaws that would later work their way into view. He loved battle and craved glory so earnestly and ardently that his fervor infected those around him. Beneath his look-at-me exterior was a leader with extraordinary inspirational powers, which he would demonstrate after receiving another promotion and a new assignment at the beginning of October.

Custer's new command of about 3,000 men was a fine, if yet undistinguished, body of troops. Officially designated the Third Cavalry Division, for months it had been known simply as "Wilson's division," after its commander, Gen. James Wilson. When Wilson received a new assignment, he handed over command to Custer on October 1. Wilson had built the Third Division and was proud of what he had made. "Every man was mounted and every non-commissioned officer and private was armed with a Spencer carbine," Wilson explained in his postwar memoirs. "By constant work, constant instruction, constant attention to the details of discipline and equipment and by the gradual perfection of their armament they had become, without bravado or bluster, model American cavalry, fully competent to grapple with any military task that might confront them."[21] The men in ranks had confidence in themselves, but lacked the animating spirit

20 Wert, *Custer*, 233-35, 262-63.

21 Wilson, *Under the Old Flag*, 1:564-65. Wilson exaggerated the preponderance of the excellent Spencer carbines in the Third Cavalry Division. Many men still carried Burnside carbines. A more accurate statement would be that most men carried a carbine and most of those were Spencers. John D. McAulay, *Carbines of the U.S. Cavalry* (Woonsocket, RI, 1997), 52-55.

needed to rise to the fame and reputation they craved. They grumbled about living in the shadow of Merritt's First Division, and complained that Wilson had lacked the dash and élan to use them properly. All that would change with the arrival of Custer.

As one approving Pennsylvanian put it, "the boys liked Custer, there was some get up and get to him." A member of the 1st Vermont recognized that a page had been turned, that a new chapter in the history of the division was about to be written, and made clear that the men had no illusions about what lay ahead. The troopers understood that service under the aggressive Custer "meant mounted charges, instead of dismounted skirmishing, and a foremost place in every fight."[22] All of that the glory-starved soldiers of the Third Division eagerly accepted. On the other hand, the men of his old command, the Michigan brigade, lamented their loss. Colonel Peter Stagg of the 1st Michigan Cavalry wrote in his official report for September 1864 that despite very active service and being engaged numerous times, the most severe loss that month was the transfer of General Custer.[23]

*   *   *

The strength, efficiency, and the *esprit de corps* in the Federal cavalry contrasted sharply with the horseman serving under Jubal Early. Immediately after the defeat at Winchester on September 19, Early wrote to General Lee about "the enemy's very great superiority in cavalry and the comparative inefficiency of ours." A few days later, he informed Lee that "The enemy's immense superiority in cavalry and the inefficiency of the greater part of mine has been the cause of all my disasters."[24]

Two understrength divisions comprised Early's entire mounted arm. The stronger of the two divisions belonged to Maj. Gen. Fitzhugh Lee, a

---

22 Rodenbough, *18th Regiment,* 65; James. J. Brown memoir, private collection; G. G. Benedict, *Vermont in the Civil War: A History of the Part Taken by the Vermont Soldiers and Sailors in the War for the Union, 1861-5,* 2 vols. (Burlington, VT, 1886-1888), 2:661.

23 *OR* 43, pt. 1, 463. The Second Cavalry Division, the smallest of Torbert's three divisions, was led by Col. William Powell, who had been in command little more than a week. Powell would lead his men on a tour of destruction through the Luray Valley, a sub-section of the Shenandoah Valley, and would take no part in the fighting that would occupy Merritt and Custer in the days ahead.

24 Ibid., 554, 558.

capable and respected officer, and his troops were likewise skilled and experienced. Fitz Lee's cavalry had contributed significantly to the success of the Army of Northern Virginia. Only since August had Fitz Lee and his troopers been away from the main army and serving in the secondary theater of the Shenandoah. If Fitz Lee's command belonged to the Confederacy's "first-team" cavalry in Virginia, Early's other division was a gang of underachievers with a bad reputation.

When Early complained about "the inefficiency of the greater part" of his cavalry, he was referring to a division known as "the Valley Cavalry," or sometimes "the western cavalry," because many of its regiments had been raised and had operated in the Valley or in the western counties. The new commander of this division, Maj. Gen. Lunsford Lindsay Lomax, had the unenviable task of trying to squeeze more value out of these wild, weak, and woeful regiments.

Lomax's command was understrength, badly armed, and poorly mounted. By 1864, disease, malnutrition, and battle casualties had depleted the South's pool of healthy cavalry mounts, and the horses ridden by the Southern troopers that fall were pitiable creatures compared to the splendid beasts that had been one of the Confederate cavalry's advantages two years earlier. Southern horsemen had never been as well armed or equipped as their Northern counterparts, but the disparity by the last fall of the war was greater than ever. An officer from the Confederate Inspector General's Office examined Lomax's division in October 1864 and found the division's horses worn down, and the men inadequately clothed and lacking shoes. Especially worrisome was the lack of proper weapons. "Very few of the men have any arms, except long Rifles, which cannot be handled on horseback," reported the officer. "[It is] owing entirely to this fact, that this division is generally overpowered by the enemy, when engaged in an open country. The troops of the enemy having from seven to twenty two shots to each man whilst our men have but one long Rifle, and that very unwieldy on horseback." The officer concluded Lomax's command "cannot properly be termed Cavalry."[25]

---

25 The inspection was two weeks after the engagement at Tom's Brook. Inspection Reports and Related Records Received by the Inspection Branch in the Confederate Adjutant and Inspector General's Office, M935, 9/3-J-39, National Archives, Washington, DC.

Lomax, however, faced a more serious problem than feeble mounts and inferior armament. Months of poor leadership by officers at almost every level had led to widespread disorganization and demoralization. Many of the officers were so ineffective at maintaining discipline that criminal behavior was almost commonplace in the ranks. Brigadier General Bradley Johnson, who served under Lomax, submitted a startling indictment of the state of the behavior of the men in the Valley Cavalry, including those in his own brigade. Acts of assault, drunkenness, vandalism, looting, robbery, extortion, burglary and battery, were common, he wrote, and "every crime in the catalogue of infamy has been committed, I believe, except murder and rape." One man had stopped a preacher who was on his way to Sunday services and robbed him of his gold watch. An officer, reported Johnson, "knocked down and kicked an aged woman who has two sons in the Confederate army, and after choking the sister locked her in a stable and set fire to it. This was because the two women would not give up horses he and his fellow thieves wished to steal." Johnson admitted the men were beyond his control: "I tried, and was seconded by almost every officer of my command, but in vain, to preserve the discipline of this brigade, but it was impossible." He went on to state that the men were so ill-disciplined not only because the officers let them get away with too many illicit acts, but because the actions of the officers themselves set such a poor example.[26] Robert E. Lee, who was well aware of this problem, agreed with Johnson that the fault lay not with the men, who constituted good raw material, but with their officers. "The want of efficient officers," Lee wrote, "& the absence of proper discipline & and instruction has been its ruin."[27]

Though the poor discipline in the Valley Cavalry manifested itself most spectacularly in such criminal behavior, far more damaging to military effectiveness were the less sensational and more widespread absences without leave (AWOL). Many of the men in the cavalry regiments raised in western Virginia claimed they had enlisted to defend against the invasion of their home region. Their loyalty was of a very practical nature—to their neighborhoods and neighbors rather than to the idea of the Confederate States of America. Many objected to being sent miles away to fight, and

26 *OR* 34, pt. 1, 7-8.

27 Lee to secretary of war, October 31, 1864, Thomas L. Rosser (CSR). M331, roll 216.

some simply left and went home to where they believed they were more sorely needed. A pervasive laxity—the "license" in Bradley Johnson's words—resulted in epidemic absenteeism. In the 20th Virginia Cavalry, for example, about 30 percent of the men deserted or went AWOL for an extended period. In the 19th Virginia Cavalry, about 20 percent went "over the hill," and in the 46th and 47th Virginia Battalions combined, an astonishing 35 percent had either deserted at least once or remained AWOL for a prolonged period. In October 1864, no company in the 46th Battalion could muster more than 11 men, and although Company A carried the names of 90 men on its roll, only three were present for duty. These AWOL rates far exceeded the average of 10 to 15 percent in Virginia regiments as a whole, and made much of Early's cavalry almost useless. Throughout the Valley Cavalry, too many men were absent from their regiments on too many pretexts, and Lee and Early believed this laissez-faire atmosphere existed because the officers permitted it.[28]

Early certainly knew the leadership was poor. From a practical standpoint, even if it were possible to turn poor officers into good leaders during active campaigning, the process of doing so would be a long one. Because he believed the Valley Cavalry existed in a state of continual demoralization, Early thought the better solution was to wipe the slate clean and simply disband the useless commands. "It would be better if they could all be put into the infantry," he explained, "but if that were tried I am afraid they would all run off."[29] Seeking a better solution, Lee appointed the unflamboyant Lomax.

Unlike Custer, the 28-year-old Lomax did not radiate personal magnetism or exude a commanding presence. One unimpressed officer thought him "soft & youthful looking." Lomax's style of leadership, much like Wesley Merritt's, did not call great attention to itself. As a consequence, Lomax, like Merritt, gained a smaller share of renown. He might even have carried his reticence to an extreme. As one former Confederate snidely put it,

---

28 John Harper Dawson, *Wildcat Cavalry: A Synoptic History of The Seventeenth Virginia Cavalry Regiment of the Jenkins-McCausland Brigade in the War Between the States* (Dayton, OH, 1982), 66; Richard L. Armstrong, *26th Virginia Cavalry* (Lynchburg, VA, 1994), 68; A. Sheehan-Dean, "Desertion (Confederate) During the Civil War," in *Encyclopedia Virginia*, retrieved from www.encyclopediavirginia.org/Desertion_ Confederate_during_the_Civil_War.

29 *OR* 43, pt. 1, 559.

Reticent by nature, Gen. Lunsford Lindsay Lomax avoided flamboyance, but both Robert E. Lee and Jubal Early appreciated his abilities. His conspicuous energy on the battlefield earned him respect among the rank and file. *USAMHI*

"nobody ever heard of Lomax doing anything good or bad."[30] Those who could see into matters more deeply with more informed perspectives, however, saw value in Lomax. After all, he was a West Point-trained former Regular Army officer and well respected by his peers. Lee and Early trusted him to correct the problems in the Valley Cavalry and bring the regiments to some level of effectiveness.[31]

Lomax's record and the testimony of his colleagues bear witness to his competence, but as with many other officers, his performance sometimes fell below Early's expectations. Late in September, while Early regrouped his army near Staunton after the defeats at Winchester and Fisher's Hill, he was desperate for news about Sheridan's movements and intentions. According to a staff officer, Early was "disgusted" by the paltry information brought to him by the cavalry. On October 1, Lomax's troopers moved northward from Staunton on the Valley Pike in the belief that they were pushing toward the enemy's rear, only to learn they were moving on Early's rear! That same

30 Alexander Hunter to Thomas L. Rosser, June 6, 1884, Papers of Thomas L. Rosser and the Rosser, Gordon and Winston Families (hereafter cited as Rosser Papers), Acc. 1171-a, Box 1, Correspondence of Thomas Lafayette Rosser 1884-1904, Special Collections, University of Virginia.

31 Edward O. Guerrant, *Bluegrass Confederate: The Headquarters Diary of Edward O. Guerrant*, William C. Davis and Meredith L. Swentor, eds. (Baton Rouge, LA, 1999), 566; Jed Hotchkiss, *Virginia*, in Clement Evans, ed., *Confederate Military History*, 12 vols. (Atlanta, 1899), 3:628-30.

morning, Early had moved his headquarters and his infantry from the vicinity of Waynesboro, east of Staunton, to Mt. Sidney 10 miles to the north—without the cavalry commanders being aware of it. In effect, Early had stolen a march on his own cavalry. Staff officer James Ferguson stated the obvious when he wrote that Early and Lomax were not communicating well, and that there was "no concert of action" between them.

Early surely had a right to expect more energy and circumspection from his cavalry commanders, and it was in that hope that he looked forward to the imminent arrival of an additional officer, a cavalryman of long experience with a reputation as a fighter: Brig. Gen. Thomas Lafayette Rosser.[32]

32 Ferguson "Memoranda," frame 399; OR 43, pt. 1, 577.

CHAPTER THREE

The Savior of the Valley

"There is the Enemy, Boys. Ride Over 'Em!"

On the night of November 27, 1900, at a meeting of a political club in Charlottesville, Virginia, former Confederate general Thomas L. Rosser objected to the speech of a colleague and attacked him.

Rosser was convening with his fellow members of the McKinley-Roosevelt Club, whose goals were to promote the policies of the Republican Party. Rosser, a lifelong Democrat, had recently switched his allegiance and was a newly minted Republican. According to a newspaper account, the 64-year-old Rosser found the remarks of the speaker disagreeable and repeatedly demanded that he desist. When the man persisted, Rosser "took instant offence," seized the object of his displeasure by the throat and dragged him from the room into the corridor "where a knock-down-and-drag-out fight ensued." After order was restored, the speaker withdrew to his home. General Rosser, as was his custom, had taken matters into his own hands, forcefully impressed his will upon circumstances and driven an opponent from the field. After the altercation in Charlottesville, a newspaper editor concluded, "General Thomas L. Rosser appears to constantly carry a chip around on his shoulder." Few who knew Rosser would have been surprised by his actions.

During the three and one-half decades since the end of the war, Rosser's name had often appeared in newspapers in connection with some controversy. The gray-haired former general brawling in Charlottesville had battled his way through life; he had mellowed little from the days in his

Thomas L. Rosser at age 27, soon after his promotion to brigadier general.
Mt. Sterling Library Association Photographic Collection, 2005AV2,
Special Collections Research Center, University of Kentucky

youth when he was removed from a boarding school in Texas because he fought too much. Tom Rosser had fight in his blood.[1]

When Rosser sat down in his old age to write his memoirs, he introduced the dominant theme of his life on page two: Honor and the necessity of fighting for it. After praising the societal codes in the antebellum South that

1   "Politicians in a Fight," *The Times* (Washington, DC), November 29, 1900, p. 2, col. 5; *The Times* (Richmond, VA), November 30, 1900, p. 4, col. 3.

emphasized the importance of honorable manhood, Rosser lamented the passing of the "code duello," which required any gentleman who felt insulted to defend his manhood by challenging and facing the offending party on the field of honor.[2] Although the record is silent as to whether Rosser ever fought a formal pistols-at-10-paces duel, his own testimony records that for more than five decades, he fought repeatedly with his fists, his words, his pen, or his sword. He fought when he believed his honor required it, and he fought, some acquaintances thought, because he liked to fight.

A Virginian by birth, Rosser shouldered much responsibility as a boy. When his parents decided to relocate to Texas, Rosser was just 13 years old. The young teenager helped move the family half way across the continent, much of it by wagon. The family settled in 1849 in Panola County, near the hamlet of Carthage. Rosser spent most of his teen years on 640 acres near Six-Mile Bayou, a tributary of the Sabine River. He wrote he was the second son and the ninth of 17 children—"a big, robust, well-developed" 13-year-old who labored beside his brothers, sisters, parents, and the family slaves to clear the ground on which they would raise cotton, build a two-story cabin and several log outbuildings, and feed themselves by garden plow and hunting rifle. Decades later, Rosser would blissfully recount the joys of growing up in the Sabine country and particularly of tracking game through the east Texas forests with his brothers.[3]

At age 18, Rosser attended a boarding school in Mt. Enterprise, Texas, where he claimed he and books "got along first rate." Rosser had less success getting along with fellow students. The schoolmaster, Mr. Campbell, established a debating society called the Neodelphians. During one debate, young Rosser managed to so offend a classmate that the two ended up debating their assertions with their fists rather than their eloquence. Rosser claimed he "badly whipped" his opponent in the fight, but the defeated boy's two brothers took up the quarrel, as did "the town gang" of pugnacious young men. "I soon had so many fights on my hands and was kept in such hot

2 Untitled manuscript fragment, Rosser Papers, Acc. 1171-g, Box 12, folder Reminiscences of Gen. Thomas L. Rosser, 2-4. Hereafter cited as Rosser Reminiscences.

3 Thomas L. Rosser, "Autobiographical Sketch," in Rosser Papers, 1171-g, Box 12, folder Miscellaneous Writings by and about Gen. Thomas L. Rosser, 5; Rosser Reminiscences, 2, 12-13.

water," Rosser recalled, "that my father was requested by Mr. Campbell to take me from his school, which was well, for had I remained pistols would have taken the place of fists, and serious trouble would have grown out of it."[4]

The following year found Rosser at West Point, New York preparing to enter the U.S. Military Academy. An aspiring cadet's career began in the summer with an encampment, where according to tradition, the upperclassmen did their best to rid the incoming class of the weak and the unworthy. In the summer of 1856, physical and psychological abuse of the novices was not only sanctioned but was routine. One ritual, called "pulling out," consisted of two or more upperclassmen—usually sophomores, or "yearlings," as they were called—ambushing a newcomer while he slept. The assailants would reach under the edges of the sleeper's tent, grab his ankles, and drag him out into the street while shouting and creating a ruckus intended to bring the camp guards to the scene of the action. The perpetrators would slink away in the darkness, leaving the hapless, often naked, victim to face the humiliation of being marched before the officer of the guard to explain why he was violating orders by being out of his tent after dark and out of uniform as well. According to Rosser, he had not been intimidated when a big, red-headed yearling named Alanson Randol, "with whom I did not enjoy the most cordial relations," told him to expect a nocturnal visit sometime soon. Rosser replied, "You're not man enough to pull me out and I dare you to try it." At a muscular and athletic six foot one and a quarter inches, the 19-year-old Rosser had the physical strength to back up his dare.[5]

When they came for him, Rosser realized he was so outnumbered that he bore the trial stoically—until Randol kicked him. The next day, Rosser formally challenged Randol to a fight, but the yearling replied, correctly, that since Rosser was not even a cadet yet, he had no standing in the community and no right to issue challenges. Rosser persisted, however, and eventually the cadets at large agreed that though the "pulling out" was sanctioned behavior, the kick was not. Rosser met Randol in Kosciuzko's garden, the place traditionally used by cadets to settle their differences, and a large audience of cadets attended. Randol had training as a boxer and, as the

4 Rosser, "Autobiographical Sketch," 7.

5 Rosser Reminiscences, 21.

larger man, managed to hold the Texan in a headlock while punching his face and knocking out one of Rosser's teeth. Rosser later admitted he was badly worsted through most of the fracas but insisted that he never gave up. He claimed he won the fight by conserving his energy while Randol exhausted himself through punching, and then unleashing his wrath on the worn-out cadet. According to Rosser, both combatants wound up in the post hospital.[6]

Rosser's days of strife at the academy were just beginning. Because of his devotion to his personal sense of honor, he would not accept one of the fundamental principles of military life: rank. He rebelled against the concept of subordination. "As a Cadet," he wrote, "I did not find the Academic or physical instruction difficult at the Military Academy, but my training at home had not prepared me for the rigid discipline and the arbitrary military dictum of snobs, whose only claim to respectability were their shoulder straps and brass buttons." Rosser admitted he was punished "frequently" for disrespectful conduct toward superior officers and for insubordination. At the beginning of his second year, Rosser assaulted, with a drawn sword, the senior cadet captain of the Corps of Cadets and faced a court-martial on charges of "mutinous conduct" and "conduct to the prejudice of good order and military discipline." The court sentenced him to official reprimand and four months of solitary confinement in the cadet prison whenever he was not on duty.[7]

---

6   Rosser "Autobiographical Sketch," 11; see also Rosser Reminiscences, 9, 19-25. The records of the post hospital show Rosser was admitted on July 2, 1856, for "contusio" (bruising) and released two days later, but they do not bear out Rosser's statement that Randol was admitted as well. Record Group 94 Records of the Adjutant General's Office, 1762-1984, Series: Field Records of Hospitals, 1821-1912. Entry 544, New York, U.S. Military Academy, 109. Hereafter cited as Records of Hospitals.

7   Rosser, "Autobiographical Sketch," 10; Special Orders No. 139, September 26, 1857, U.S. Army Adjutant General's Office, War Department, Washington; National Archives and Records Administration Record Group 94 (NARA RG94) Records of the Adjutant General's Office, 1762-1984, Series: Records relating to the U.S. Military Academy, Monthly Class Reports and Conduct Rolls, 1831-1866, Box 3, Monthly Consolidation of Weekly Class Reports Including the Conduct Roll of the Cadets of the U.S. Military Academy for the month of September 1857. Hereafter cited as Weekly Class Reports. Rosser struck Senior Cadet Captain William C. Paine, who would graduate first in the Class of 1858. He was a grandson of Robert Treat Paine, a signer of the Declaration of Independence. The War Department, Adjutant General's Office, Washington, Special Orders No. 139 dated September 26, 1857; George W. Cullum, *Biographical Register of the Officers and Graduates of the U.S. Military Academy at West Point, N.Y., from its*

West Point was at that time an enclave of machismo in which high-spirited young men competed in mind, body, and spirit not merely for acceptance but for dominance, seniority, and a larger share of success. In this highly competitive atmosphere, the young men were trained to excel and become leaders. In some cases physical attributes mattered as much or more in the development of leadership ability than did academic prowess. The vigorous, athletic, frontier-bred Rosser, with his blunt words and ready fists, made a strong impression among his fellow cadets. Records indicate that, aside from a serious bout with gonorrhea in his third year, his constitution was strong.[8] In his academic work and in his conduct, however, he compiled a poor record. Because he did not finish his fifth and final year, records of Rosser's performance at West Point are incomplete, but by the end of his fourth year, he ranked 42nd in his class—ahead of just eight students. In that 50-man class, only 10 cadets earned more than Rosser's 456 demerits over those four years.[9] Two of his close friends achieved similar records: Roommate and future Confederate hero John Pelham ranked 34th in the class, and in the room next door lived the bumptious George Custer of Ohio, who was generally considered to be the worst student at the school.[10]

Legend holds that Rosser and Custer were classmates, or roommates, or best friends or all three while they were at the academy, but such claims are more myth than fact. Custer arrived at West Point in the summer of 1857, after Rosser had completed his plebe year. The two were never in the same class, nor did they room together. In addition to being a year ahead of Custer, Rosser was more than three years older. They did have much in common, however, and certainly moved in the same social circle. As high-spirited,

Establishment, in 1802, to 1890. 3 vols. (Boston, MA, 1891), 2:699-700; Sarah Cushing Paine, *Paine Ancestry. The Family of Robert Treat Paine, Signer of the Declaration of Independence, Including Maternal Lines* (Boston, MA, 1912), 43, 47, 50, 272-75.

8 *DAB*, 16:181-82. In late September 1858, Rosser registered at the post hospital with symptoms that were diagnosed as gonorrhea. The symptoms were severe enough to keep him on the sick list for the entire month of October. Records of Hospitals, ledger page 212; Weekly Class Reports, October 1858; U.S. Military Academy, *Official Register of the Officers and Cadets of the United States Military Academy, West Point, New York* (New York, NY, editions 1857-1861).

9 Ibid.

10 Rosser Reminiscences, 56; Thomas O. Beane, "Thomas Lafayette Rosser," *The Magazine of Albemarle County History*, XVI, 1957-1958, 27.

athletic young men, they were pulled toward the physical side of being a cadet. They found their great pleasures not in lecture rooms or in solving engineering problems or in competing for high class standing, but in physical contests and camaraderie. Custer excelled in horsemanship, and Rosser displayed an aptitude for handling artillery. Both were highly intelligent, but neither was bookish. Their strengths and inclinations lay in the power of the spirit and the force of will rather than the brilliance of mind. Both preferred action to contemplation, and both were born leaders. It would have been strange if two such kindred spirits had not been on friendly terms in a community as small as the Corps of Cadets in the 1850s. Any claim their relationship was exceptionally close, however, suffers for lack of evidence. In the recollections of life at the academy written by contemporaries, Custer is mentioned prominently, Rosser is mentioned infrequently, and any suggestion of a unique bond between the two is not mentioned at all. In Custer's brief published memoir of West Point, Rosser's name appears only in a list of cadets who joined the Confederacy. Rosser relates many details of his years at West Point in his unpublished memoirs, but he does not mention Custer at all.[11]

In the years just before the Civil War, cadets at West Point warmly debated the momentous questions dividing the country. Like Pelham and many other Southerners, Rosser believed in the principles that led several states to secede from the Union, and like Pelham and many other Southerners, Rosser stayed true to his principles by severing his connection to the U.S. Army on the cusp of graduation from the military academy with the class of May 1861. He resigned on April 22, 14 days before graduation.[12]

Rosser joined the Washington Artillery of New Orleans as a lieutenant. While serving with the Confederate army in Virginia, he performed beyond the satisfaction of his superiors, and his abilities, coupled with his West Point background, made him a young man to watch. He attracted the notice of Brig. Gen. James Ewell Brown (Jeb) Stuart, himself a rising star in the

---

11 Custer, "War Memoir," 448. One of Custer's many biographers claims that during long route marches beyond the confines of the post at West Point, Custer and Rosser went AWOL together, scheming to place themselves at the end of the column and then to disappear to a nearby tavern for a few drinks before rejoining the march. The biographer cites no source, and the sensationalistic character of the book makes the reliability of such claims suspect. D.A. Kinsley, *Favor the Bold*, 2 vols. (New York, NY, 1957), 1:10-11.

12 Weekly Class Reports, April 1861.

cavalry, and Stuart would become Rosser's most staunch and influential supporter. As Stuart rose in rank and influence, so did Rosser's prospects. As early as April 1862, Stuart took the unusual step of writing to Jefferson Davis, the president of the Confederate States of America, to recommend the promotion of Rosser, who was still a mere captain of artillery.[13] Thanks to Stuart's persistent efforts, that June Rosser was promoted to colonel and given command of the 5th Virginia Cavalry regiment.

Many young men in Rosser's position would have been pleased with a colonel's commission and grateful for the avid support of a superior; they would have been pleased with the opportunity to win fame and glory with a regiment of cavalry. Not Rosser. He decided to take offense. Unlike his friend Custer, who in his final weeks at West Point had written to his sister, "It is my duty to take whatever position they assign me," Rosser believed he had some right to choose his assignments.[14] He wished to remain in the artillery and, to the astonishment of some observers, refused both the promotion and the transfer to the cavalry. According to Rosser, Secretary of War George W. Randolph summoned the 25-year-old junior officer and explained to the young man that he did not have a say in the matter and that the government wished for Rosser to take command of the cavalry regiment. Rosser felt his indignation rise at such "highhanded" treatment, and he again declined. Secretary Randolph explained that the assignment was an order, not a request, and that the only way Rosser could decline it was to resign his commission in the Confederate service. Well in the grip of his passion, Rosser declared that he would resign and left the room. Stuart mollified Rosser, convinced him not to step down and smoothed things over with the secretary, but Rosser remained resentful and contentious. Decades later he still believed he had been treated shabbily.[15]

At the end of August 1862, while Stuart was leading a raid on Catlett Station in northern Virginia, Colonel Rosser's 5th Virginia Cavalry had,

---

13 Stuart to Davis, April 4, 1862, in Rosser Compiled Service Record, *Compiled Service Records of Confederate Generals and Staff Officers, and Nonregimental Enlisted Men.* NARA microfilm publication M331B NARA RG109, Roll 216. Hereafter cited as Rosser CSR; Stuart to A&IGO, January 13, 1862, Rosser CSR.

14 George A. Custer and Elizabeth Bacon Custer, *The Custer Story; the Life and Intimate Letters of General George A. Custer and his Wife Elizabeth,* Marguerite Merington, ed. (New York, NY, 1950), 10.

15 Rosser, "Autobiographical Sketch," 29-30.

through some insignificant confusion, advanced to the head of the column. Knowing Rosser's regiment was armed only with obsolete lances and wishing a better armed regiment at the head of the column, Stuart directed Rosser to let another command pass to the front. Rosser later admitted that Stuart had given the command good naturedly and that the order seemed reasonable, but he felt "to yield the post of honor, although it had accidentally fallen to my lot, would have disgraced me and my regiment, and I declined to do it."[16] Stuart repeated the order, this time in what Rosser thought was "a very peremptory manner." "My whole nature revolted!" Rosser admitted. "I could not submit." Rosser rose in his stirrups, and "in the most defiant manner" told the chief of cavalry that he would not comply with the order.[17] "My place is in the front and here I am. To yield it to another regiment would disgrace me and my regiment," argued Rosser, "and it would be better that I and my entire regiment should fall to the fire of the enemy, than to fall in disgrace, and I will not yield my position to anybody." Stuart explained that he would be sure Rosser suffered no disgrace and repeated his order a third time. "But I was mad," continued Rosser, "and set in my determination, and refused to yield."[18] Stuart, according to Rosser, let the matter drop.

Rosser clashed with men in his own regiment as well. Upon taking command, he had alienated many of the officers. According to Rosser, the previous commander, Lt. Col. Henry Clay Pate, who had raised most of the companies in the regiment, bridled at being superseded by an outsider. Rosser stated Pate "became non-cooperative and really an obstruction to harmony and discipline, and finally I had to arrest him for disobedience of orders and conduct prejudicial to good order and military discipline in the regiment."[19] Some officers took the opposing view and supported Pate because they believed Rosser took disagreements personally and tended to define insubordination too broadly. Lieutenant William Staehlin, of the 5th Virginia, for example, wrote that Rosser displayed "petty spite and mean disposition," and declared "I believe he would resort to any mean & low act

16 Rosser Reminiscences, 176.

17 Ibid., 176-77.

18 Rosser, "Autobiographical Sketch," 42-43.

19 Ibid., 31.

to gain his insatiate ambition & gred [sic] for office and promotion."Rosser's aggressive remedy of bringing charges against Pate ended unsatisfactorily for Rosser when the court-martial board exonerated Pate.[20]

Pate was not the only subordinate officially vindicated in a public conflict with Rosser. In the autumn of 1864, Rosser brought charges against Col. Reuben Boston for alleged misconduct in action. After reviewing the evidence, a court found Boston innocent. Likewise, during the final winter of the war, Rosser had a disagreement with Col. Thomas T. Munford and brought charges of sedition against him. Munford had been serving as a colonel of cavalry for almost three years, was staunchly loyal to the Confederate cause, and was highly regarded as an officer, but he had made his personal dislike for Rosser plain. Munford believed the charges had no merit, and the court agreed. Once again, Rosser's charges were dismissed.[21]

As the months passed, Rosser's strengths and weaknesses revealed themselves, and his superiors, principally Stuart and R. E. Lee, had to consider how best to take advantage of Rosser's abilities. Despite Rosser's tempestuous nature, he was, as army commander General Lee stated, "an excellent officer in the field, who is prompt, cool, and fearless."[22] Lee issued these words of praise in support of Rosser's promotion to brigadier general in late 1863, but his careful use of the phrase "in the field" might suggest a subtle distinction in Lee's mind. Throughout 1862 and 1863, Rosser proved himself an asset to Stuart's cavalry in action, but when he was not "in the field," Rosser tended to clash with men around him. Furthermore, throughout 1863, Rosser became increasingly focused on his personal advancement, and his agitation created problems that festered. Rosser's

20 Robert J. Driver, *5th Virginia Cavalry* (Lynchburg, VA, 1997), 34.

21 Records of Confederate courts-martial are rare, and no records regarding Rosser's case against Boston or Munford have come to light. Regarding Boston, see *Daily Dispatch* (Richmond, VA), November 23, 1864, p. 1, col. 6. Regarding Munford, Rosser suggested that the court gave Munford a letter of reprimand, but no evidence supports that claim. Munford and Early both stated that the court exonerated Munford. Early said that had he not been absent from his headquarters on business he never would have let the case go to trial. Thomas T. Munford, "Reminiscences of Cavalry Operations, Paper No. 3," *Southern Historical Society Papers* (Richmond, VA, 1885), 13:144; Rosser letter dated January 25, 1884, to *The State* (Richmond, VA), Unidentified clipping [January 1885] in Elizabeth W. Rosser Scrapbook 1877-1902, Rosser Papers, Acc. 1171-a , Box 2, 40. Hereafter cited at Rosser Scrapbook 1877; Early to Editor of *The State* (Richmond, VA), April 28, 1884.

22 *OR* 29, pt. 2, 772.

dissatisfaction with the slowness of promotion led to disappointment and to threats of resignation. After nine months as a colonel, Rosser was hungry enough for advancement that he wrote to Congressman Alexander R. Boteler. "I have been a Col. for a long time," Rosser observed in asking the congressman to use his influence to help him make the step to brigadier. Rosser threatened he was so impatient for promotion that he would leave the cavalry and shift to the infantry, if necessary. Stuart believed that Rosser possessed all of the qualities of a successful cavalry general, and worked to keep him in the mounted arm and get him promoted to general.[23] The Confederate War Department eventually promoted Rosser to brigadier, but within months he was pining for yet another promotion. Late in the summer of 1864, Rosser told the chief of cavalry that he would resign if he were not soon promoted to major general.[24]

Within reasonable bounds, ambition fuels achievement. Rosser's superiors did not weigh the headstrong young man's striving heavily against him, for a man with such drive could be of great benefit to the Confederacy. During the winters, while many commanders took furloughs or spent time quietly in camp, Rosser executed raids against enemy outposts. In the winter of 1863-1864 and again a year later, for example, he led men through frigid weather and deep snows to surprise Federal garrisons in the mountains of West Virginia. These raids demonstrated that Rosser possessed many of the traits most desirable in a commander. Not only was he active and eager to get at the enemy, but he could plan and execute successful independent operations. One of his more admirable traits was physical toughness, which earned him the respect of the men he led. His raids made valuable contributions to the Confederate war effort, and he often spoke of them with pride.

Stuart and General Lee naturally put a high value on such an officer and looked upon his ambition as enterprise. Both men found it easy to overlook Rosser's temperamental over-sensitivity because he was an asset in the field. Lee, of course, had spent his entire adult life in the army and perfectly

---

23 Rosser to A. R. Boteler, March 15, 1863, Rosser CSR; Stuart endorsement on unidentified correspondence, n.d., (Mss1 ST923 d 1-107), Jeb Stuart Papers (1851-1864), Section 1, Virginia Historical Society, Richmond.

24 Rosser to wife, September 1, 1864, Rosser Papers 1171-c, Box 1; Elizabeth W. Rosser *Scrapbook 1861-1865*, Rosser Papers, Acc. 1171-a, Box 2.

In this rare image, probably taken at the time of his wedding in May 1863 when he was 26 years old, Rosser appears as his superiors wished to see him: a self-assured, professionally trained leader "eminently fitted to exert great influence over men."

Holsinger Collection, Albert and Shirley Small Special Collections, University of Virginia

understood what made a successful officer. Stuart, though only three years older than Rosser, possessed managerial skills and political savvy that made him seem older than his years. His effective handling of the Confederate cavalry early in the war and his maturity in working with his superiors fueled Stuart's rise to prominence. Generals Lee and Stuart also knew how difficult it was to find men with the right temperament to command cavalry. Stuart tried to instill the spirit he believed should animate every horse soldier: "An attack of cavalry should be sudden, bold and vigorous; to falter is to fail." He saw in Rosser a man who needed no instruction in vigorous offensive movements. Rosser later claimed that the only speech he made before any engagement was always the same: "There is the enemy, boys. Ride over 'em!" Men of enterprise and energy who willingly endured hardships and eagerly struck at the enemy were men in high demand in Robert E. Lee's army.[25]

But Rosser's inner drive also worked against him. His ambition went beyond rational bounds and drove him to act unreasonably. Since 1861, Stuart had been Rosser's most important benefactor. He had successfully pushed hard for his advancement. In January 1863, Stuart wrote to the Adjutant and Inspector General's Office to praise Rosser as "vigilant, active and accurate in his conclusions . . . a bold and dashing leader . . . a rigid disciplinarian." In other public documents, Stuart declared that "no officer I have met within the Confederacy combines in a more eminent degree the characteristics of the Cavalry Commander than Colonel Rosser. He is an officer of superior ability, possesses in an extraordinary degree the talent to command and the skill to lead with coolness and decision of character." Privately, Stuart once referred to Rosser as "my right hand man," and wrote to Rosser, "There is no difference of opinion with General officers under whom you have served that upon the field of battle, in coolness + capacity to 'control happening events' + wield troops, you have no superior"[26] Even while praising Rosser, Stuart had, like Lee, made a distinction between Rosser on the field and off of it. Stuart repeatedly preached patience to Rosser, and assured him promotion would come.

Although chief of cavalry for the Confederacy's most successful army, Stuart could wield no magic wand to eliminate political considerations. Brigadier generalships were few, and men with powers as great as or greater than Stuart's also wished to see their own protégés promoted. Rosser's discontent grew as the weeks passed. Despite the cavalry chief's vigorous support of his advancement, Rosser believed the delay suggested Stuart was not doing enough and was therefore somehow misleading him. "Stuart has been false to me as he has ever been to his country and to his wife," Rosser wrote to his own wife. He explained that in public, he put on a cheerful face and treated Stuart as he always had, but he swore, "I will never give him another opportunity of deceiving me again." Rosser grew ever more firm in

25 Untitled manuscript, Rosser Papers Acc. 1171-g, Box 13, folder Speeches of Gen. Thomas L. Rosser: Rosser speech re: the "Laurel Brigade," the Civil War.

26 Stuart to A&IGO, January 13, 1863, Rosser CSR; Adele H. Mitchell, ed., *The Letters of Major General James E. B. Stuart* (1990), 275, 279; Stuart to Rosser, September 30, 1863, Rosser, Papers, Acc. 1171-a, Box 1.

his belief that Stuart had mistreated him. "I cannot respect Stuart as a gentleman," he declared to his wife, "and I think that the sooner I leave him the better for us all."[27]

Rosser at long last received his promotion to brigadier general but continued nursing an unreasoning grievance against his commander. In February 1864, Stuart sent Rosser a long letter full of cordial advice and suggestions, but by March Rosser was convinced Stuart was "hostile" toward him.[28] When Rosser decided to disregard one (or perhaps more) of Stuart's orders regarding three men from the 12th Virginia Cavalry who were wanted at headquarters to serve as scouts, Stuart chastised Rosser and sent a long lecture on obedience. Rosser replied aggressively and lectured his superior in return:

> Your communication of [April] 25th inst. has just been handed me. I will send Sgt. McCleary to you as ordered but I do it under protest. I am not reconciled to the justice of such a detail by your letter upon the subject. Whilst I will never again hesitate to obey any order you may give me, I will never be convinced that it is right and proper for a Commanding officer to make a detail as you have made this choosing the individual yourself mentioning him by name—Thus assuming a prerogative which alone is mine if not by regulation it certainly is made so by Custom and courtesy requires that certain forms be observed.
>
> If you desire men (Scouts) for a peculiar and particular purpose, I think it due to me that fact be mentioned and I be allowed to select the men myself. I feel that in a case of this kind I am more competent to judge than you are.
>
> I certainly would treat my Cols. with more respect in a case of this kind than you have extended to me.[29]

The bitter response revealed the worst characteristics of the "off the field" Rosser: a prickly pride and the unreasoning impetuous petulance that

---

27 Rosser to wife, September 15, 16, 24 and 26, 1863 (see also letter of October 5, 1863), Rosser Papers, Acc. 1171-c, Box 1.

28 Stuart to Rosser, February 10, 1864, Rosser Papers, Acc. 1171-a, Box 1; Rosser to wife, March 14, 1864, Rosser Papers, Acc. 1171-c, Box 1, folder 1864.

29 Rosser to Stuart, April 27, 1864, Henry B. McClellan Papers, Virginia Historical Society, Richmond, VA; Stuart to Rosser, April 25, 1864, Rosser Papers, Acc. 1171-c, Box 1, folder 1864.

led him so often into conflict. Rosser admitted that, "by regulation," Stuart had a right to give him any order he wished, but Rosser felt Stuart had overstepped some social boundary. His objection was not based on the rule of law, for he knew the order was perfectly legal. His complaint was based upon the vague grounds of "custom and courtesy" and the importance of "certain forms." In essence, Rosser's argument was that while Stuart's order was legal, it was discourteous.

Rosser's history of insubordination from his days at West Point onward demonstrates that he was quick to take offense at perceived slights. Perhaps he still bore a grudge over how Stuart had forced him into the cavalry. What is certain is that in his anger in early 1864 Rosser dismissed as irrelevant more than two years of Stuart's ardent support of his career. He considered Stuart a foe, and there the matter rested when Stuart was mortally wounded in battle in May 1864.

When Maj. Gen. Wade Hampton eventually replaced Stuart as cavalry chief of Lee's army, Rosser found reason to believe that Hampton, too, mistreated him. Like Stuart, Hampton genuinely valued Rosser's abilities and frankly told him so. Unlike Stuart, Hampton was a South Carolinian, and when he advocated the promotion of a deserving young general, it was not Rosser but Mathew C. Butler, a fellow South Carolinian and an officer of much merit. Rosser, however, could not accept the result in good grace. "Hampton will not do me justice," Rosser complained to his wife. "I am unwilling to serve under Butler or with any S.C. troops in the Cav'y."[30]

More than two years had passed since the secretary of war had explained to Rosser that he could not choose his assignments, but Rosser still believed he could somehow benefit by fighting the powers above him. "I am very unwilling to remain where I am," he informed his wife, "and have told Hampton that I would resign before I would serve under Butler. . . . Hampton has acted in bad faith toward me and I would like to leave the Cavalry even if [it] would require a transfer from this army to the West or even to the Trans-Mississippi. This I know you will object to—but my darling you must not interfere with my interests."[31]

30 Rosser to wife, September 1, 1864, Rosser Papers, Acc. 1171-c, Box 1, folder 1864.

31 Rosser to wife, August 28, 1864, and September 1, 1864, Rosser Papers, Acc. 1171-c, Box 1, folder 1864.

*   *   *

Beginning in his teens and continuing until his final decade, Rosser lived his life as a controversialist, moving from one disagreement, provocation, or instance of offended honor to the next. The contentious lifestyle was not a result of accident or bad luck, but rather of philosophy. When he was 49 years old, Rosser advised his son about what should be the guiding principles in his life:

> Your father is with you in all quarrels, and I don't care with whom they are, my confidence in you is such that I know you can do no cowardly act, but I wish to say that the bravest of men are cool, and go slowly and as I am an old and an experienced man, loving you better than I do my life, you had better consult me in all questions of honor. . . . But Tom, my dear son, fight on the spot if you are insulted, even if it costs you your life. Dead a brave man is better than live a coward and life is too short that all we can do is to give our name and reputation to the world and generation after generation will hang your portrait in their parlor and in pride say, 'that is my relative who died as he lived, a Brave and Honest man.'[32]

Few could disagree with Rosser's advice to his son about the importance of personal honor, bravery, and honesty, but Rosser's death-before-dishonor approach to life, coupled with an innate aggressiveness and impetuosity, led to a life of conflict. Rosser embraced conflict. For him it was both a means to an end and, apparently, a source of pleasure. As a newspaperman who had observed Rosser during and after the war put it, "he fought as if he loved it."[33]

Many cultures in which war holds a dominant place give high social standing to successful warriors. The virtues of warriors—physical strength and courage, loyalty to king and to fellow warriors, willingness to sacrifice self—become motivating principles. Such was the case in Anglo-Saxon Britain, for example, where a man could hope for no greater reward than to be honored as a successful warrior. These ideas, these underpinnings of warrior culture, were very much alive in America in the mid-19th century, especially in the Southern states. The code duello, or the system of ideas that

32 Rosser to Thomas L. Rosser, Jr., March 12, 1886, Rosser Papers, Acc. 1171-g, Box 2.

33 Staunton *Spectator and Vindicator* (Staunton, VA), April 8, 1910, p. 2, col. 1.

promoted and governed personal duels, emphasized a man's courage and a willingness to die out of loyalty to an idea. Rosser revered this code. The U.S. Army was itself a warrior culture in which soldiers were taught to fight for and swear loyalty to their country. Cadets at West Point, including Rosser and Custer, were immersed in that culture. The Confederate States of America, born out of conflict and existing wholly in a time of war, was by necessity a warrior culture in which true Confederates valued the ideals of courage, honor, loyalty, and sacrifice above life itself.

For warriors like Rosser, the greatest prizes in life were attainable only in one place: the battlefield. Only on the battlefield could they measure themselves against other men for the highest stakes. Only on the battlefield could a warrior prove his commitment to his highest ideals and earn the respect of other brave men and the love of their people. To earn such love and respect through sacrifice was to achieve a measure of immortality and glory. The battlefield, therefore, was a place of terrible joy and happiness for warriors like Rosser and Custer and many others.

William H. F. Payne served as a brigade commander under Rosser, and because he, too, saw himself as a warrior and embraced all of the virtues of the warrior code, Payne understood the foundations of Rosser's combativeness. Payne understood that Rosser fought because he enjoyed fighting and craved glory. After the war, having returned to his career as an attorney, Payne in 1866 wrote an admiring letter to his former commander in which he attempted to articulate the appeal of Rosser's warrior spirit. "I always see you, figure you, ready to rush into battle," he explained. "Cheerful, daring, full of expediency, knowing no difficulties, arbitrary and despotic too. Loving and admiring brave deeds and brave men so highly as to set all law and precedent aside to show your admiration. Restless, ambitious, but on the battlefield, with more of the 'Gaudia certaminis' than any man I ever knew."[34]

The Latin phrase *gaudium certaminis* can be translated as the joy of the fight. Anyone who has felt the excitement of competing and facing up to challenges—whether in athletics or in academics or in business or in war—can understand the concept of *gaudium certaminis*. The combatant exults in the opportunity to engage challenges, meets the endeavor joyfully and is filled with confidence and a desire for victory. Rosser had on many

---

34 Payne to Rosser, March 29, 1866, Rosser Papers, Acc. 1171-g, Box 1.

fields shown his affinity for battle and had been wounded at least four times during the war. Clinton Gallaher, a teenager who served as a courier for Rosser, observed that the general was always in harm's way and was "brave as a lion." Rosser, Gallaher wrote, "expected everybody around him to be in the thickest of the fight, carrying orders to the front, and to be with him and at his side whatever the danger and he had no use for any other kind." Rosser was severely wounded in the leg at Trevilian Station in June 1864. While the fight continued around him, soldiers lifted the injured general from his horse and lay him on the ground. A private at his side later recorded in his diary that the bleeding Rosser raged with combativeness and remained absorbed by the fight, declaring "that he could whip Sheridan with His Gallant Brigade, that GOD never placed better men on earth."[35]

Off the battlefield, Rosser was still drawn to the joy of the contest. After the war he proved to be a gifted writer capable of mounting persuasive arguments. He delivered speeches on the political issues of the day, and frequently published letters in newspapers to express his opinions or to dispute the statements of others. The feuds in the public press—and there were many—and Rosser's repeated willingness to participate in them bear out Payne's astute observation that Rosser by nature craved the joy of the fight.

*　*　*

As September 1864 drew to a close, Jubal Early, at work in his headquarters in the Shenandoah Valley, wrestled with the problem of increasing the effectiveness of his cavalry. His thoughts turned to Thomas Rosser. Early was finding, as Robert E. Lee had on a broader scale, that the longer the war continued, the more difficult it became to find competent commanders. At the Third Battle of Winchester, Early lost an important

---

35 Gabriel Adeleye and Kofi Acquah-Dadzie, *World Dictionary of Foreign Expressions: A Resource for Readers and Writers* (Mundelein, IL, 1999), 154; "A Missionary in the East, 'Gaudium Certaminus,'" *The Christian Church: A Journal in Defense of Christian Truth*, vol. 3 (London: S. W. Partridge and Co., 1883), 161; DeWitt C. Gallaher, Jr. ed., *A Diary Depicting the Experiences of DeWitt Clinton Gallaher in the War Between the States while Serving in the Confederate Army* (privately published, 1961), 12; Charles McVicar diary. Hanley Regional Library Archives, Winchester VA; Jack D. Welsh, *Medical Histories of Confederate Generals* (Kent, OH, 1995), 189.

collaborator when a bullet hit Maj. Gen. Fitzhugh Lee in the left thigh.[36] Not only had Fitz Lee served as the leader of Early's best division of cavalry, but he had held the position of chief of cavalry, in which he exercised supervisory control over all of Early' mounted arm. While Fitz Lee recuperated, Early hoped to replace the lost leadership and almost certainly requested the services of Rosser and his brigade.[37]

Months earlier, Rosser had served under Early in the Valley during the cold winter of 1863-64. The two had clashed, notably when Rosser left his command without permission to visit his wife. Like Stuart and Hampton, Early overlooked, and would continue to overlook, Rosser's willfulness in favor of his usefulness.[38] Early had strongly supported Rosser's candidacy for higher rank and told R. E. Lee that he had "a very high opinion of him as a cavalry officer."[39] When Early needed a cavalry leader in late 1864, Lee saw Rosser and his brigade as the obvious choice, especially because many of the men in the brigade called the Valley home.

Rosser, however, had no fondness for Jubal Early, a man he described as "perverse and mean," and "a miserable old Rascal."[40] As he had clashed with many of his superiors, so would Rosser clash with Early. The rift that had opened between the two men in the Shenandoah Valley in late 1863 would deepen in 1864. For years afterward, Rosser nursed a grudge that in time led to a public feud with Early so intense and personally offensive that some observers thought the two men would end up on a dueling ground with pistols in their hands.[41] In October 1864, however, the open hostility between the two lay far in the future, and as the two worked together in the Valley, Rosser would tolerate Early while focusing his aggression on the Northern invaders.

---

36 Welsh, *Medical Histories*, 132.

37 Next in seniority behind Lee stood Brig. Gen. Williams Carter Wickham, who temporarily assumed command of Fitz Lee's division. Wickham would leave the army early in October to take his seat in the Confederate Congress, leaving the command position of Fitz Lee's division vacant.

38 Rosser to wife, January, 1864, Rosser Papers, Acc. 1171-c, Box 1, folder 1864.

39 *OR* 33, 1166-67.

40 Rosser to wife, January 25, 1864, Rosser Papers, 1171-c, Box 1, and December 14, 1864, 1171-g, Box 1.

41 Alexandria *Gazette*, June 24, 1887, and St. Paul *Daily Globe*, June 24, 1887.

By October 1864, Rosser had been in command of his brigade for about a year. Almost all of the men in the three regiments and one battalion that made up the brigade were from Virginia. Most had served well since the outbreak of the war and had helped make their original leader, Col. Turner Ashby, one of the heroes of the Confederacy. The brigade had built a solid reputation before Rosser arrived to lead it, and its members readily accepted him based on his record as a fighter. As one officer put it, "Rosser in personal appearance, by education and experience and by a reputation for courage and dash already acquired, appealed to the [men's] soldierly instincts." Superiors, including R. E. Lee and the secretary of war, had formally praised Rosser after he led the brigade on a successful raid that had added "fresh laurels to that veteran brigade." As the laurel plant was a traditional symbol of victory, Rosser began referring to his command as "the Laurel Brigade," and he ordered that its battle flags be trimmed with laurel and that soldiers wear on their uniforms a badge of three or five leaves. The men readily adopted the proud *nom de guerre*, and Rosser acted to ensure that the brigade would continue in its winning ways. Rosser demanded aggressiveness. The standard procedure in the Laurel Brigade would be to charge enemy cavalry on sight. General Stuart assured Rosser that he believed the Laurels to be one of the best brigades in the army.[42]

After receiving orders to join Early, Rosser traveled ahead of his brigade and arrived at Early's headquarters at Mt. Sidney on October 2, 1864.[43] Though well known in the army, and especially in the cavalry, Rosser would be working with many men who would be forming judgments based for the first time on personal experience. At first, many saw the erect, strongly built frame and the intelligent good looks and formed a favorable impression. "He impresses you in his physical presence as a man of great strength and endurance," noted a new acquaintance. "In conversation his voice is never

42 William N. McDonald, *A History of the Laurel Brigade, Originally Ashby's Cavalry of the Army of Northern Virginia and Chew's Battery* (1907, rpt. Frederick, MD, 1987), 196, 229-230; *OR* 33, 46; Frank M. Myers, *The Comanches: A History of White's Battalion, Virginia Cavalry* (Baltimore, MD, 1871, rpt. Marietta, GA, 1956), 340-341; Thomas D. Ranson reminiscence with cover letter to John W. Daniel, March 17, 1909, Lewis Leigh Peters Collection, U.S. Army Military History Institute, USAHEC, Carlisle, PA. Hereafter cited as Ranson Reminiscence; Stuart to Rosser, February 10, 1864, Rosser Papers, Acc. 1171-a, Box 1.

43 *OR* 43, pt. 1, 578. The Laurel Brigade moved by a long march across the state and rejoined its commander on October 5, 1864.

pitched on a high key, but is deliberate without being slow, and energetic without being demonstrative. He is one who is eminently fitted to exert great influence over men, and to retain a hold on their confidence."[44] For some, however, the initial spell soon wore off. One officer in the 3rd Virginia Cavalry complained that Rosser surrounded himself with sycophants "who would black his boots if necessary."[45] Rosser's "countenance denoting self-confidence," as one officer described it, combined with his tendency toward blunt speech and his decisive manner to leave an impression of arrogance. Captain George Booth, a staff officer serving Brig. Gen. Bradley Johnson, recalled meeting Rosser at an informal gathering of commanders that October soon after Rosser arrived in the Valley. Rosser spoke openly of the success he and other cavalry commanders had enjoyed against the Federals in eastern Virginia and then, in a jocular fashion, ungraciously began mocking the cavalrymen from the Valley, who had been notably unsuccessful. According to Booth, Rosser asked "why we had been permitting the federal cavalry to misuse us so terribly?" Rosser went on to declare that "he would now show us how it ought to be done."[46]

As Rosser put all of his self-confidence on display, so too did he apply his force of character to the new task before him. According to an officer of the 35th Battalion of Virginia Cavalry, Rosser arrived in the Shenandoah declaring that he was going to "run over everything in the Valley."[47] A Federal officer recalled that Rosser issued a proclamation and had it printed up as a circular for distribution through the Valley:

Patriots of the Valley:

Once more to the rescue of your homes and firesides! Dream not of peace or submission as long as the feet of Northern vandals desecrate your own, your native soil! Temporary reverses have befallen our arms in this department; despair not: the

44 William F. Phelps, education pioneer and writer from New York, recorded these impressions when he met Rosser in 1873. "Custer and Rosser," *The Daily State Journal* (Alexandria, VA), October 31, 1873, p. 3, col. 1.

45 Mark T. Alexander to "My Dear Mother," November 15, 1864, Mark Alexander Papers, Swem Library, College of William and Mary, Williamsburg, VA.

46 McDonald, *Laurel Brigade*, 196; George Wilson Booth. *Personal Reminiscences of a Maryland Soldier in the War Between the States, 1861-1865* (Baltimore, MD, 1986), 152.

47 Myers, *The Comanches*, 335, 341.

government of your choice has declared its speedy redemption paramount to its present existence and final triumph, and confidently appeals to the patriotic impulses of the masses. Rally! Organize! And report, mounted, to Rosser, Major-General.[48]

Someone in those early days of October dubbed Rosser "the Savior of the Valley." Who bestowed the name is not clear. It may have been a citizen or a newspaper correspondent, but some, including Jubal Early, believed the self-assured Rosser conferred the *nom de guerre* on himself. Word of the brazen moniker spread, and it both raised expectations for Rosser's performance and irritated many of the men who had been serving in the Valley for months—Jubal Early among them. The nickname became well enough known for both Phil Sheridan and George Custer to use it mockingly.[49] A Confederate staff officer summed up a general opinion of Rosser when he wrote that the cavalryman was "one of the bravest and most enterprising of our cavalry commanders, given albeit to perhaps an undue amount of boasting, owing to a superabundance of self-esteem, but withal a soldier of considerable merit." Even Col. Thomas Munford, who would later stand with Rosser's most severe critics, saw much to praise when Rosser arrived in the Valley "with fresh energy" and "full of confidence, eager to redeem the cavalry mishaps in the Valley."[50]

48 Bean, "Sheridan in the Shenandoah." Though the document projects the brash confidence Rosser brought to the Valley, the authenticity of the text is suspicious because of the phrase "Major-General." Rosser was not promoted to major general until November 1864.

49 Early later wrote that he thought Rosser engaged in self-promotion with his "ridiculous vaporing" and that he resented the implication that the Laurel Brigade would "show the rest of my command how to fight." "Generals Early and Rosser," Philadelphia *Weekly Times*, May 17, 1884; *OR* 43, pt. 2, 327. In a letter to his wife, Rosser referred to himself as "the Savior of the Valley" on November 15, 1864, but the name had been in common use well before that date. Rosser Papers, Acc. 1171-c, Box 1, folder 1864.

50 Booth, *Reminiscences*, 152; Munford, "Reminiscences . . . No. 3," 13:137.

CHAPTER FOUR

No Quarter on the Back Road

"When he Entered a Battle it Was to Kill."

In the early days of October, Jubal Early struggled to regroup his beaten army and return to action against Philip Sheridan. Foremost in Early's mind was his role in General Lee's strategic plan.

Early's letters to Lee show that he clearly understood that his army operated in the Valley to divert the Federals' attention and resources from Richmond and Petersburg. With his small army, Early was to keep Sheridan and his 40,000 men from leaving the Valley and moving eastward across Virginia to cooperate with Gen. U. S. Grant against Lee. Early also understood the critical importance Lee placed on protecting the fertile valley and its harvests. If the Confederate armies defending Petersburg and the capital were to survive, the men would have to eat. The produce of the farms of the Shenandoah had become essential to the survival of the Confederacy. Early, then, had two tasks that were almost impossible to achieve simultaneously because success in one endeavor advanced defeat in the other. He was to protect the Valley from the Federals while at the same time trying to prevent the Federals from leaving the Valley.

What Early required more than anything in that first week of October was information about Sheridan's intentions and movements, and he would rely on Rosser and Lomax to obtain it. Early's two cavalry divisions together numbered fewer than 3,500 men, who would have to be spread across hundreds of square miles to cover the Valley's roads, fords, and mountain gaps to try to track the movements of Sheridan's more numerous troops.

When Rosser arrived, Early presented him with a promotion of sorts by giving him more responsibility without increasing his rank or pay. Early directed Rosser to temporarily assume command of the wounded Fitz Lee's cavalry division and to operate against the western portion of the Federal position. The Federal cavalry occupied a line along the North River, stretching eastward from Bridgewater and the Harrisonburg-Warm Springs Turnpike to Mt. Crawford and the Valley Pike and onward toward Port Republic. Rosser formed his command just south of Bridgewater. The Federal commander in that sector was George A. Custer. Lunsford Lomax formed his division on the Valley Pike opposite Mt. Crawford.

Rosser commanded about 1,400 cavalrymen. Lomax's division numbered about 2,000 men but was broken into segments. The largest detachment was sent to the Luray Valley, a sub-region of the Shenandoah Valley, to track Federal movements, occupy passes in the Blue Ridge Mountains, and gather information.[1] Lomax, meanwhile, remained at Mt. Crawford with just two brigades of the troubled Valley Cavalry and a battery of artillery. Marylander Bradley T. Johnson, a brigadier general of considerable experience, was perhaps the lone pillar of stability upon which Lomax could lean, and Johnson commanded about a third of Lomax's men. The other, larger brigade belonged to Col. William L. Jackson of the 19th Virginia Cavalry, but he had gone down in August with a leg wound. William P. Thompson, a lieutenant colonel in the 19th Virginia, assumed command in his absence.[2] Lieutenant John R. McNulty's Baltimore Light

1   OR 43, pt. 1, 612. Early directed that Brig. Gen. John McCausland's brigade be posted to monitor the roads through Brown's Gap and Swift Run Gap through the Blue Ridge. Lomax would also send John Imboden's brigade to the Luray Valley. See Appendix B for a discussion of the strength of Rosser's and Lomax's command.

2   Richmond issued orders on September 27, 1864, for Brig. Gen. Henry B. Davidson to replace the wounded Jackson in command of the brigade. No evidence suggests Davidson had reported for duty by October 9. An anonymous letter printed in a Richmond newspaper gives evidence that Thompson was in command of the brigade at Tom's Brook. See OR 43, pt. 2, 880 and A Soldier, "The Cavalry – Letter From 'A Soldier,'" Richmond Sentinel, November 10, 1864. After the war, Thompson achieved vast wealth as a financier and corporate executive. He served as a vice-president of Standard Oil. "William P. Thompson: Financier, connected with Standard Oil." Wheeling Intelligencer, Feb. 4, 1896. Ohio County Public Library. Obituary in New York Times, February 4, 1896. See also Robert K. Krick, Lee's Colonels (Dayton, OH, 1991), 371. For a synopsis of Thompson's service record, see Richard L. Armstrong, The 19th and 20th Virginia Cavalry (Lynchburg, VA, 1994), 134, 175-76. The comparison of the relative sizes of the brigades is based upon Lomax's statement that he commanded about 800 men and Armstrong's revelation, based

Artillery, also known as the Baltimore Battery, commanded six three-inch
Ordnance Rifles that had been captured from the Federals in an earlier fight,
but Lomax reported that only three of the guns were serviceable.[3] When all
were present in this force of six regiments, four battalions, and the lone
three-gun battery, Major General Lomax commanded only 800 men, or
about what a colonel of cavalry might have hoped to command two years
earlier.[4]

Rosser's and Lomax's men skirmished with the Federals daily along the
North River while Early, at his headquarters near Mt. Sidney, tried to discern
Sheridan's intentions. At the end of September, Grant wished Sheridan to
cross east of the Blue Ridge and begin destroying the railroads and the James
River Canal, which were important in feeding Lee's army around Richmond
and Petersburg. Sheridan, however, was concerned about his own supply
line and explained that with his army in the upper Valley, his supply lines
passed northward through miles of guerilla-infested country, and he would
have to use too much of his own army simply to defend the supply route.
Because Early's army was "completely broken up and is dispirited," argued
Sheridan, almost all that Grant had desired had been accomplished. He
explained that Lee's army had been supplied from the counties in the
northern part of the Valley, but that all of the grain and forage in the rich
country around Staunton farther south had been stockpiled for the use of
Early's army, and that its destruction "would be a terrible blow to them."[5]
Sheridan proposed that he finish up the work of destruction, leave the Valley
a wasteland, and then move on to the next task. "I think that the best policy

---

on brigade returns, that Jackson's brigade numbered 528 men, aggregate present, on
October 25, 1864, two weeks after the battle. Armstrong, *The 19th and 20th Virginia
Cavalry,* 80.

3 McNulty had little experience leading a battery in action. The outfit's commander, Capt.
William Griffin, was in a Federal prison, and McNulty, too, had spent more than five
months as a prisoner of war. After his release in February 1864, McNulty spent six months
away from the battery serving on Bradley Johnson's staff. Kevin C. Ruffner, *Maryland's
Blue and Gray* (Baton Rouge, LA, 1997), 311, 318.

4 *OR* 43, pt. 1, 612-13. The 2nd Maryland Cavalry Battalion of Lomax's division might
serve as an example of the chaos worked by steady attrition. The outfit had lost most of its
officers and had acquired a reputation as a troublesome unit. Fewer than 100 men were
present for duty in late September 1864, and the name of the commander remains elusive.
Ruffner, *Maryland's Blue & Gray,* 207, 306. See Appendix A.

5 *OR* 43, pt. 1, 429-30.

will be to let the burning of the crops of the Valley be the end of this campaign," he wrote to Grant on October 1, "and let some of this army go somewhere else."[6] Grant acceded to Sheridan's plan to retrace his steps northward, and Sheridan issued his orders for the devastation of the Valley.

Sheridan's primary tool in the ruin of the Valley would be his cavalry. Mounted troops could cover vast areas far more quickly and thoroughly than could infantry, so while Sheridan managed the withdrawal of his foot soldiers and artillery, he left the conduct of the devastation to his cavalry chief, Alfred Torbert. With rear guards holding the line along the North River, Torbert ordered his cavalry to begin the destruction in Rockingham County south of Harrisonburg. According to Lt. Charles Veil of the 1st U.S. Cavalry, Torbert directed his troops "to lay the valley in waste and drive off every hoof of stock we could find, burn all grain and hay and not to spare barns or buildings housing grain. So we stretched a line of cavalry across the Valley and started down, carrying out the orders to the letter. Cornfields with the corn in shock were set on fire," he continued, "hay and grain stacks were burned, barns that had hay or grain in set on fire so that the entire Valley was ablaze, and the smoke settled over like a cloud. It was pretty severe medicine."[7] Orders explicitly prohibited burning dwellings and any barns near them, or even from torching barns in a position that might endanger a house by reason of the direction of the wind. In fact, Federal officers verbally cautioned subordinates "to take great care" to see that dwellings were not endangered.[8]

On October 3, however, the death of a single soldier changed the situation significantly. Near dusk, three Federal soldiers rode east on the Swift Run Gap Road near the town of Dayton. One of them, an officer, rode alone a short distance ahead of two enlisted men serving as orderlies. They were returning to Sheridan's headquarters at Harrisonburg from Custer's headquarters near Bridgewater. Ahead of them through the gray, rainy twilight, they saw three mounted strangers wearing rubber overcoats also riding eastward, but at a very slow pace. Since Dayton lay nearly four and a

---

6   *OR* 33, pt. 2, 249.

7   Charles H. Veil memoir, Civil War Miscellaneous Collection, U.S. Army History Education Center (USAHEC), Carlisle, PA.

8   Charles J. Seymour, "Sheridan Defended from Charge of Cruelty," *Burlington Weekly Press*, May 27, 1887.

half miles behind the front lines, the Federals assumed the men were fellow
Northerners and approached unwarily. Suddenly, one of the trio seized the
officer's reins, and his two partners attempted to do the same to the Federal
orderlies. Taken by surprise and confronted with a revolver, the officer,
according to one of his orderlies, exclaimed, "I surrender, I surrender." One
orderly recalled that the three mystery riders ignored the officer and started
shooting. The officer fell dead with a bullet in the head and another in the
chest. One orderly was captured, but the other fled on foot to Custer's
headquarters.[9]

The dead officer was 22-year-old Lt. John R. Meigs, who was not only
the son of Maj. Gen. Montgomery C. Meigs, one of Abraham Lincoln's
closest military advisors, but also chief engineer to, and a personal favorite
of, Philip H. Sheridan.[10] The killing of Meigs, and the reaction to it,
illustrates the grim nature of the war in 1864 and how drastically
circumstances had changed since the armies had fought in the Shenandoah in
1862.[11]

Rules and ideas that in 1861 and 1862 had defined "civilized warfare"
were by late 1864 largely ignored. After living with war and all its cruelty at
their very doorsteps for more than three years, many Southern men decided
to stand by no longer. Throughout the South, thousands of men, including
civilians, soldiers home on leave or with disabilities, deserters, or men or
boys too old or young to be conscripted, joined the fight while staying at
home. They did so without regard for such conventions as uniforms or
official military status. They operated with varying degrees of organization
and with tactics that differed widely. Some acted as individuals and used the
ancient methods of the highwayman to waylay unsuspecting soldiers in blue.
Others banded together into small units and attacked picket posts or wagon
trains and cut telegraph wires. The Confederate government called them
"partisans" or "irregulars." The Federals called them guerrillas or
"murderers, thieves and cutthroats," or, most often, "bushwhackers." Many
Southern women joined the fight as well. The more reckless would,
according to the accounts of Federal soldiers, fire shots out of open windows

---

9   Mary A Giunta, ed., *A Civil War Soldier of Christ and Country: The Selected
Correspondence of John Rodgers Meigs, 1859-1864* (Urbana, IL, 2006), 241-43.

10 Cullum, *Biographical Register*, 2:866.

11 *OR* 42, pt. 2, 318.

at passing Yankees. Many more women, however, supported the Southern war efforts by providing food and safe havens for the partisans who worked on farms by day and rode against the invaders by night.

Many of the rules of civilized warfare had been agreed upon across cultures and over centuries to protect the innocent. The rules existed to distinguish between combatants and non-combatants. When combatants and non-combatants in 1864 America decided to ignore the rules, the difference between combatant and non-combatant became more difficult to determine. In the past, a man who surrendered was usually taken prisoner and treated as a non-combatant. Likewise, dwellings were considered the homes of non-combatants. When civilians began waging war as guerillas or partisans, however, many Federal commanders decided that the rules had changed. Sheridan characterized the bushwhackers as "cowardly" for hiding among non-combatants. The guerrillas were responsible for involving the innocent in their lawless behavior. "The ultimate results of the guerrilla system of warfare," read one of Sheridan's orders:

> is the total destruction of all private rights in the country occupied by such parties. This destruction may as well commence at once, and the responsibility of it must rest upon the authorities at Richmond, who have acknowledged the legitimacy of guerrilla bands. The injury done this army by them is very slight. The injury they have inflicted upon the people, and upon the rebel army, may be counted by millions.[12]

Like Sheridan, Custer also refused to recognize the sanctity of a civilian home that harbored bushwhackers. Just weeks earlier, on August 18, Custer's Michigan Brigade was camped east of Berryville, Virginia. That night at picket posts around the encampment, Pvt. Alpheus Day of the 5th Michigan Cavalry was killed, another man of the regiment wounded, and two men from the 7th Michigan taken prisoner. Survivors stated the attacks came from men wearing civilian clothes. The next morning Custer ordered 50 men of the 5th Michigan to burn four homes in the area—one home for each soldier killed, wounded or taken. The houses designated for destruction belonged to "well-known secessionists."

12 *OR* 43, pt. 1, 56.

The attacks on the pickets the night before, however, had not been carried out by civilians but by Confederate soldiers belonging to Maj. John S. Mosby's cavalry command. Mosby's men, who used guerrilla tactics and did not always wear uniforms, did as much as any military organization in Virginia to blur the line between combatant and non-combatant. After Custer's Michiganders began to fulfill their orders, smoke from the burning homes attracted Mosby's men, who attacked a detachment of the house burners in the lane leading to the home of a Colonel Morgan. A short time later, part of the 5th Michigan Cavalry arrived and found a massacre scene: Twelve Michigan men lay dead and three wounded, two of whom would soon die. The wounded survivors claimed they were shot after surrendering and that Confederates dressed in civilian clothes had ridden around the field firing additional rounds into each fallen Federal. Most of the men had been shot in the head, including the sole survivor, Pvt. Sam Davis, who said he had turned over his weapons and stood with his hands up before being shot in the face. Mosby's men had served notice that house burners would not be granted prisoner-of-war status.[13]

About a month later, the Federals sent a similar message in the streets of Front Royal, Virginia. After a brief skirmish with some of Mosby's men, Wesley Merritt's Federals executed six prisoners. Torbert, Merritt, and Custer were all present, but as the senior officer Torbert bore ultimate responsibility. Outraged Southerners, including Mosby himself, nevertheless fixed blame on Custer. Mosby determined to kill an equal number of prisoners—but only men from Custer's command. Both Robert E. Lee and Secretary of War John Seddon approved the proposal, and in November Mosby ordered seven of Custer's men executed near the town of Berryville.[14]

With these recent events as prologue, the situation in the Valley in October following the killing of Lt. John R. Meigs was especially volatile. General Montgomery Meigs described the killing of his son as "murder." Sheridan considered it an "assassination," and reasoned that because it occurred behind Union lines and the perpetrators were reportedly not wearing Confederate uniforms, the killers were bushwhackers. "Since I

13 William J. Miller, "Demons That Day," *Civil War Magazine*, Issue 59, December 1996, 46-55.

14 Jeffry D. Wert, *Mosby's Rangers* (New York, NY, 1990), 213-15, 245-49.

came into the Valley, from Harpers Ferry up to Harrisonburg," Sheridan wrote Grant, "every train, every small party, and every straggler has been bushwhacked." In retribution, Sheridan ordered all the homes in a five-mile radius around Dayton burned. He gave the job to Custer, who climbed into his saddle and replied, "Look out for smoke." Though Sheridan countermanded his order before the job was finished, the Federal commander had made his point: Civilians would pay for enabling bushwhackers. Within days, Rosser's Confederates would counter with a strong reply of their own. [15]

*   *   *

On the night of October 5, Southern cavalrymen stood in their camps south of the North River and saw the sky to the north alight with an orange glow. The fires had been burning in Union-held territory for the past few days, but the Confederates could not yet see the extent of the destruction to one of the most productive agricultural areas in the Confederacy. The people of the Shenandoah came to know the names of Sheridan, Merritt, and Custer well, and the Northerners' campaign of ruination became known simply as "The Burning." The next morning, Sheridan's infantry divisions moved northward on the Valley Turnpike while the cavalry brought up the rear, ranging across the Valley with torches in hand. [16]

For four days, Federal cavalry filled the fields with fire and the skies with smoke, sowing sorrow and misery across one thousand square miles. Federal infantry, meanwhile, plodding northward through the center of the Valley on the turnpike followed the movements of their mounted colleagues by the black columns rising into the sky from burning haystacks, barns, mills, fields, and even dwellings. A New Yorker stood on a rise near Mt. Jackson and counted 167 pillars of smoke. [17]

15 *OR* 43, pt. 1, 30; James E. Taylor, *With Sheridan Up the Shenandoah Valley in 1864. Leaves from a Special Artist's Sketch Book and Diary* (Dayton, OH, 1989), 434.

16 Newel Cheney, *History of the Ninth Regiment, New York Volunteer Cavalry, War of 1861 to 1865* (Jamestown, NY, 1901), 226.

17 James R. Bowen, *Regimental History of the First New York Dragoons During Three Years of Active Service in the Great Civil War* (Battle Creek, MI, 1900), 243.

Federal cavalry during The Burning, based upon a sketch by field artist Alfred Waud,
whose succinct caption read: "The 3rd Custer div. on the 7th of Octr. retiring and
burning the forage Etc. Somewhere near Mt. Jackson." *LOC*

After three days of destruction, Sheridan reported to Grant:

I have destroyed over 2,000 barns filled with wheat, hay, and farming implements;
over seventy mills filled with flour and wheat; have driven in front of the army over
4 [thousand] head of stock, and have killed and issued to the troops not less than
3,000 sheep. This destruction embraces the Luray Valley and Little Fort Valley, as
well as the main valley. A large number of horses have been obtained, a proper
estimate of which I cannot now make.[18] Merritt claimed his division alone drove off
3,300 animals and confiscated or destroyed property worth more than three million
dollars.[19]

18 *OR* 43, pt. 1, 30-31.

19 *OR* 43, pt. 2, 443.

The cold detachment with which Sheridan could cite the numbers was a luxury his men ordered to ride onto peaceful farms and burn, destroy, and confiscate did not share. Many Federal troopers later lamented having to discharge "this disagreeable and demoralizing duty," and recorded episodes they could not forget. As the 2nd Massachusetts rounded up livestock, a trooper watched a barefooted young woman run beside Lt. Col. Caspar Crowninshield's horse pleading with him to leave the family's cow. Crowninshield ignored her and rode on in stony silence. The woman delivered her final, fruitless words to his back: "Take her, god damn you and go to hell with her." A Michigan officer could not bear to watch the sobbing of families in one village as their buildings burned. "It was too much for me and at the first moment that duty would permit, I hurried away from the scene," he admitted. "General Merritt did not see these things, nor did General Sheridan, much less General Grant." Thirty-year-old Roger Hannaford, an Englishman who had grown up in Ohio and started a family there, rode in the ranks of the 2nd Ohio Cavalry, and The Burning made a lifelong impression on him. He understood and did not dispute the reasoning Grant and Sheridan used for desolating the Valley, but he confessed, "it was to me most terrible." As he rode through the smoke and the stench and looked upon the weeping women and children and saw whole families packing up and leaving their land to escape the coming hunger, he felt disgust. "My soul loathed it," wrote Hannaford, "and earnestly did I desire to escape having any lot or part in it." He hoped he would not be ordered to join one of the torch-bearing details and be forced to actually burn a family's farm because he knew he could not disobey the order. Hannaford later wrote that though the desolation was exaggerated in some of the press accounts, and though he witnessed acts of humanity amid the barbarism, the whole operation was appalling to him: "God knows it was terrible, terrible even still."[20]

An officer from New York recalled that the destruction triggered an exodus: "Many families were moving out of the valley. Every supply train carried back families going north. The destruction of all grain, flour, feed and taking all farm stock by the army left the people nothing to subsist on

---

20 Moses Harris, "With the Reserve Brigade," *Journal of the United Stated Cavalry Association,* 3 (1892) :15; Kidd, *Personal Recollections*, 399; Roger Hannaford memoir, Civil War Papers, Cincinnati Historical Society Library, Cincinnati, OH, Box 1, folder 6.

during the approaching winter." Sheridan reported that 400 wagons carried refugees northward from the area of Harrisonburg. Most of these people were German Baptist Brethren, conscientious objectors commonly known as "Dunkers." Many of the civilians rode north in empty army wagons likely returning to supply depots at Winchester and elsewhere. Other refugees overloaded any vehicle with wheels, from two-wheeled dog carts to heavy farm wagons pulled by six-horse teams.[21]

As the Federal troops culled through the farms, Federal officers tried to make practical use of the grain and livestock, taking what they could use before destroying what they could not move away. Such economical instincts, however, were considered secondary to the prime objects of desolation and waste. Colonel James Kidd of the 6th Michigan recalled an episode in which he postponed the burning of several grist mills while Federal commissary officers set men to grinding flour and meal to distribute to nearby regiments. During the delay, General Merritt rode up in a state of agitation. "Merritt was provoked," explained Kidd. "He pointed to the west and one could have made a chart of Custer's trail by the columns of black smoke which marked it. The general was manifestly fretting lest Custer should appear to outdo him in zeal in obeying orders." Kidd assured the general that the mills would never grind again, and the buildings were soon ablaze.[22]

After the war, Merritt remained firm in his belief that the destruction was necessary. Almost four years of war led the Federals to adopt harsh policies that would have been unthinkable at the outset of the conflict. The goal in 1864 was to end the war as soon as possible, and for Merritt and the rest of Sheridan's cavalrymen, that meant destroying or taking anything that could be of value to the Confederacy. "It was a severe measure," admitted Merritt, "and appears severer now in the lapse of time; but it was necessary as a measure of war." The Shenandoah, he continued, was "the paradise of bushwhackers and guerrillas." The Burning was intended to remove the Valley as an asset to the Confederacy as an area of military operations and a region of agricultural plenty. "The Valley from Staunton to Winchester was

21 *OR* 43, pt. 1, 30; Cheney, *History of the Ninth Regiment*, 226; Edwin Havens to "Dear Nell," October 9, 1864, Edwin Havens Letters, Archives and Historical Collections, Michigan State University.

22 Kidd, *Personal Recollections*, 397-98.

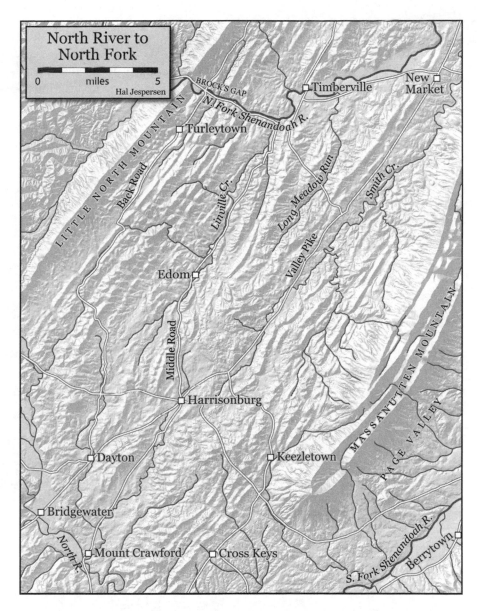

North River to North Fork

0   miles   5

Hal Jespersen

BROCK'S GAP · New Market · Timberville · N. Fork Shenandoah R. · LITTLE NORTH MOUNTAIN · Back Road · Turleytown · Linville Cr. · Long Meadow Run · Smith Cr. · Valley Pike · Edom · Middle Road · MASSANUTTEN MOUNTAIN · PAGE VALLEY · Harrisonburg · Dayton · Keezletown · Bridgewater · North R. · Mount Crawford · Cross Keys · S. Fork Shenandoah R. · Berrytown

completely devastated," Merritt wrote, "and the armies thereafter occupying that country had to look elsewhere for their supplies." Merritt denied the campaign of destruction left civilians destitute: "There is little doubt, however, that enough was left in the country for the subsistence of the people, for this, besides being contemplated by orders, resulted of necessity from the fact that, while the work was done hurriedly, the citizens had ample time to secrete supplies, and did so."[23]

Henry Kyd Douglas, one of Jubal Early's staff officers, disagreed. Douglas argued that Merritt and Sheridan studiously ignored the suffering of the civilians by failing to mention "the private dwellings which their troops drunk with their license to burn, laid in ashes, and the unspeakable suffering and horrors they brought on innocent women and children. It is almost impossible to believe that a soldier with the reputation and distinction of General Wesley Merritt could have been an actor in such inhumanity."[24]

More than 30 years after The Burning, a Confederate officer from Maryland who witnessed the Federal campaign of devastation, remained adamant that such brutality must never be accepted, even in war:

> Time is a great physician, and after the lapse of more than a third of a century many a wound then received has healed and many an indignity has been forgiven; but while we are human and life lasts—nay, while the world has a conscience and detests unnecessary cruelty and crime—these diabolical deeds, perpetrated under the guise of military necessity and with fiendish delight, will ever be reprehended and the promoters held up to the detestation and scorn of the good and true, not only of our own, but of all generations to come.[25]

*   *   *

As the Federals burned through the country between Harrisonburg and Port Republic, Early worried that Sheridan might be preparing an attack. He also knew a retrograde movement by the Federals was just as possible. In his insatiable desire for information, Early urged Rosser to be vigilant. "Be on the look out & prepare for anything which might happen," he ordered. "If the enemy move back I wish you to follow him at once & do what you can to annoy him."[26] As dawn broke on October 6, Rosser's alert pickets

---

23 Wesley Merritt, "Sheridan in the Shenandoah Valley," in *Battles and Leaders of the Civil War*, 4 vols. (New York, NY, 1887-88), 4:513.

24 Henry Kyd Douglas, *I Rode with Stonewall* (Chapel Hill, NC, 1940), 315.

25 Booth, *Reminiscences,* 151.

26 Margret Ann Vogtsberger, *The Dulanys of Welbourne: A Family in Mosby's Confederacy* (Charlottesville, VA, 1997), 226-27.

discovered the Federals withdrawing northward from Bridgewater. Rosser put his division on the road at once to follow his friend Custer on the Harrisonburg-Warm Springs turnpike and the Back Road. According to one man of the 2nd Ohio Cavalry, not five minutes after the last Federal lookouts pulled out of position to join the northward movement, they heard Confederate bugles sounding "boots and saddles"—the call to pack up and get ready to move.[27] Merritt's men began withdrawing northward at the same time, and Lomax's Confederate troopers followed through the heart of the Valley along the turnpike and the Keezletown Road. Early assuaged his concern about Sheridan's intentions by ordering Lomax to detach a brigade and send it northward through the Luray Valley. If Sheridan's plan was to leave the region and head eastward, he might do so through the Luray. Early was leaving no stone unturned in his search for clues to Sheridan's intentions.[28]

Though Rosser's Confederates had seen the results of The Burning in Augusta County surrounding Staunton, and they had seen the smoky glow from fires in Rockingham, not until they crossed the North River and moved into "the burnt district" between Bridgewater and Harrisonburg did they see for themselves the vast devastation. A man of the 11th Virginia Cavalry recorded in his diary that he and his comrades spent the day riding past smoking dwellings and hearing the newly homeless recount how the Yankees allowed the families to remove their furniture from the houses then burned the homes, and in some cases the furniture as well. Scarcely a barn on the road remained standing.[29] Rosser knew many of the men in his ranks lived in the Rockingham and Shenandoah counties and that their homes lay in the path of the Federal army. He could see they were animated by rage and hatred.[30] An officer in the Laurel Brigade recalled years later, after time had dulled his passions, that, "On every side, from mountain to mountain, the

27 Hannaford memoir.

28 *OR* 43, pt. 1, 612.

29 Alfred Moore Diary, University of Notre Dame Rare Books and Special Collections. Manuscripts of the American Civil War: Diaries and Journals. Accessed September 22, 2014, www.rarebooks.nd.edu/digital/civil_war/diaries_journals/moore/MSN-CW_8010-42.shtml.

30 Thomas L. Rosser, "Annals of the War: Rosser and His Men," *Philadelphia Weekly Times*, March 22, 1884.

flames from all the barns, mills, grain and hay stacks, and in very many instances from dwellings, too, were blazing skyward, leaving a smoky trail of desolation to mark the footsteps of the devil's inspector-general, and show in a fiery record, that will last as long as the war is remembered, that the United States, under the government of Satan and Lincoln, sent Phil. Sheridan to campaign in the Valley of Virginia."[31]

Colonel Thomas M. Munford reflected on what it must have been like for men like those in Rosser's command contemplating their families sitting unknowingly at home while the terror and destruction moved toward them. He theorized that many would not have been able to resist going AWOL to ride home and see to the safe removal of their families.[32] As the Confederate cavalry pressed hard on the heels of the Federal incendiarists, a man in the Laurel Brigade admitted they were "impelled by a sense of personal injury."[33]

The smoke from burning farms mixed with cold mists on that cloudy, drizzly October 6th. The western side of the Valley, close by the foot of Little North Mountain, was a country of high ridges and hills, and narrow glens and hollows. The ridges funneled rainwater on to the Back Road, and the rough and stony road bed bruised the feet of the thousands of cavalry horses passing over it.[34] Progress was often slow. James E. Taylor, an artist traveling with Custer's column on assignment for Frank Leslie's Illustrated Newspaper, noted the routine along the Back Road: "The main body in column of fours was in the rear detaching parties to the right and left to burn every mill, barn and haystack to be seen. Ordinarily the rear guard followed at a slow walk, the greater part deployed as skirmishers; when the enemy pressed too close, the men would halt and face about, a brisk fullisade would last a few moments, when the graycoats would be off, then trotting on, the rear guard would halt at the edge of the next hill or belt of woods to repeat the operation."[35]

31 Myers, *The Comanches*, 335-336.

32 Thomas T. Munford, "Annals of the War: Munford on Rosser," *Philadelphia Weekly Times*, May 17, 1884.

33 McDonald, *Laurel Brigade,* 303.

34 Perkins, *Three Years,* 289.

35 Taylor, *With Sheridan,* 449.

Just north of the hamlet of Turleytown, the North Fork of the Shenandoah River flows eastward out of the mountains between the steep and picturesque faces of Turley Mountain and Gap Rock. The area was known as Brock's Gap, or perhaps even more commonly as Cootes' Store. Seventy-one-year-old Samuel Cootes, a veteran of the War of 1812, kept a store at the mouth of the gap where the Back Road forded the river and intersected the road to Timberville and New Market.[36] The North Fork was a substantial obstacle for Custer, burdened as he was with the hundreds of head of livestock he was driving northward. To give the long column time to cross, he deployed a strong rear guard on the south side of the river and his artillery on the high ground above the north bank. After the division and its impedimenta crossed the river, Custer prepared to send his men into camp. Having corralled the cattle and sheep, most of the Federals settled down on the high ground north of the river.[37]

With a zeal for vengeance quickening their pace, however, the head of Rosser's column struck the Federal rear guard near Turleytown about 4:00 p.m. Colonel Munford dismounted the 2nd Virginia Cavalry and sent the troopers forward as skirmishers. The Federals moved back steadily and accelerated their pace after the 4th Virginia Cavalry moved up to hasten them along.[38] Using the ample cover on the south bank, Rosser wisely formed his men in column of fours (a column composed of four-men abreast). The Confederates charged in their narrow columns with Munford's 2nd Virginia Cavalry angling westward toward the gap. The 5th New York Cavalry and 18th Pennsylvania Cavalry bore the brunt of the blow, and Rosser's men cut off about 75 of the New Yorkers, who fled westward into the mountains. The Federals fended off the Southerners and restored order at the ford, but Rosser's men had made an impression, and Early's orders to "follow him at once & do what you can to annoy him" had been faithfully obeyed.

36 Carolyn Cootes, "Samuel Cootes of Rockingham, Co., VA," RootsWeb Cootes-L Archives. Accessed June 2, 2002, http://cootes.com/samuel/obituary.htm.

37 Hannaford memoir.

38 Notebook of Beverly Whittle, 2nd Virginia Cavalry Regiment, Co. C, September-November 1864, Papers of Beverly Kennon Whittle, 1863-79. Acc. 7973, Special Collections, University of Virginia, Charlottesville, VA, Box 3, mss notebook folder: "1864 Sept. 12- 1865 Feb 18."

An officer of the 2nd Ohio admitted the aggressiveness of the Confederates created an atmosphere of "considerable uneasiness" in the Federal camps on the night of October 6. So anxious were the Federal officers on this first night of their withdrawal that they kept at least the 2nd Ohio Cavalry and the 5th New York Cavalry on picket all night. The 75 stray troopers who had been cut out of the 5th New York meandered through the dark woods and returned to the fold that night, while troopers of the 2nd Ohio lay in line of battle in a cornfield.[39] With campfires forbidden and orders for silence strictly enforced, the Buckeyes slept on the ground at the head of their saddled horses with their bridle reins in their hands. The night was exceedingly and unseasonably cold, and few of the men had overcoats or a thick blanket. Without fires, the men did without even the small comfort of hot coffee.[40]

South of the river, the Confederates, too, spent an uncomfortable night. In addition to the cold, they were hungry and on short rations. Trooper Beverly Whittle of the 2nd Virginia Cavalry noted they existed in a cloud of haze and breathed the stench of smoke. The air, he recalled, "is impregnated with the smell of burning property." Somewhere along the line of march Whittle found a pointed message left behind by a Federal who had not forgotten the Confederates' fiery visit to Pennsylvania that July when some of Early's men had ransomed and burned the town of Chambersburg. Scrawled on a plank were the words: "Remember Chambersburg."[41]

*   *   *

During the day, Merritt's column moved northward along the Valley Pike, paralleling Custer's route a few miles to the west. According to a staff officer at Merritt's headquarters at Timberville, Rosser's attack at Brock's Gap, news of which had reached Merritt before sundown, convinced the Federals to take more heed of their pursuers. Merritt strengthened the support for the rear guard and heightened security around the livestock herd,

---

39 *OR* 43, pt. 1, 102; Louis N. Beaudry, *War Journal of Louis N. Beaudry, Fifth New York Cavalry*, Richard E. Beaudry, ed. (Jefferson, NC, 1996), 176.

40 Luman Harris Tenney, *War Diary of Luman Harris Tenney 1861-1865* (Cleveland, OH, 1914), 131; Hannaford memoir.

41 Notebook of Beverly Whittle.

which had already grown to enormous proportions. After just a single day of sweeping through prosperous Rockingham County, Merritt's troopers had gathered more than 2,500 beeves and uncounted numbers of horses, mules, sheep, goats, and swine. Keeping the herds under control would only grow more difficult as the army moved northward and confiscated more animals, but already the unhappy creatures, displaced from their homes and goaded into a forced march, were singing a cacophonic song of woe. A Pennsylvanian recalled the uproar of the animals' first night away from their homes:

> Imagine, if you can, dear reader, the thunder of dozens of majestic bulls and bullocks, goring each other indiscriminately by way of being acquainted; the bellowing of a 1000 cows whose calves had been carelessly lost by the way, or were now being slaughtered before their eyes by the hungry soldiers herding them . . . . Add to this the hideous noise that mules and jacks only can make, the sharp squealing porkers . . . the bleating of the droves of sheep, the plaintive cry of goats, while on every hand you were beset by beseeching men and women, who had followed the herdsman into camp, in the hope of identifying their only cow, their only horse, mule, sheep, hog or goat, as the case may be, and you can form an [idea] of the character of our camp at Timberville, on the night of October 6, 1864.[42]

Following the path of misery spread by the Federals, Confederate cavalrymen encountered nothing but anger and grief. The fields and livestock pens on the smoking farms stood empty. The blue-clad troopers, their uniforms blackened and reeking of smoke, delivered a powerful message to people for whom the future was bleak: The Southern armies could no longer defend the Southern people, and Confederate defeat was inevitable. The prohibition against destroying homes was crucial in defining the nature of the operation Grant wished Sheridan to undertake. General David Hunter, who earlier in the summer had commanded Federal troops in the Valley, acquired a reputation for burning houses. He purposely ordered his troops to burn the Lexington home of Virginia Governor William

---

42 Bean, "Sheridan in the Shenandoah."

Letcher. Jubal Early recalled seeing the ruins of many other homes in the region after Hunter's army passed through.[43]

One of the reasons Grant sent Sheridan to replace Hunter in the Valley was that the latter's actions seemed to some merely indiscriminate brutality. Grant did not wish the destruction in the Valley to be a campaign of cruelty or terror or punishment, but rather a rational attempt to achieve the specific military goal of denying food and supplies to Robert E. Lee's Confederate army. When Sheridan, infuriated by the killing of Lt. John Meigs, had ordered the burning of houses around Dayton, however, he had acted irrationally. Sheridan had unwittingly but fundamentally undercut Grant's rational purpose when he decided to use the torch to "teach a lesson" to the people of Rockingham County who might be feeding and sheltering bushwhackers.[44] To the Southerners, the burning of 100 barns likely meant less than the burning of a single house, and whatever message Grant originally intended to convey, Sheridan's actions ensured that the Southerners received a different message altogether: The Yankees were burning houses.

According to Sheridan, only "a few" houses had been torched near Dayton before he countermanded the order, but throughout the days to follow, and despite orders to the contrary, more dwellings burned. "That houses were sometimes burnt was doubtless true," admitted a trooper in Custer's division, "but it was only when they caught from the barn." In cases where barns stood so close to dwellings that sparks and flying ash might endanger the houses, soldiers sometimes helped citizens remove furniture from the residences before igniting the barns.[45] Not all of the Federals were so tender hearted. Lieutenant Veil of the 1st U.S. Cavalry remembered an encounter with a citizen:

> I was in charge of a portion of the line that day and, as I came to a fine barn and farm residence, I saw a venerable old gentleman standing at the gate. As he saw I was an officer he beckoned me to come up. When I reached him, he said: "My dear sir, I

43 Edward A. Miller, Jr., *Lincoln's Abolitionist General* (Columbia, SC, 1997), 210-11; Jubal A. Early, *A Memoir of the Last Year of the War for Independence* (Lynchburg, VA, 1867), 48.

44 Sheridan, *Personal Memoirs,* 2:52.

45 Hannaford memoir.

see what you are doing. My barn is full of grain. I have a lot of women, children and slaves here that will starve if you destroy my barn; not only that, but you will burn my house. My men are all in the army. I have eighteen hundred dollars in gold in my cellar. Take the gold and spare my barn.

Veil saw that his men were already at the barn, and with the jaded air of a soldier merely following orders, he did nothing to stop them. "I sympathized with the old gentleman," he wrote, "but rode off and left his gold. The barn was burned and probably the house too; I did not wait to see."[46] Any time a house burned, whether through accident, or cruelty, or indifference like Lieutenant Veil's, the Confederates' hunger for vengeance sharpened. Confederates took revenge on Federal prisoners.

After the war, Confederates who had been with Rosser's command wrote openly about a public execution of Federal prisoners in a meadow along the Back Road. Their accounts differ in some details—whether the number was four or five, or whether the event occurred on October 6 near Linville Creek or October 8 north of Mill Creek—but the witnesses agreed that a large portion of Rosser's command attended at least one formal execution of prisoners. Sergeant William Brent of the 7th Virginia Cavalry appears to have played a role in the killing. Brent, like most veterans in 1864, was a realist. He was one of four brothers who had enlisted in the Confederate cavalry, and one of the three still alive. His older brother had been killed in battle a year earlier. A younger brother, Hugh, also in the 7th Virginia Cavalry, rode nearby and still carried a Federal bullet in his leg from two years earlier. William had been wounded at least four times, twice seriously, and had also spent time in a Northern prison. The 22-year-old veteran had no illusions about war and no love of Federal soldiers. He recalled that early on an October morning someplace on the Back Road, a handful of Federal prisoners were herded into a clearing. The spot had been chosen because it was in view of Federals occupying a picket post not far away.[47] The Confederates' intention was to execute these few barn burners

---

46 Charles H. Veil memoir.

47 William A. Brent memoir, unpaginated typescript, private collection; P. J. White, "'The Bloody Fifth' Cavalry," *The Times-Dispatch* (Richmond, VA), November 8, 1908; Myers, *The Comanches*, 336; Fred Swarker, "Wants to Know the Reason Why," *Richmond Dispatch*, January 1, 1883; William B. Conway, "The Hanging of Four of Sheridan's

in full view of their fellow barn burners, and thereby send a message of their own: burning and looting would be punished.

"There were five of these unfortunates," wrote Brent, "one of them was a Sergeant, and when I saw him the evening before, had been quite a fine looking fellow, with his new and clean uniform and generally neat and gentlemanly appearance. When I saw him shot [the next day] I would hardly have recognized him for the same man." The Confederates had taken the newer clothes of the doomed men and dressed them in tattered Confederate outfits. A squad of men that had been detailed to shoot the prisoners stood ready. The sergeant, Brent thought, spoke eloquently and even evoked pity. He said he could prove that he had saved houses on previous days by driving off rogue soldiers eager to pillage and burn. The man appealed to an officer present, but to no avail. "While the Sergeant was still pleading," continued Brent. "two were quietly shot down, two broke and ran and were shot and fell dead before they had gone fifty yards. The Sergeant now being the only one left, the crowd appealed for him, but in vain. Finally he said, 'If I must die, I wish to die like a man,' closed his eyes, and said 'Lord have mercy on my soul, now fire.'"[48]

Postwar accounts identified Maj. James Breathed as an executioner of prisoners during these days on the Back Road.[49] The 25-year-old Breathed commanded all of the horse artillery in Early's army and had earned a reputation during the war for ferocity. Breathed was a true believer in the cause of Confederate independence. A fellow officer thought Breathed "fought the Yankees because he hated them . . . . When he entered a battle it was to kill." Just a few days earlier, Breathed had joined in a cavalry charge during a skirmish at Bridgewater. A Confederate colonel saw him return from the charge with blood dripping from his sword and a fire of excitement

---

Cavalrymen," *Richmond Dispatch*, January 15, 1883; Marcellus French, "Another Account," *Richmond Dispatch*, January 15, 1883; George Baylor, *Bull Run to Bull Run: Four Years in the Army of Northern Virginia* (1900, rpt. Washington, DC, 1983), 249.

48 William A. Brent memoir.

49 "T. D. R" [Thomas D. Ranson], "The Reason Why," clipping from *Richmond Dispatch* [unknown month] 1892, Rosser Scrapbook 1877; White, "The Bloody Fifth." The Federals were well aware of these executions. Thomas D. Ranson of the 12th Virginia Cavalry wrote that after he was captured at Tom's Brook, Federal officers informed him that they planned executions in retribution. Ranson reminiscence.

The extraordinarily aggressive Maj. James Breathed, whom witnesses linked to the execution of Federal prisoners along the Back Road.

Wise's *The Long Arm of Lee*

lighting his eyes. Breathed was exultant as he exclaimed that he had personally killed three enemy soldiers by running them through.[50]

In the execution described by Brent, the 7th Virginia Cavalry was drawn up in formation nearby under the eyes of Lt. Col. Thomas Marshall. Brent's account also states Col. Reuben Boston of the 5th Virginia Cavalry was present. Soldiers belonging to the 4th Virginia Cavalry and to the 35th Battalion wrote they either witnessed the event or participated in it. The presence of witnesses from four different regiments representing all three of the brigades under Rosser suggests this was no "back-room" proceeding, and the presence of the field officers further indicates the executions were sanctioned by high-ranking commanders, and probably by Rosser as well.[51]

The killing of prisoners became less formal and almost routine. Not far from New Market, a few hapless blue-clad soldiers were caught trying to burn a mill and, according to an officer in the Laurel Brigade, "were instantly shot."[52] Sergeant Brent recalled another incident in which he chased a

50 Ferguson, "Memoranda," frame 399; William H. F. Payne to H. H. Matthews, May 22, 1902, in H. H. Matthews, "Pelham-Breathed Battery, Appendix," *St. Mary's Beacon*, 1904-1905, quoted in David P. Bridges, *Fighting with Jeb Stuart: Major James Breathed and the Confederate Horse Artillery* (Alexandria, VA, 2006), 15, 314-17; *Robert J. Trout, "The Hoss": Officer Biographies and Rosters of the Stuart Horse Artillery Battalion* (United States, 2003), 13-16.

51 William A. Brent memoir.

52 Myers, *The Comanches*, 336.

handful of fleeing Northerners. "We were running them," he later wrote, "and I was trying to kill a fellow that I had singled out for that purpose." The flying Northerner jumped from his racing horse and landed face first just as Brent caught up with him. Brent was not sure if the man was dead, injured, or playing possum, but it did not matter. "I went back, took his gun from his sling, a 'Spencer Seven-Shooter' and shot him with it through the head."[53] A Confederate staff officer recalled standing with a young woman beside the remains of her father's burned barn near Mill Creek. On the ground before her lay a wounded Yankee, and officer urged her to shoot the man.[54]

The Confederates met brutality with brutality. Men on both sides realized that putting up hands in surrender no longer guaranteed their safety; for many, flight became the best option. A Confederate artilleryman recalled seeing dead soldiers dressed in blue lying here and there along the Back Road, and for them he had no sympathy. "Just at dusk this evening," he wrote in his diary, "I saw a Federal soldier lying on the field; from all appearances he was mortally wounded. He was piteously lamenting his condition and said, 'Oh, I want to see mother; I wish I would have stayed at home.' I wished so too."[55]

53 William A. Brent memoir.

54 Ferguson, "Memoranda," frame 399.

55 George M. Neese, *Three Years in the Confederate Horse Artillery* (New York, NY, 1911), 319.

CHAPTER FIVE

General Sheridan Loses Patience

"No Half Measures . . ."

After the fight at Brock's Gap on the night of October 6, Thomas Rosser made his headquarters at Turleytown at the home of Joseph Zirkle, who, according to an astonished staff officer, weighed more than 300 pounds.[1] With the chance to rest, Rosser found time to look back on the day, and despite the satisfaction of driving off Custer's men in the skirmish that evening at the gap, he was not pleased. The long pursuit of more than 25 miles through the burnt landscape had taxed him and his men physically and emotionally, and every step of the way Rosser had carried the additional burden of command responsibility. Through no fault of his own, he had begun the day unprepared for events. The Federals pulled out of their positions on the North River suddenly, before Rosser and Lomax could receive full instructions from Jubal Early. Though both cavalry commanders had immediately led their men forward to give chase, neither general knew precisely what Early expected or desired. From Zirkle's, Rosser wrote to ask for instructions.

Early was moving his headquarters northward from Mt. Sidney, and spent parts of the 6th and 7th in transit on the Valley Pike. Though Rosser was only eight miles west of the pike, a courier would have to travel much farther while navigating the complex series of paths and byroads between

---

1 Ferguson, "Memoranda," Frame 399.

the two headquarters. Early replied on the morning of the 7th, but there is some evidence his message miscarried, and its full contents remain unknown. Early wrote to Rosser again that evening:

New Market 7 p.m.
October 7th 1864

General

Your courier did not reach me until sunrise this morning, + I immediately wrote to you to follow the enemy + endeavor to do all the damage you could. I thought I wrote you full instructions by Mr. Calloway on yesterday. I wish you to continue the pursuit + harass the enemy as much as possible. Lomax is following down The Pike having passed this place at 10 o'clock this morning. It is possible that Sheridan may cross the mountains to the East side + go to the Rappahannock or he may go to send a part of his force to Washington to be shipped to Grant. I wish to ascertain what he intends + I shall remain here tomorrow, to get the information, so that I may move across the mountains myself if necessary. You must continue on + go as far as Winchester – if you can. Lomax has sent a brigade down the Luray Valley. If you find a chance to strike a blow do so, without waiting instructions.

Respectfully,

J. A. Early
Lt. General[2]

After writing out "full instructions" on October 6, Early repeated them twice the next day. Only the third message survives, a significant point because the content of his orders to Rosser would become the focus of a bitter dispute. Rosser would criticize Early for issuing orders that did not allow him enough discretion. These orders of October 7, however, give Rosser great flexibility. Early wrote that if Rosser could strike a blow, he should do so. If Rosser could push on to threaten Sheridan's supplies or his line of communication at Winchester or some other point, Early desired it done. Nowhere does Early compel Rosser to do anything but follow and harass, and look for opportunities to hinder Sheridan. Early asked Rosser to

---

2   Early to Rosser, October 7, 1864, Rosser Papers, Acc. 1171-a, Box 1.

be vigilant, active, and relentless in causing difficulties that would preoccupy Sheridan, but he left the details to his cavalry commander. Knowing Rosser's natural energetic combativeness, Early had reason to believe Rosser would deliver what was needed.

Early's orders also make clear that his prime concern was the possibility that Sheridan might slip away from them and abandon the Valley. If Sheridan were to shift his army eastward out of the Shenandoah, Early would have to go after him and try to bring him to battle. With these orders, Early was clarifying for Rosser the principle underlying their broad mission: The reason they were in the Valley was to keep Sheridan from combining with General Grant against R. E. Lee, and to accomplish that goal they had to know Sheridan's location at all times as well as to strive to discover his intentions. Early wished Rosser's cavalry to maintain continuous contact with Sheridan's army until the Confederate commander could find a favorable opportunity to strike it. Rosser's subsequent actions, however, suggest he did not have a firm grasp of the broad picture so clear in Early's mind.

One of the chief complaints against Early, which Lomax voiced immediately after the fight at Tom's Brook and that Rosser would still be repeating 40 years later, was that he did not appoint a chief of cavalry to replace the wounded Fitz Lee. Early sent Lomax's division and Rosser's division to follow the Federals without the unifying tether a chief of cavalry would have provided. Lomax was senior to Rosser and was the logical choice to exercise overall command. Early never explained why he did not designate Lomax cavalry chief, but he may have thought Lomax had enough to do in managing his ill-disciplined troops during the operation. Perhaps Early thought that the two generals, who would be operating just a few miles apart, would use their initiative to cooperate as necessary, and that Lomax could be trusted to use his judgment to assert his right to take overall command when a situation warranted it. Possibly Early thought two West Pointers with years of experience as cavalrymen could conduct what he saw as an uncomplicated operation: vigorously harass the Federals and gather and report as much information as possible. Despite their later criticism of his instructions, neither Rosser nor Lomax could fault Early for a lack of trust. If anything, his instructions might have left them too much discretion rather than too little. Rarely do subordinates complain about being given too much independence, yet Rosser and Lomax would do so.

* * *

Through the keen air and sunshine on the morning of October 7, at least part of Custer's column moved eastward, away from the Back Road, through Timberville and Forestville. This neighborhood in the Valley, as indicated by the names of the villages, was wooded and lacked the long splendid vistas of the open farm country to the south, east, and north. Forestville reminded a Federal artilleryman of a shipwreck—"a forlorn village cast away on a rocky lee shore."[3]

Colonel Alexander Pennington's Federal brigade moved briskly, passing most of the confiscated cattle and sheep that filled the road for miles. The Federals found that the country in this section of the Valley was not as suitable for farming as was the fertile land they had passed through the previous day. Fewer farms meant fewer barns to burn, so the columns moved at a better rate.[4]

Rosser's men followed Custer to Timberville, then Forestville, and on northward closely enough that the leading elements of the Confederate column may have heard the music from the mounted band Custer customarily had "tooting defiantly" in the rear of his column.[5] Below Forestville, the Northerners' main column wound northwesterly to return to the Back Road, and Custer's thoughts certainly included what figured to be one of the day's major challenges: crossing Mill Creek.

Though neither broad nor deep, Mill Creek could not be easily crossed at any point. The creek ran out of Little North Mountain on the west to cut clear across the Valley for nearly 10 miles before emptying into the Shenandoah River near Mt. Jackson. As Custer approached the stream from the south, his problem was to get his scattered division, its trains, and the confiscated livestock across the creek as quickly and efficiently as possible. To avoid a traffic jam at the Back Road ford, Custer attempted to find additional crossings at other points. The shallow creek wound eastward though low meadows for more than a mile and a half to Mt. Clifton (also known as Clifton Mills). Within that distance, low banks and a firm bottom offered

---

3 Perkins, *Three Years*, 289.

4 Hannaford memoir; Pennington relieved Lt. Col. George Purington of command of the first brigade in Custer's division on October 7. *OR* 43, pt. 1, 102.

5 Rodenbough, *18th Regiment*, 60.

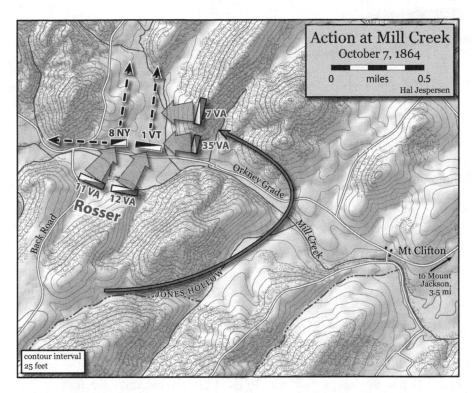

Action at Mill Creek
October 7, 1864

0   miles   0.5
Hal Jespersen

7 VA
8 NY 1 VT
35 VA
11 VA 12 VA
Rosser
Orkney Grade
Mill Creek
JONES HOLLOW
Back Road
Mt Clifton
to Mount
Jackson,
3.5 mi

contour interval
25 feet

multiple possible crossing places, most notably the ford at Clifton Mills itself, which was fed by three country roads. Custer's division, along with the herds of livestock and the long caravan of refugees, crossed the creek successfully. Once on the north side of Mill Creek, however, at some point in the afternoon, Custer's column mysteriously stopped moving, and portions of the livestock herds were corralled.[6]

The halt permitted Rosser enough time to close up on Custer's rear and plan an attack. Rosser's artillery, rolling with Munford's brigade, had not yet arrived, but Rosser refused to wait.[7] From the high ground south of Mill Creek, he wolfishly looked for a way to get at the Federals. Custer's rear guard continued to hold the ford at the Back Road, so Rosser ordered Col. Richard Dulany to take a mounted detachment through a hollow to the left, cross to the north bank somewhere downstream, then swing upstream to

6 Hannaford memoir.

7 Notebook of Beverly Whittle.

outflank the defending Federals and to open the ford for the rest of Rosser's troops. With the 35th Virginia Battalion and Capt. Dan Hatcher's squadron from the 7th Virginia Cavalry—perhaps 220 men total—Dulany easily crossed and moved upstream. Riding in the lead, Captain Hatcher ran into a group of Federals coming directly at him, and, as was the custom in the Laurel Brigade, he immediately ordered his men to charge. The Federals fled, and Hatcher continued on to a high hill overlooking the ford Rosser wanted opened. Dulany halted his little command on the hill to survey the situation.[8]

Below spread plenty of Federals—New Englanders and New Yorkers, most of whom belonged to Lt. Col. John Bennett's 1st Vermont Cavalry. The ranks of the 1st Vermont had recently been replenished, and the regiment numbered 400 officers and men. More than a third of them were raw recruits, and they were in for a harsh baptism at Mill Creek.[9] Bennett's men had been holding the ford for hours while the rest of Custer's regiments, batteries, and wagons, along with the refugees and the cumbersome livestock herd, processed northward. Nothing noteworthy had happened until around 2:00 p.m., when delays ahead in the column forced the tail of the division wagon train to halt. Bennett did not know the cause of the delays, but he knew his assignment was to hold his ground until the train began moving. Meanwhile, Confederate activity at the ford increased, and Bennett had his hands full maintaining his position against Rosser's spirited harassment. Bennett sent calls for help—three of them—but only a small part of the 8th New York Cavalry and a few dozen men of the 1st New Hampshire Cavalry came to the Vermonters' relief. It was at this point that Dulany's Confederates appeared on a hill just to the east, and Bennett likely realized he was in for serious trouble.[10]

On the hill sat the 35th Virginia Battalion, six companies of Virginians and Marylanders, some of whom had been born and raised not far away. The battalion coveted the nickname "the Comanches," bestowed by Rosser after he watched them in a ferocious charge in the fight at Parker's Store a year

8 Myers, *The Comanches*, 336

9 Benedict, *Vermont*, 2:661.

10 *OR* 43, pt. 1, 544-45.

earlier.[11] According to Capt. Frank Myers, who commanded the battalion on October 7, Colonel Dulany sat on the hill and studied the scene for so long that the Federals opened an accurate rifle fire. Myers spoke up: "Colonel, give us orders and let us do something quick." Dulany, a gentlemanly horse breeder from Northern Virginia, merely replied, "Be cautious." Myers knew Dulany was hard of hearing and thought perhaps the colonel had not understood him, so he repeated his request. Dulany merely repeated his reply. Thinking the best opportunity to attack had already passed, Myers could no longer bear to idly watch the moments fly by. Taking matters into his own hands, he ordered his 200 or so Comanches to charge.

Meyers saw three groups of Federals, only one of which was formed to meet his charge. True to their name, the Comanches continued pressing the attack regardless of the odds. "No halt was intended or attempted," Myers wrote. Bennett's Vermonters stood quietly awaiting the Comanches—a fatally flawed tactic. The experienced Vermont officers likely knew a line of cavalry must meet a charge with a countercharge to have any hope of success, but no one issued the order to do so. Instead, the Federals stood idle until the Comanches galloped within 10 steps—and then broke. "In a very brief space," remembered Myers, "the battalion was among the Yankees, neutralizing their superiority in numbers and carbines by a very free use of their pistols and sabres." Rosser alertly seized the moment and immediately sent the 11th and 12th Virginia regiments hurtling across the abandoned ford.[12]

Lieutenant Colonel Bennett later blamed the unsteadiness of his new men—about 150 recruits who had never "drilled a day or heard a shot in earnest"—for the resulting chaos. During the scattering flight from the ford, Bennett, still hoping for help, tried to reform his broken command, but neither he nor any other officer could do anything to get the frightened men to stop. For two miles the Federals ran—past wagons, ambulances, captured livestock, and everything else. They did not stop until they reached the safety of the main body of their brigade. Rosser and his men—enraged, contemptuous, and filled with the joy of the fight all at the same time— pushed on in their pursuit. Farther ahead in Custer's column, an

11 John E. Divine, *35th Battalion Virginia Cavalry* (Lynchburg, VA, 1985), 16, 42, 76; Myers, *The Comanches*, 237-38.

12 Ibid., 336 -37.

unsuspecting trooper from Ohio recalled the strange sensation that came over him as he became aware of the chaos and fear rushing toward him from the rear. He heard "a noise like a 'mighty rushing wind'" followed by "a most terrific yelling" and a burst of musketry. Soldiers, cattle drovers, teamsters, and refugees broke and ran in many directions but mostly north. The Ohioan thought "the vision of Satan could not have added to the look of fear in their panic stricken countenances."[13]

Amid the swirling confusion, Capt. George Baylor and his men of the 12th Virginia Cavalry spurred their mounts northward from the ford and deeper into the bowels of the snakelike Federal column. The Virginians met little resistance and found that any disorganized Federals in their path preferred flight rather than surrender or combat. One Southerner thought Custer's men at Mill Creek, "could not withstand men who were seeking vengeance rather than victory." Baylor came upon many abandoned wagons, traveling forges, and hundreds of sheep. While some Confederates took charge of the captures and hastily turned them southward, Baylor and most of the 12th Virginia troopers continued pushing after the Federal fugitives. When they came upon some of Custer's men in a defensive position behind rails in a stand of woods, they charged and drove them off. The effort was meant to buy time with which to secure the captured forges and livestock. The Confederates gathered their trophies and withdrew toward the Mill Creek ford.[14]

For much of 1864, newspapers and army camps had been filled with stories of disease, starvation, frostbite, and other sufferings endured by captives in prisons. The misery and death occurred in the North as well as the South. Prisoner exchanges were stopped in 1864, so any man who surrendered knew he was heading to prison—if he were fortunate. As the Confederates had already demonstrated, they were not always accepting surrenders or offering quarter. Bands of frightened Federals fled westward from Mill Creek into the woods on Little North Mountain and made their way northward through the night to rejoin Custer's column in cheerless camps that night at Columbia Furnace. Many of the Vermonters, however, were taken so quickly they could not run. The 1st Vermont reported one

13 *OR* 43, pt. 1, 545; Hannaford memoir.

14 McDonald, *Laurel Brigade,* 303; Baylor, *Bull Run,* 249.

officer and 36 men captured or missing, and at least one of those men was reported killed after being taken captive. One of Rosser's staff officers reported the capture of nine traveling forges, a pair of caissons, several hundred sheep, "many cattle," and about 40 Yankees.[15]

After Rosser's men withdrew, Custer restored order by reinforcing his rear guard and establishing a strong point, with artillery, to prevent any more surprises. Federal pickets who remained along Mill Creek soon heard curious animal noises emanating from the woods on the south bank. Rosser, too, had men along the creek, and the Southern pickets started tossing taunts and jibes across the stream. "The Johnnies now began twitting us," recalled one Federal, "bleating like sheep + crying 'ho, ho' as tho driving cattle, calling over to us, asking where were our sheep, advising us to be careful as our rations of beef would now be cut short + all such talk, but we generally gave them as good as they sent."[16]

The talk in the Federal ranks was that Custer was furious over the embarrassing lapse at Mill Creek. Who ordered the column stopped? Who ordered the livestock corralled? Why had two hours of marching time been wasted in the middle of the day? Whether Custer ever found a culprit or doled out punishment for the fiasco is unknown, but he pushed his column on to Columbia Furnace, sending the men into camp on the steep high ground on the north side of Stony Creek.[17] There the Federals rested uneasily with their injured pride.

---

15 Beaudry, *War Journal*, 176; Charles R. Farr Diary (1st Vermont), Farr Collection, USAHEC. See also Henry Norton, *Deeds of Daring, or History of the Eighth New York Volunteer Cavalry* (Norwich, NY, 1889), 94; Benedict, *Vermont*, 2:661-62. Benedict, in his history of Vermont military organizations in the war, bases his account of this skirmish on Bennett's report, but Benedict also places this engagement "at a point five miles north of Columbia Furnace," which Bennett does not assert. Bennett, commanding the rear guard, sets the time of the fight at between 2:00 p.m. and 3:00 p.m., the same time that Captain Myers reports that his battalion attacked Custer's rear guard at Mill Creek. Custer's division did not travel north from Columbia Furnace until the next morning, October 8, so Benedict's account is erroneous as to the day and place of the engagement. *OR* 43, pt. 1, 544-45; Ferguson "Memoranda," frame 399. See Appendix B for information on casualties.

16 Hannaford memoir. Captain Baylor relates that men from the 12th Virginia were detailed to move the sheep herd into the mountains. After being put into pasture near Orkney Springs, the livestock eventually came under the control of the Confederate Commissary Department, and the herd was issued as rations to Confederate troops. Baylor, *Bull Run*, 249-50.

17 Hannaford memoir.

Among the Confederates, the small victory sent Rosser's pride surging. He was quick to make sure that word of his success reached Early at New Market. Eager to report any good news from his district, Early sent word of the successful skirmish on to Richmond. Southern newspaper editors, who for months had been laboring to cast depressing news in the best light possible, informed the public of the success. It was a small affair, but giving Custer a black eye boosted the morale of Rosser's men and of Rosser himself. Later, Early would come to think that the minor feat on the Back Road had a negative effect on subsequent events. Rosser became "elated" out of proportion to the size of the small triumphs, claimed the army commander, and "boastingly sent me word that he was going to drive Sheridan across the Potomac." Early was not alone in suggesting the success at Mill Creek may have gone to Rosser's head, making him too confident and too aggressive two days later on the banks of Tom's Brook.[18]

* * *

Along the Valley Pike and its byways on October 7, the sounds of gunshots and the high-pitched yelping of attacking Confederates mingled with the crackling of flames to fill the cold air throughout the day. The leading regiments of Lomax's column gave the Federal rear guard no rest. Lomax's men mistakenly believed the Federals were trying to burn the Confederate hospital at Mt. Jackson, and the Virginians pushed the Federal rear through the streets of the town and northward. Along the pike itself, Federal infantry joined in the destruction of anything that could be of use to the Confederacy.

At Edinburg, events took a dramatic turn after the Federals set fire to the Grandstaff Mill on Stony Creek. The pleas of two young women successfully penetrated the hard heart of a Federal officer—some say it was Sheridan himself—who ordered the mill spared. Northern soldiers joined townspeople in dousing the flames.[19] Nevertheless, the invaders found no

18 Munford, "Reminiscences . . . No. 3," 135; "Relating to the Annals. General Early Criticises the Recent Contributions of General Rosser," *Philadelphia Weekly Times*, May 17, 1884; George E. Pond, *The Shenandoah Valley in 1864* (New York, NY, 1883), 204.

19 John L. Heatwole, *The Burning: Sheridan's Devastation of the Shenandoah Valley* (Charlottesville, VA, 1998), 208.

gratitude or goodwill in the hearts of the people of Edinburg. A Federal staff officer recalled the "universal manifestation of hate and contempt" with which the people of Edinburg treated the Federals as they moved through town. The citizens eagerly awaited the arrival of the Southern cavalry, which was not far behind the Federals, and the white-haired old men of Edinburg had all dressed in gray or butternut to show their support. "The fair sex of the town," the Northerner wrote, "were done up in their very best attire, for the purpose, as they contemptuously informed us, of saving at least one suit, believing as they alleged, that we intended to burn out the place, but really for the purpose of giving a cheerful welcome to their friends in gray, whom they momentarily expected to dash into town." Even the children of the village joined in the cheers for Jefferson Davis and General Lee to taunt the hated "Yankee Vandals" as they rode out of town.[20]

After the Federals went into camp on the evening of October 7, Capt. Theodore W. Bean, a Pennsylvanian, saw hundreds of refugees continue northward. Many of them, he explained, were Mennonites or "Dunkers" —pacifists who would not support either side in the war. With the loss of their farms, they headed north to seek churches of their faiths in Pennsylvania, where they might find assistance through the coming winter. Sheridan provided wagons to the refugees, but the families could not take everything with them and had no choice but to leave many of their possessions behind. The Federal soldiers riding from farm to farm burning and destroying did not hesitate to help themselves to the abandoned goods. "It was no infrequent sight," Captain Bean recalled, "to see our soldiers casting off boots, socks and underclothing, in exchange for the better and cleaner that would be freely offered them by these distressed people, from the abundance that they were leaving behind them." The Federal troopers were living high on the butter, soft bread, chickens, mutton, ducks, pork, apple butter, and beef they gathered each day. Each morning, after the invaders moved out and left beside their cold campfires whatever they could

---

20 Bean, "Sheridan in the Shenandoah." Soldiers and mapmakers frequently labeled the town "Edenburg." John Wayland, a prominent historian of the Valley, wrote that "the name of the town has sometimes been written 'Edenburg,' and was explained as a comparison of the locality to the Garden of Eden." John W. Wayland, *The Valley Turnpike, Winchester to Staunton and Other Roads*. Typescript (Winchester-Frederick County Historical Society, vol. VI, 1948), 28; John Milton Hoge, "A Journal by John Milton Hoge, 1862-5," Mary Hoge Bruce, ed., privately published.

not carry or consume, the non-refugees—the newly destitute residents of the area—entered the abandoned camps to scavenge amid what had recently belonged to them or their neighbors.[21]

On the morning of October 8, the Federals pulled out of their camps amid snow squalls. The air was cold enough to set many men wishing for an overcoat, but most troopers had only the warm weather gear they had been wearing all summer, and so they shivered.[22] In the morning chill under a ragged gray sky that set a dreary tone, Merritt's men continued the work of destruction along the Valley Pike. Colonel Thomas C. Devin reported that his brigade, specifically the 9th New York Cavalry and the 1st New York Dragoons, burned 115 barns and 21 mills, more than 200 stacks of hay and grain, 60 acres of corn, and 18,000 bushels of wheat—in addition to herding away 684 head of cattle, sheep, and hogs. At Woodstock, the New Yorkers burned a locomotive and the railroad depot.[23] Colonel James Kidd's brigade brought up the rear, burning or driving off whatever Devin's men had missed while parrying thrusts by Lomax's pursuers.

The 1st, 6th, and 5th Michigan regiments, Kidd's three rearmost outfits, arrived at Woodstock to find the village burning. One Federal officer thought the burning and devastation had broken down order and discipline, and by October 8 the Federal troopers had become "careless, irresponsible and undisciplined." Gusting winds fanned the flames consuming the barns and the railroad depot torched by Devin's troopers, spreading them to nearby dwellings. An observer thought that if the fire had begun upwind of town instead of downwind of the town, it would have spread so rapidly that "no effort . . . could have saved the place."[24] Troopers of the 1st and the 6th Michigan regiments dismounted to help citizens fight the fires while the men of the 5th Michigan, serving that day as the rear guard, watched for the arrival of the pursuing Confederates.

21 Bean, "Sheridan in the Shenandoah"; "Some Personal Recollections of George W. Towle," *The Second Mass. and Its Fighting Californians*, accessed March 12, 2015, http://www.2mass.reunioncivilwar.com/References/Hist-Towle%20Memoirs.pdf.

22 Beaudry, *War Journal*, 176.

23 *OR* 43, pt. 1, 477. Devin's substantive rank was colonel with a brevet to brigadier general.

24 Bean, "Sheridan in the Shenandoah."

In an article meant for publication in a Massachusetts newspaper, artilleryman George Perkins wrote of what he witnessed in the streets of Woodstock as the fires spread: "I shall never forget the scene. Families turned out of house and home hurried down the street to escape the flames, fathers and mothers with arms full of helpless children, and others hanging on to their garments. Terror stamped every countenance." In an aside to the editor of the paper read by those safe in New England, Perkins added, "Let your readers be thankful they live so far from the actual scene of conflict."[25]

Lieutenant Colonel William Thompson's brigade led Lomax's column forward, and those Virginians were first to see the smoke rising from Woodstock. One furious Confederate recalled that the sight of the smoking village enraged his comrades, and, "with vengeance in their hearts for the cruel persecutors of the defenseless, they rushed with head-long speed through the burning town, carrying everything before them."[26] Colonel Kidd wrote that his Michigan men fought the flames in Woodstock willingly and energetically, "but were interrupted in their laudable purpose by Lomax's Confederates, who charged the rear guard into the town."[27] The Michiganders fled and reformed north of the village, but both brigades of Lomax's division kept coming and pitched into them. The enraged Southerners chased the Michigan men for five miles before falling back to make camp at Woodstock.[28]

On the Back Road, Rosser's angry men harassed the Federals just as fiercely. At sunrise on October 8, Rosser had his men in the saddle and moving. Colonel William H. F. "Billy" Payne's small brigade led the way, followed by Rosser's Laurel Brigade. As Custer's men broke camp at Columbia Furnace and continued northward, the rear guard composed of the 18th Pennsylvania Cavalry set fire to the iron furnace and its outbuildings. Payne's men followed so closely that the buildings were still blazing when they rode by.[29]

25 Perkins, *Three Years*, 300.

26 A Soldier, "The Cavalry." Textual evidence establishes that the correspondent served in Jackson's Brigade.

27 Kidd, *Personal Recollections,* 400.

28 Hoge, *A Journal;* A Soldier, "The Cavalry"; Kidd, *Personal Recollections*, 400.

29 Rodenbough, *18th Regiment*, 60; Neese, *Three Years,* 319.

Payne's men were active and aggressive, just like their leader. At 34, Payne combined learning, intelligence and a warrior's heart. He had such complete confidence in himself and his men that he claimed he never expected to lose a fight. Billy Payne attended the Virginia Military Institute before studying law and rising to Commonwealth's attorney in Fauquier County, Virginia. After enlisting as a private at the beginning of the war, he rose to colonel while compiling a record of audacity. In the battle at Williamsburg in May 1862, a bullet tore through Payne's face and mouth, smashing out teeth, fracturing his jaw, and cutting his tongue in half. He did not bleed to death only because a surgeon happened to be nearby to pinch with his fingers the arteries in Payne's mouth. During recuperation, Payne could only consume fluids. He feared his broken jaw would never "unite." His weight dropped to 100 pounds, and he communicated only by mumbling out of the corner of his ravaged mouth.[30] Many men would have sought peace after enduring such an ordeal, perhaps thinking they had done their share. Not Payne. After months of recovery, he went again in search of battlefields as soon as he was able. Badly wounded again and captured during the movement to Gettysburg, Payne spent months in a Federal prison camp. As soon as he was exchanged, he again went in search of combat. Payne fully embraced the warrior ethos of courage, patriotism, and self-sacrifice, and he was devoted to his country, which was Virginia. A bronze plaque on his grave proclaims that loyalty was the essential motivation of his life: "His love for his state was the absorbing passion of his life, the motive of every action, the inspiration of every

---

30 W. H. F. Payne to father, June 19, 1862. Hunton Family Papers, Virginia Historical Society.

feeling. He loved Virginia with a love brought from out the historic past. There was no pulse in his ambition whose beatings were not measured from her heart." After experiencing combat and seeing how it affected men, Payne admitted to some puzzlement that he had never been in the paralyzing grip of fear. "I used to be amazed at the clearness & energy of my thoughts & feelings," he wrote after the war without a hint of boastfulness. "I never was in doubt on a battlefield. I never remember to have hesitated about the right thing to be done." The joy he had known on the battlefield was sublime, and his postwar writings contain hints of disappointment that he had survived. He believed that to perish upon the battlefield would have been "The death of all deaths—in the arms of brave men, with the roar of the guns & the rush of the Cavalry and the shout of victory, (that voice of the Gods) as the last sound which was heard before entering the presence of the Gods."[31] Such was the *gaudium certaminis*—the joy of the fight—that Payne believed was the chief soldierly virtue that animates all true warriors.

Payne and his men pressed northward on the Back Road looking for an opportunity to attack. Around noon, about three miles south of Tom's Brook, they came upon the Federals where the terrain was favorable for a charge. Payne ordered his troopers to drive in close and use their sabers.[32] Riding with Payne's cavalrymen were three irrepressible artillery officers— Maj. James Breathed, Capt. John Walton Thomson, and Lt. John "Tuck" Carter. Breathed had helped lead the charge across Mill Creek the day before, shouting for the men to use their sabers rather than their guns. Breathed found kindred spirits in 20-year-old Thomson and Carter, both of whom had reputations for reckless courage. All three, when their duties to their batteries would permit, routinely volunteered to ride with the cavalry whenever they whiffed the prospect of a fight.

A Virginian by birth, the remarkable Breathed spent his formative years near Hagerstown, Maryland. When still a teenager, he began intern work with a local physician and at the age of 21 completed studies at the School of Medicine of the University of Maryland. High-spirited and adventurous, Dr.

---

31 Richard M. McMurry, *Virginia Military Institute Alumni in the Civil War* (Lynchburg, VA, 1999), 186; Hotchkiss, *Virginia*, 647; Kenneth L. Stiles, *4th Virginia Cavalry* (Lynchburg, VA, 1985), 130; Welsh, *Medical Histories*, 164-65; Lewis Marshall Helm, *Black Horse Cavalry* (Falls Church, VA, 2004), 295, 296.

32 Ferguson, "Memoranda," frame 399.

Breathed became an early follower of Jeb Stuart and a lieutenant in the Stuart Horse Artillery Battery when it was formed in 1861. He had no training as an artillerist, but his eagerness to learn, his energy, and most of all his aggressiveness earned him rapid promotion and widespread respect. The cavalry officers with whom his battery served marveled at his enthusiasm and prized Breathed for his fearlessness. "The sound of his guns excited him to madness," wrote one officer, who added with some hyperbole, "He fought artillery as if it was a side-arm. He considered any distance except muzzle to muzzle as being too far off." Major Breathed often slept beside his guns, and though he commanded all of the horse artillery in Rosser's division, he habitually helped aim and direct the fire of the pieces in battle. Breathed was riding with Rosser's column, and specifically with the brigade of the combative Payne, because he wished to be in on the action. He knew that if they could get close enough to the enemy, Payne would attack.[33]

According to one Federal trooper, for the rest of the day the rear of Custer's column was "menaced considerably" as Payne charged repeatedly. The 18th Pennsylvania Cavalry formed Custer's rear guard and had more than it could handle, so the 2nd New York Cavalry was sent back to help.[34] "In all the hard service which the regiment did," declared Maj. John Phillips, the commander of the 18th Pennsylvania, "it had no harder day's work than that of the 8th of October, 1864. It was one continued running fight." The Pennsylvanians lost four killed, seven wounded, and five missing— significant losses for mere skirmishing.[35]

The frantic work of the Pennsylvanians staving off attacks on the rear allowed the rest of Custer's column some rest. Part of Col. Alexander Pennington's brigade was watering horses in Tom's Brook and resting on the hills near the hamlet of Mt. Olive. It would have been a lovely spot had the sun been a little warmer. Twenty-six-year-old Alexander Cummings McWhorter Pennington, Jr., may have been basking nonetheless in the warm

---

33 Ferguson, "Memoranda"; Bridges, *Fighting with JEB Stuart*, 314-17, 15; Trout, "The Hoss," 13-16; Untitled memoranda, Munford-Ellis Papers, Box 17, folder "Writings: Civil War Mss. of Thos. T. Munford (Rosser-Munford Dispute) 4 of 4."

34 Beaudry, *War Journal*, 176; Rodenbough, *18th Regiment*, 60; *OR* 43, pt. 1, 540.

35 Rodenbough, *18th Regiment*, 28. See also A.B. Nettleton, "How the Day Was Saved at the Battle of Cedar Creek," in *Glimpses of the Nation's Struggle: A Series of Papers Read Before the Minnesota Commandery of the Military Order of the Loyal Legion of the United States*, vol. 1 (St. Paul, MN, 1887), 1:260. Nettleton served in the 2nd Ohio Cavalry.

Artist Alfred Waud sketched dismounted troopers of the Federal rear guard shaking out a skirmish line to oppose the pursuing Confederates. Waud's caption, "Rosser attacking the rear—Oct. 8th 1864 nr. Harrisonburg. Shenandoah Valley," seems to be general rather than specific since Rosser's men were more than 30 miles from Harrisonburg on October 8. *LOC*

glow of his recent promotion. A West-Point classmate of Wesley Merritt, and a close friend of George Custer, Pennington had spent all but one week of the war in the artillery, where he had proved himself exceptionally proficient and earned much respect among the men with whom he worked. For the past year and more his battery had been attached to Custer's Michigan Brigade, playing an important, but unsung, role in Custer's rise to prominence. Pennington particularly distinguished himself at Gettysburg, where the extraordinary accuracy of his battery's fire drew admiring comment not only from his brother officers but from Confederate officers as well. One superior declared that Pennington was "always ready, always willing," and Custer prized him for his efficiency and professionalism.[36] He was from the powerful Penningtons of New Jersey, with two governors and a congressmen featuring prominently in his family tree, including his father, who had sat in Congress while his son studied at the military academy. In September 1864, the colonelcy of the 3rd New Jersey Cavalry stood vacant, and Pennington suddenly found the path to advancement open to him. He lay down on September 30 a brevet captain in the 2nd U.S. Artillery, and the

36 *OR* 27, pt. 1, 994.

A. C. M. Pennington, posing early in the war in the uniform of a lieutenant of artillery. He received his first cavalry command just eight days before leading a brigade in action at Tom's Brook. *LOC*

next day found himself a colonel of cavalry. October 1 also happened to be George Custer's first day as commander of the Third Cavalry Division, which, by chance, included the 3rd New Jersey. Even more fortuitous for Colonel Pennington was that the brigade to which his New Jersey regiment belonged had no brigadier general to command it. Just six days later, General Custer appointed him to lead the First Brigade of the Third Division, completing Pennington's nearly miraculous rise from commanding a few guns and artillerymen to commanding a brigade of five regiments, a battalion, and a battery in less than eight days' time.[37]

Toward noon on October 8, as Pennington's men watered and washed in Tom's Brook, the day turned pleasant. The brook flowed out of the mountains just a quarter-mile to the west and bubbled eastward over a stony bottom between rocky banks. The ground south of the brook rose in a long, picturesque slope to a plateau, which the locals referred to as Coffman's Hill.[38] A few weeks earlier, a group of Federal prisoners had rested by Tom's Brook, which one Connecticut Yankee thought possessed astonishing restorative powers. Perhaps because he was a Romantic disposed to see the world as a great poem, or perhaps because he was a prisoner of war and arrived there thirsty after a long, hot march—or more likely because he was both—the captive Yankee felt himself entranced and wrote, "Never was nectar more delicious than the water of this stream, nor downy pillow more welcome than the sod on its banks."[39]

Pennington's men likely also enjoyed their brief rest by the brook, but they were jarred from their repose when another attack hit the rear guard less than a mile south on the Back Road. The attack was a strong one, and some of the Pennsylvanians from the rear guard came scrambling in great haste down Coffman's Hill and across the brook. Pennington's men quickly

---

37 *Biographical Directory of the United States Congress.* Pennington, Alexander Cumming, McWhorter, (1810-1867), accessed October 4, 2014, http://bioguide. Congress. Gov/scripts/biodisplay.pl?index=P000213 and http://bioguide.Congress.gov/scripts/bio display.pl?index=P000214; Francis B. Heitman, *Historical Register and Dictionary of the United States Army: From its Organization, September 29, 1789, to March 2, 1903,* 2 vols. (Washington, DC, 1903), 1:782.

38 Some postwar writers describing the action at Tom's Brook have referred to this elevation as "Spiker's Hill." See Appendix C for a discussion of the name of the hill.

39 Homer B. Sprague, *Lights and Shadows in Confederate Prisons, A Personal Experience, 1864-5* (New York, NY, 1915).

formed in line of battle across the Back Road as Federal wagons continued moving northward on the road at a trot, but the Confederates did not push their advantage. Instead, they "blustered," or tried to put on a show of strength atop Coffman's Hill. Pennington's men sat on their mounts in line of battle and calmly watched, but after an hour Pennington saw through the charade and ordered a withdrawal. The Northern regiments remained in battle formation during the retrograde movement to discourage the Southerners from growing too bold, occasionally halting and turning to face the enemy. Payne's Confederates, also in line of battle, followed at what one Federal trooper considered "a most respectful distance."[40]

Philip Sheridan likely did not yet know of Payne's vigor on the Back Road, but he had reached the limit of his patience with what was happening along the Valley Pike. He had the impression that only a few hundred Confederate cavalry had been "dogging at Merritt all day." Riding southward, the commanding general encountered Merritt on the pike and, according to a startled staff officer, used "exceedingly severe" language in demanding an explanation for why the "dogging" rebels had not been punished.[41] Ten minutes before noon on October 8, Sheridan wrote to Alfred Torbert to inform the cavalry commander that he wished the Confederate harassment stopped. "I want General Merritt to turn on them," Sheridan ordered, "and follow them with either the whole or such portion of his force as he may deem necessary. This will be done to-day."[42] Sheridan was clearly annoyed by the necessity of having to order what he believed Torbert should have done on his own. Torbert had fallen into his commander's bad graces two weeks earlier during the Fisher's Hill operations. There, Sheridan had sent Torbert on a long flanking march up the Luray Valley in an attempt to get in Jubal Early's rear at New Market. Sheridan had hoped the move would result in the destruction of Early's already badly thrashed army. Torbert's movement there had been, in Sheridan's words, "an entire failure," and Philip Sheridan did not long tolerate subordinates who failed.[43] To another commander, Gen. William Averell, he had spelled out exactly what he

---

40 Hannaford memoir.

41 Bean, "Sheridan in the Shenandoah."

42 *OR* 43, pt. 2, 320.

43 *OR* 43, pt. 1, 28-9.

demanded from his cavalry leaders: "I want you to distinctly understand. I do not advise rashness, but I do desire resolution and actual fighting, with necessary casualties."[44] Even Averell, who was one of the more experienced cavalrymen in the Union army, could not please Sheridan, who fired him. Torbert could have had no doubts that he might be next.

After watching Pennington's brigade withdraw on this October day, Colonel Payne halted his brigade and waited for the rest of Rosser's division to arrive. When Thomas Munford and his Virginians reached the scene, the two brigades followed in the wake of the Federals more than a mile north of Tom's Brook. Pennington's brigade and the rest of Custer's men had withdrawn to the north of the Tumbling Run, while Payne and Munford, accompanied by Rosser himself, halted not far from the Barb House, a brick home between the South Fork of Tumbling Run and the main course of Tumbling Run a little farther north.[45] Not far away were the earthworks dug more than two weeks earlier by Confederate infantry prior to the disastrous battle at Fisher's Hill. From the high ground east of the Back Road, Rosser's scouts could see flags of the Federal signal station on Round Hill, a prominent mound of wooded sandstone rising conspicuously 300 feet above the Valley floor. The Yankee signal flags wagged vigorously, sending word, no doubt, of Confederate cavalry advancing toward Tumbling Run.[46]

Rosser was now in a very lonely position. He had orders from Early to press the enemy vigorously, and he had done so. In his order of October 7, Early had directed Rosser to go on to Winchester "if you can." Rosser had pushed forward so far that he was close to the pickets shielding the main body of Sheridan's army, which was in camp north of Round Hill. The Federal cavalry had disengaged and drawn off. The path seemed open for Rosser to advance farther northward toward the rear of Sheridan's army and

---

44 Ibid., 505. Sheridan relieved Averell on September 24, 1864. Ibid., 28-9, 49.

45 Ferguson, "Memoranda," frame 399.

46 Tumbling Run crosses the Back Road about four and a half miles north of Tom's Brook. Two tributaries of Tumbling Run (South Fork of Tumbling Run and a smaller unnamed rivulet) also cross the Back Road at lesser distances from Tom's Brook. Sergeant Haden of the 1st Virginia states that Munford's brigade advanced no farther north than Tumbling Run, but, as might be expected, soldiers, and others, were not meticulous in their use of the name "Tumbling Run," and thus imprecision hinders interpretation of accounts of activity in this area. Rosser, "Annals," March 22, 1884; B. J. Haden, *Reminiscences of J.E.B. Stuart's Cavalry* (Palmyra, VA, 1993), 35.

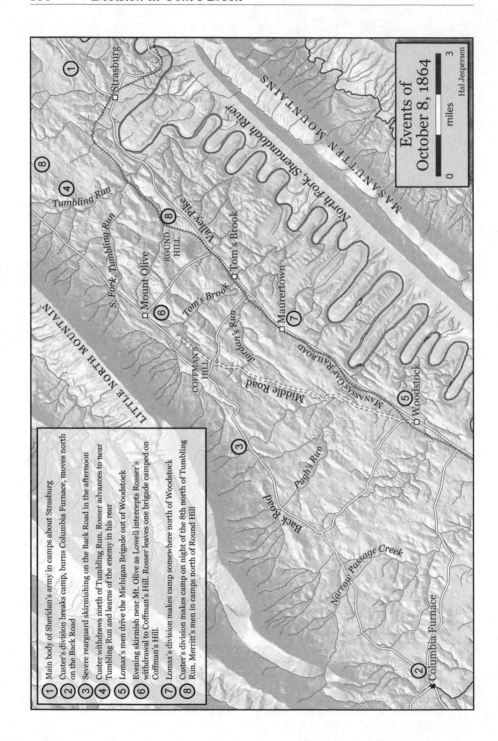

Events of
October 8, 1864

Hal Jespersen

0   miles   3

① Main body of Sheridan's army in camps about Strasburg

② Custer's division breaks camp, burns Columbia Furnace, moves north on the Back Road

③ Severe rearguard skirmishing on the Back Road in the afternoon

④ Custer withdraws north of Tumbling Run. Rosser advances to near Tumbling Run and learns of the enemy in his rear

⑤ Lomax's men drive the Michigan Brigade out of Woodstock

⑥ Evening skirmish near Mt. Olive as Lowell intercepts Rosser's withdrawal to Coffman's Hill. Rosser leaves one brigade camped on Coffman's Hill.

⑦ Lomax's division makes camp somewhere north of Woodstock

⑧ Custer's division makes camp on night of the 8th north of Tumbling Run. Merritt's men in camps north of Round Hill

even on toward Winchester. Rosser understood continuing north from that point would at best take him farther from Early's army, and at worst take him and his men into a trap behind enemy lines. Rosser had reached the moment of decision: Was it possible, in his judgment, to push on to Winchester?

Here, near Tumbling Run, the weight of Early's three-word qualifying phrase "if you can" became heavier than it had been when Rosser first read it the day before many miles to the south. Only Rosser could decide what was possible or advisable and what was not, and only he would be responsible. An important factor in his decision was that the day's pursuit had strung his command out over several miles. With the Laurel Brigade and the trains far to the rear, his division was spread over too much ground. He had only half of his division with him and none of its artillery.

While wrestling with his decision, Rosser received news that altered his situation and gave him a reprieve. An old citizen came to him with news that Federal cavalry was moving from the east upon Rosser's line of withdrawal up the Back Road. Rosser instantly understood that going forward was no longer possible, and he wisely ordered a withdrawal to rejoin the Laurel Brigade. Sergeant Jerry Haden of the 1st Virginia Cavalry recalled that he and many of his comrades had felt anxious being so far forward. "We tarried there longer than most of us thought prudent," he wrote after the war. "I remember very well that Colonel Munford seemed very much relieved when we started to retire."[47]

The old citizen's information was accurate. After Sheridan lost his patience and ordered Torbert to do something about the Confederate harassment, Col. Charles R. Lowell was ordered to take his brigade, along with Lt. Frank Taylor's horse artillery battery, and move across country from the Valley Pike toward the Back Road. As Lowell led his men into the vicinity of Mt. Olive, he alertly realized he had arrived on Rosser's escape route. Seeing the opportunity to drive into the Confederate rear, Lowell pressed northward down the Back Road toward Tumbling Run just as the Southerners retraced their steps southward on the same road.[48] Rosser and his vanguard drew swords and charged. Though descriptions of this encounter are few and lacking in detail, several participants mentioned its

47 Haden, *Reminiscences,* 35.

48 In this part of the Valley, the Back Road was sometimes referred to as the Cedar Creek Grade.

severity. Rosser and his men cut their way through Lowell's regiments and dashed to safety on the high ground south of the brook.[49] The action continued beyond the initial saber charge, for a soldier two miles away on the Valley Pike heard "quite severe" cannon fire toward the Back Road in what sounded to him like a "heavy engagement."[50] One of Lowell's men, trooper George Towle of the 2nd Massachusetts Cavalry, recalled that his squadron was deployed in reserve when it attracted the attention of Confederate artillery. A shot struck the ground short of the squadron's formation and bounded over the heads of the mounted men, creating some consternation in the ranks. Towle, like many soldiers, felt the anxiety of being under fire was greatest when forced to remain idle. "Much to my personal relief," he admitted, "we were ordered to deploy as skirmishers and shortly after that to advance." An officer informed brigade commander Lowell that the 2nd Massachusetts was practically out of ammunition, to which Lowell laconically replied, "That makes no difference, advance." The regiment went forward, and, perhaps as Lowell had suspected, the Confederates withdrew. Years later, Confederate brigade commander Colonel Munford remembered this short, sharp fight because of the loss of five young troopers of his 2nd Virginia Cavalry—five of "the very best boys . . . all of them beardless boys."[51]

*   *   *

To the east on the Valley Pike, meanwhile, Torbert complied with the letter of Sheridan's noon directive, but not with its spirit. As always, Sheridan expected a vigorous response, but Torbert merely ordered Merritt to send a force to learn the Confederates' strength. Merritt sent James Kidd's tired men to retrace their steps on a reconnaissance southward to Woodstock.[52]

---

49 Kidd 446, 460, 465; McDonald, *Laurel Brigade,* 303; Ferguson, "Memoranda," frame 399.

50 Perkins, *Three Years,* 290.

51 "Recollections of George W. Towle"; Munford, "Reminiscences . . . No. 3," 136.

52 *OR* 43, pt. 2, 320.

Since finding Woodstock in flames earlier in the afternoon and charging into the streets to force the Federals out, Lunsford Lomax had pressed northward. When nearing Maurertown, he feared he was too far ahead of Rosser's progress on the Back Road and halted. Lomax eventually withdrew nearer Woodstock and sent word to Early of his location and the presence of the enemy. Not wishing to push forward blindly, Lomax decided to wait until he had more information and ordered his men to make camp. Soon, however, Lomax heard gunfire from the Back Road—the sharp skirmish between Lowell's men and Rosser's. Understanding immediately that the enemy might be concentrating on Rosser, Lomax ordered his men back into their saddles and led them forward to attack the Federals and prevent them from converging on Rosser. Lomax once again struck Kidd's Michiganders, the same men he had chased out of Woodstock earlier in the day. Kidd recalled that about a mile south of Tom's Brook, the Confederates came on him in force on both sides of the turnpike. Major Smith H. Hastings and his men of the 5th Michigan Cavalry performed heroic work turning back three of Lomax's charges before retiring to an established defensive line at Tom's Brook at dark.[53]

That evening, the Federal cavalry brigades made camp near Round Hill.[54] The weather took a turn for the worse after dark. The temperature dropped and sleet lashed the camps of both armies.[55] Though Merritt's men might have gained some shelter northeast of Round Hill, Custer's men, in the open fields near Tumbling Run on the Back Road, and Rosser's men on the hills and ridges south of Tom's Brook, struggled to find repose beside their wind-whipped campfires.[56] Munford's and Payne's troopers especially must have found rest difficult. Munford established his headquarters on Coffman's Hill, the high ground just south of where the Back Road crossed Tom's Brook, and posted pickets at the ford and videttes toward Mt. Olive. To Munford's right, closer to the Valley Pike, Payne also put pickets out to

53 *OR* 43, pt. 1, 612.

54 Ibid., 446-47. One regiment each from Devin and Lowell accompanied the reconnaissance. See also Hillman Hall, *History of the Sixth New York Cavalry (Second Ira Harris Guard), Second Brigade, First Division, Cavalry Corps, Army of the Potomac, 1861-1865* (Worcester, MA, 1908), 231.

55 Perkins, *Three Years,* 289-90; Ferguson, "Memoranda," frame 399.

56 *OR* 43, pt. 1, 430.

the north.[57] The Federals, too, sent pickets out toward Mt. Olive, and as the Confederates looked upon a disconcerting number of Yankee campfires they realized, perhaps for the first time, the length of the odds against them in the sparring matches that had filled their days.[58]

Sheridan, too, found rest elusive. After his noon dispatch to Torbert, the Confederate harassment of his army's rear had somehow increased, and his own cavalry seemed unable or unwilling to stop it. "Tired of these annoyances," he wrote in his memoirs, "I concluded to open the enemy's eyes in earnest."[59] Captain George B. Sanford, a Regular Army officer serving on Torbert's staff, recalled that Torbert was summoned to Sheridan's headquarters that night. Sanford thought well of both generals, and of Sheridan he astutely observed:

> He was a wonderful man on the battle field, and never in as good humor as when under fire. This pre-supposes, however, that everyone about was doing his duty as he deemed it should be done. If he judged the contrary one might as well be in the path of a Kansas cyclone. Explanations were not in order, and the scathing torrent of invective that poured out, his shrill voice rising ever higher as his anger grew, while his piercing eye seemed absolutely to blaze, was a sight once seen not likely to be forgotten.[60]

Torbert and Sanford might have guessed that a summons to headquarters was a cyclone warning, and when they arrived Sanford stayed outside while his general went in to meet with the army commander. "I heard a portion of the conversation—as much of it as I deemed it advisable to hear," recalled Sanford. "Then I rode off a short distance and waited for my Chief. I can testify quite freely that Sheridan was 'mad clear through' and was quite willing that everybody should know it. Among other things that he said to Torbert was: 'I want you to go out there in the morning and whip that Rebel cavalry or get whipped yourself.'"[61] The commanding general also made

57 Ferguson, "Memoranda," frame 399.

58 McDonald, *Laurel Brigade*, 304; White's Battalion drew picket duty for the Laurel Brigade on the night of the 8th. Myers, *The Comanches,* 338.

59 Sheridan, *Memoirs*, 2:56.

60 George B. Sanford, *Fighting Rebels and Redskins; Experiences in Army Life of Colonel George B. Sanford, 1861-1892*, E. R. Hagemann, ed. (Norman, OK, 1969), 269.

61 Sanford, *Fighting Rebels,* 283.

clear to his subordinate that he would be literally under the boss's eye, Sheridan declared he would ride to the peak of Round Hill to watch Torbert's performance.[62]

Accompanying Torbert through the blustery night back to cavalry headquarters, Sanford saw that his general was also "mad," but Torbert held his anger to himself. Neither man said anything at all as they rode through the darkness.[63] Torbert dashed off orders to his two division commanders. Merritt was to have his men in the saddle ready to move at 6:00 a.m. Custer would, by that time, be moving southward toward Tom's Brook, where the skirmish with Rosser earlier in the evening had ended indecisively. Custer was to communicate with Merritt so the two could coordinate their advance. Torbert also explained that although they did not know where to find the main body of the Confederate cavalry, they knew it had been on the Back Road the night before. Merritt, therefore, was to move toward the Back Road. Merritt would thus establish a link with Custer after scouring the intervening country for Confederates. At the same time, Merritt was directed to send "a strong reconnaissance" southward on the Valley Pike to find the enemy and learn his strength. Torbert closed his orders by making clear to Merritt that there must be no half measures: "You must put every available man in the fight."[64]

62 A postwar account by John Danby, who served as a scout for Torbert, offers a different version of circumstances of Sheridan's angry order to Torbert. Danby states that Sheridan found Torbert and his staff in a nearby home feasting on a large turkey dinner and that the army commander berated his cavalry chief there in front of his staff. In a newspaper item published more than 23 years after the incident, Sheridan is quoted as saying that he found Torbert at a farmhouse but that he spoke to him outside and told him if Torbert did not "clean out" Rosser then he (Sheridan) would take Torbert's "Division" and do it himself. In his memoirs, Sheridan includes the famous phrase "whip that Rebel cavalry or get whipped yourself!" Both Sanford and Danby include the phrase in their versions, but it is notably missing from the Sheridan version as printed in the newspaper. Sheridan's statements quoted in the newspaper seem to have been made informally to a reporter and do not agree with those in Danby's article or with Sanford's account. John Danby, "Torbert in the Valley," in W. C. King and W. P. Darcy, *Camp-fire Sketches and Battle-field Echoes of the Rebellion* (Springfield, MA, 1887), 361-68; "Sheridan on Rosser," New Ulm *Review* (MN), May 11, 1887; Sheridan, *Memoirs,* 2:56.

63 Sanford, *Fighting Rebels,* 283.

64 *OR* 43, pt. 2, 320-21.

CHAPTER SIX

Decision at Tom's Brook

"We Must Bust Him up Today."

In the camp of the 1st Virginia Cavalry not far from the Back Road on the night of October 8, Sgt. Jerry Haden permitted his men to perform a simple but unusual act: He let them remove their saddles from their weary horses. Sergeant Haden made a point of noting this mundane act because it was a departure from the norm. Unsaddling, he explained, "was rarely ever done when in such close proximity to the enemy."[1] The animals were tired after covering more than 50 miles in three days of skirmishing, and out of pity the troopers thought it safe enough to take the risk of unsaddling so close to the enemy.

Rosser also was confident, and he had reason to be so. After the punishment of Custer's rearguard earlier in the day followed by the successful charge through Lowell's men to gain safety that evening, all on the heels of the success at Mill Creek the day before, Rosser could be pleased. He had followed his orders and been a thorn in Sheridan's side, which is what Early had hoped for. As Rosser considered his plans for the next day, he undoubtedly looked upon the future in light of the immediate past. For three days, he began each day in the role of the aggressor and ordered his men to mount up and move forward after the Federals. All

---

1 Haden, *Reminiscences*, 35.

through those three days it had been Rosser's men who had provoked engagements, and he had little reason to expect the pattern would be broken. In fact, he apparently had no desire that it be broken. Some of his officers tried to persuade him to withdraw in the morning. Though he apparently expressed misgivings, Rosser followed his natural disposition and maintained an aggressive posture. He was concerned that he stood 26 miles ahead of any support or assistance and knew that just a few miles away slept a powerful enemy, though just how powerful he did not know. According to staff officer Capt. William McDonald, however, Rosser "determined to stay where he was, thinking that if pressed by an overwhelming force on the morrow, it would be quite easy to retire in good order."[2] On the night of October 8th, Rosser sent a note to General Lomax on the Valley Pike informing him of his intention to advance at dawn. He may also have written to Early, who years later recalled that in the afterglow of the successes at Mill Creek and elsewhere Rosser had written to say he was going to "drive him [Sheridan] across the Potomac." Early stated he wrote to Rosser "to caution him against rashness," but Rosser never gave any indication he received such a note.[3]

Rosser was mistaken in his belief that he would again dictate circumstances in the morning. The change in routine began as soon as the troopers in the Federal camps rolled out of their blankets. Morning twilight began filtering light into the Shenandoah Valley a few minutes before 6 a.m. on October 9, and the pack animals and wagon train of Custer's division headed north on the Back Road away from the field of the coming engagement. By sunup at 6:20 or so, Custer's men were preparing to move southward on the Back Road. Pennington's brigade, accompanied by Capt. Charles Peirce's battery of the 2nd U.S. Artillery, would move first. Colonel William Wells's brigade would follow. Some of the Federal regiments had been issued an extra 60 rounds of ammunition, so the men had no illusions about what lay ahead.[4]

---

2   McDonald, *Laurel Brigade,* 305.

3   *The State* (Richmond), April 28, 1884. See also Martin F. Schmitt, "An Interview with General Jubal A. Early in 1889," *The Journal of Southern History,* Vol. 11, No. 4 (November, 1945), 560.

4   Tenney, *War Diary,* 133. Peirce's command consisted of the remnants of Batteries B and L of the 2nd U.S. and contained two light 12-pounders under Lt. Samuel B. McIntire and

Since Rosser had camped two miles to the rear, much depended on Colonel Munford, whom Rosser had left on Coffman's Hill. Munford, like all the men in his family, was wholly devoted to the Confederate cause. Older brother William had been in uniform since the beginning of the war and served as a private in a Virginia battery. Younger brother Ellis, also an artilleryman, was killed on the deadly first day of July 1862 at Malvern Hill. Their father, George Wythe Munford, was the Secretary of the Commonwealth of Virginia and as such had verified the governor's proclamation of secession in June 1861.[5]

A small man and a neat dresser with dark, bright eyes, Thomas Munford was a Virginia Military Institute graduate and a capable officer. That Munford did his job well made it all the more strange that he had been wearing the uniform of a colonel of Confederate cavalry for almost two-and-a-half years—longer than any man in the army. Cavalry chief Jeb Stuart had at least twice recommended Munford for promotion to general, and Robert E. Lee supported Munford's elevation as well. Long after men who had been junior to him in rank were promoted over him, Munford continued in command of his 2nd Virginia Cavalry while only occasionally exercising temporary brigade command. Rosser, one of those elevated over Munford, had been a mere lieutenant at the Battle of First Manassas in July 1861 while Munford was then already a lieutenant colonel. By October 1863, Munford had been promoted one step to full colonel, but Rosser had been raised five grades in rank to brigadier general! Though Jeb Stuart supported Munford's advancement, he did so rather tepidly. In Stuart's eyes, at least, Munford lacked something as a cavalry commander, and it may well have been the dash, the élan, and the forcefulness of character Rosser possessed in abundance. Munford did not lack ambition, however, so in October 1864 he looked upon Rosser as a rival. Nor could Munford retain the self-respect

---

two rifled guns under Lt. Edward Heaton. *OR* 43, pt. 1, 550. See also Heitman, *Historical Register,* 1:669, 519. Though Custer and others reported the division advanced at 6 a.m., Captain Peirce reported leaving camp at between 8 and 9 a.m. *OR 43*, pt. 1, 520, 549, 543, 545; W. G. Cummings, "Six Months in the Third Cavalry Division Under Custer," in *War Sketches and Incidents as Related by Companions of the Iowa Commandery Military Order of the Loyal Legion of the United States,* vol. 1 (Des Moines, IA, 1893), 298.

5   American Civil War Research Database, Duxbury, MA, Historical Data Systems, Inc. http://www.civilwardata.com/index.html; Staunton *Spectator*, June 25, 1861, image 1, col 5.

Col. Thomas Munford in a brigadier general's uniform (circa 1875) commanded the
brigade holding the left of Rosser's position at Tom's Brook.

Anne S.K. Brown Military Collection, Brown University Library

necessary to command troops while accepting that he had been justly passed over for promotion. Munford was a good soldier, a competent commander, and a loyal Confederate, and he bore no great affection for Thomas Rosser.[6]

In the pre-dawn chill of October 9, Munford sent scouts from the 4th Virginia Cavalry out toward the Federals at Tumbling Run. Levi Pitman, a cabinetmaker in Mt. Olive, was up early and watched the Southerners ride by his home headed north. Not many minutes later he heard gunfire and watched them return in considerably more haste.[7] The riders brought Munford word of Federal activity. This meant trouble, for the pattern of the last few days had been broken. Munford called for the bugler to sound "boots and saddles" and sent a messenger to Rosser—the first of "several" he claimed to send that morning. The colonel then visited his picket line along the brook at the foot of the hill and reinforced it with the rest of the 4th Virginia.[8]

Staff officer James Ferguson recorded the ominous sound of artillery fire reached Rosser's camp, and the general went forward, leaving orders for the Laurel Brigade and the four guns of Capt. Philip Johnston's battery to follow as soon as possible. Rosser took with him a section of two guns from Capt. Jimmie Thomson's horse artillery. Major Edward McDonald of the 11th Virginia recalled meeting Rosser riding toward the sound of the firing. Rosser asked McDonald what he thought of his position, and the major offered no false encouragement: "I told him I thought he was too far away from his support and that I feared he would have a hard time of it."[9]

---

6   Ferguson, "Memoranda," frame 399; Schmitt, "Interview," 558; Letterbook, Jeb Stuart Papers, Virginia Historical Society, Richmond, 19, 37-9; McMurry, *Alumni*, 178. Munford was never promoted to general. In the final week of the war, Fitzhugh Lee would name Munford a brigadier, but the appointment was not binding. In an era of ringing rhetoric and elaborate praise for comrades, Lee's description of Munford as "in many respects a good officer. . . ." seems extraordinarily tepid. Copy of undated letter from Fitzhugh Lee to Marcus J. Wright, John Bolling Papers, Civil War Times Illustrated Collection, USAHEC.

7   Levi Pitman Diary, Levi Pitman Papers, 1831-1892, Special Collections, University of Virginia, Charlottesville, VA.

8   Munford, "Annals"; Munford, "Reminiscences . . . No. 3," 136.

9   Ferguson, "Memoranda," frame 399. The firing may have come from the Valley Pike, where Lomax's troops were about this time moving northward; Edward H. McDonald, *Reminiscences of the War Between the States*, McDonald Papers, Acc. 2131-2, University of North Carolina, Chapel Hill, NC, 115.

Capt. James Thomson, age 20, fought with a portion of his artillery battery in the center of the Confederate line on Coffman's Hill.

Wise's *The Long Arm of Lee*

Whatever ill feeling existed between Munford and Rosser that morning would increase with the passage of time. The mutual dislike was probably natural, for the two men differed in temperament and personality, and those differences manifested themselves in how each man commanded troops. Rosser, of course, was relentlessly active and aggressive. Munford was more deliberate. Munford weighed alternatives. Rosser sought to control events. A rule of thumb commonly employed when measuring the intangible qualities of a commander balanced the man's "dash" against his "discretion." A good officer needed both, and too much of either quality would negatively affect the commander's overall performance. Recklessly aggressive officers were dismissed as possessing "more dash than discretion," yet too much deliberation could make a commander a passive victim of circumstances—a pawn to fate. Munford thought Rosser too prone toward rashness. Rosser thought Munford too timid. Twenty years later, both men would write accounts of what transpired on Coffman's Hill, and neither account can be considered the testimony of an unbiased man.

Munford was willing to give credit where it was due and believed that in the days before Tom's Brook, Rosser "had done first rate" in managing the pursuit of Custer's division.[10] Ever afterward, however, Munford would see Rosser's decisions on Coffman's Hill as the epitome of rashness. He remembered Rosser riding up that morning and "in a vaunting manner asked

10 Munford to Jed Hotchkiss, October 12, 1897. Hotchkiss Papers, Library of Congress, microfilm roll 49, frame 240.

me 'What was the matter?' I replied, the enemy are moving up to attack us, and we can't hold this position against such odds. In the same tone and spirit he replied, 'I'll drive them into Strasburg by ten o'clock.' I then said they will turn your left—said he, 'I'll look out for that.'" According to Munford, the two men then rode to the picket line, where he had pointed to the masses of the enemy visible in the distance. Rosser himself later stated "the country was blue with them," but he did not reverse his decision to stay and fight. The Federal advance allowed no more time for discussion, and Munford rode off to reposition some of his troops.[11]

Whether Munford recalled or related the conversation accurately, the declaration "I'll drive them into Strasburg by ten o'clock" is not out of character for the belligerent Rosser, and it also supports evidence he had alerted Lomax the night before that he intended to act offensively on the morning of October 9.[12] Moreover, regardless of the words Rosser used and regardless of his manner—"vaunting" or otherwise—Munford had accurately rendered the essence of the conversation: Rosser had decided to fight. Perhaps he had decided earlier that morning, or perhaps impulsively and reflexively while in conversation with the wary Munford, but there can be no doubt that despite later protestations to the contrary, Rosser had decided to fight. Munford, or anyone else familiar with Rosser and his history, could not have found the decision surprising.

But the situation was not the same as it had been the night before when Rosser informed Lomax he would take the offensive. The Federals had turned to meet him and were advancing, so Rosser had lost any initiative he might have expected to hold. Now, he would have to wrest the initiative from the Federals. Given these new circumstances, Rosser's best option might have been to abandon Coffman's Hill while there was still time to do so and preserve the strength of his division for a fight under more advantageous conditions. Thomas Rosse, however, would have nothing to do with turning tail and decided the best option was to fight.

---

11 Munford, "Reminiscences . . . No. 3," 136; Marginalia on a typescript labeled "from Sheridan's Memoirs Vol 2 Page 56 57 ti," Rosser Papers, Acc. 1171-g, Box 12, folder Miscellaneous Writings by and about Gen. Thomas L. Rosser.

12 The sentence also echoes, in spirit, at least, the boast of driving the Federals into the Potomac that Early says he received from Rosser just before the fight at Tom's Brook. See *The State* (Richmond), April 28, 1884.

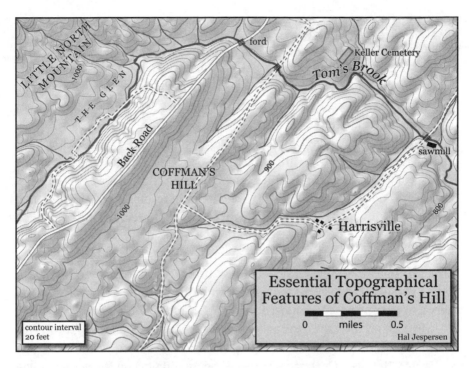

Essential Topographical
Features of Coffman's Hill

contour interval
20 feet

0   miles   0.5

Hal Jespersen

Having decided against withdrawal, Rosser had two choices: advance immediately to meet the Federal attack or prepare defensively to receive it. Rosser did not advance immediately. He deployed his troops and prepared to begin the engagement in a defensive posture. He had not, apparently, much time to acquaint himself with the ground upon which he had chosen to fight, though perhaps he had done so the night before. In either case the virtues of Coffman's Hill as a defensive position had suddenly become of the utmost importance.

As Rosser looked critically at the topography of Coffman's Hill, perhaps for the first time, the dominant terrain feature was purely scenic—the peaked ridge of Little North Mountain loomed skyward less than half a mile to the west, or on his left hand as he faced northward toward the enemy. The hill on which Rosser sat was not truly a hill but more of a bluff that sloped away from the apex in three—not four—directions. This height was the northern end of a miles-long plateau. The plateau ended about a mile south of Tom's Brook. There the ground began a downward slope that stopped abruptly at the rocky bank of the brook, which ran sideways from west to east 130 feet lower than the crest of the plateau. On the opposite side of the brook, the land rose again in a continuation of the plateau. Knolls, pastures and crop fields covered the open country on the north side, which was somewhat lower than the sloping ground where Rosser's men stood south of the brook. To the east, on Rosser's right, the Coffman's Hill plateau became a series of knolls interspersed with ravines cut by rivulets feeding the brook. A wood stood a few hundred yards east of the Back Road, but the general absence of trees made for good visibility.

The brook was not a formidable obstacle and could be crossed in most places, but the large rocks lining the banks and streambed in many places would compel cavalry and artillery to negotiate a crossing with care—a dangerous maneuver if under fire. Even as a mere hindrance for mounted troops, regardless of the uniform they wore or the direction in which they were moving, the rocky creek would direct any commander's focus toward three fords, one at the Back Road, another about 600 yards to the east and a third still farther east at the Smoots saw mill about a mile from the Back Road. These points offered the easiest and closest routes for crossing and therefore would attract the most attention during a fight.[13]

Most important, as Rosser sat on the hill he had chosen to fight for, was that the flanks of the position offered no formidable obstacles to the passage of cavalry. Between Coffman's Hill and the mountains, on Rosser's left, lay a glen—a narrow, secluded valley—with the mountains forming the western side and Coffman's Hill the eastern side. Through this glen ran Tom's Brook, which drained the mountain's slope. The brook wound northerly through the glen along the western base of Coffman's Hill, roughly parallel to the Back Road, before bending almost 90 degrees to the east, crossing the Back Road and continuing along the northern base of Coffman's Hill and on its way to the North Fork of the Shenandoah River about five miles distant. The western slope of Coffman's Hill was steep—the ground rose some 130 feet in about a quarter mile—and in some places rocks and ledges made scaling the slope very difficult for infantry, let alone cavalry. Parts of the slope, however, were less steep and could be climbed by cavalrymen—mounted or dismounted. The most noteworthy feature of the western slope of Coffman's Hill, however, was a small road looping through

---

13 War-era maps show the name of the saw mill as Smutz, Smitz's and Smith's. Unfortunately, the names of the roads leading to these fords vary in local usage. Sources, including cartographer Jed Hotchkiss, refer to the roads leading to *both* of these fords as the "Middle Road."

the glen and connecting to the Back Road in two places. This byway eased passage into and out of the glen considerably. Trees on the slope effectively screened the glen from viewers on crest, raising the possibility that a force could enter the glen without being seen from above.

Eastward from the Back Road, the high ground extended along the southern side of Tom's Brook for more than two miles toward the Valley Pike. No physical feature on the terrain stood out as a bulwark upon which to anchor a defensive position. Wherever the last soldier stood on Rosser's eastern flank, he would see open ground and no topographical obstacles.

Upon first view, especially from the north, the rising slope of Coffman's Hill seems formidable. But, upon closer examination, both flanks of the Confederate position were vulnerable. To properly cover the position, Rosser would not only have to defend his front along the brook, but also his left flank above the glen and his right on the knolls and fields in the direction of the Pike. Like every hill ever fought over since the beginning of time, the strength of Coffman's Hill as a defensive position depended entirely upon the relative sizes of the forces defending it and attacking it. A force of a few thousand men might hold the position for a considerable time, but the breadth of the hill and the accessibility of its flanks made it a perilous defensive position for a force facing an enemy of superior numbers. If Rosser deployed his forces according to standard procedure—with a strong reserve and part of his force fighting as dismounted riflemen at the standard intervals of one man every 15 feet and mounted troops in line of battle behind the riflemen—he commanded enough men to form a fighting front of about a mile. But to properly defend the position on Coffman's Hill—front and flanks—Rosser would need many more men than he had available. The position at Coffman's Hill was simply too broad to defend with 1,400 men and six guns against a numerically superior enemy.

Without breakfast, the men and horses of the Laurel Brigade and the remainder of Payne's small brigade of about 300 men went forward at a trot and arrived on Coffman's Hill at about the same time Rosser did.[14] The sun was up but cast only a pale, gray light as the same raw, gloomy weather—wind and threatening snow—chilled the men gathering on the hills above Tom's Brook. More chilling for the Confederates, perhaps, was the view of the meadows north of the creek. Twenty-four-year-old

---

14 McDonald, *Laurel Brigade,* 305; Munford, "Annals"; Ranson Reminiscence.

artillerymen George Neese "saw the fields blued all over with hosts of Yankee horsemen in full battle array in line and column."[15] Staff officer William McDonald, who had noted the night before Rosser believed he could retire if presented with a superior force, now saw that the hypothetical situation was at hand. "In the fights of the two preceding days the greatly superior number of the enemy had either not been noticed or were disregarded," he explained. "Now, as squadron after squadron deployed in full view, the inequality of the contest was manifest . . . every opening disclosed moving masses of bluecoats . . . covering the hill slopes and blocking the roads with apparently countless squadrons."[16]

As Rosser sat upon his dapple-gray horse on Coffman's Hill, the weight of command might well have pressed upon him heavily. He might have ticked off at least half a dozen reasons for not standing and fighting that morning. He was far from the nearest infantry support, and he would have to make his own decisions. He had exercised command over three brigades for precisely three days, and he did not yet know all his subordinate officers well, nor they him. He had never conducted a fight of the size and scope that now lay before him. Rosser knew Munford bore him no affection and did not know the extent to which he could count on his support. He did not know the strength of the enemy, but what he saw in the meadows north of Tom's Brook told him he was outnumbered. Rosser had, at best, only a passing familiarity with his position. He did not know where Lomax was or whether he would fight on the Pike two miles to the east. Rosser did know his own largest brigade, the Laurels, was severely weakened by fatigue after 12 days and more than 200 miles of continuous marching, much of it through hard rains. The men and horses of the Laurel Brigade, about 40 percent of Rosser's entire force, were in poor condition for a pitched battle.[17]

Finally, Rosser was in pain. He had been shot in the Battle of Trevilian Station in June—his fourth wound of the war—and the lesion on his leg had reopened on October 8—the day before—and pained him so much he confided to his wife that he wished to be at home. A staff officer declared Rosser was in poor health and few officers would have either the patriotism

15 Neese, *Three Years,* 322.

16 McDonald, *Laurel Brigade,* 305-06.

17 Myers, *The Comanches,* 333-35; Ranson Reminiscence.

or the ambition to remain in the field in Rosser's condition. "His wound which was but partially healed when he returned to duty [in August], has broken out anew, and his whole leg from the knee down is spoke of as resembling more a mammoth beet than a man's leg. His life is endangered by every day's exertion and yet he is constantly in the saddle." How all of these burdens weighed upon Rosser or what effect they had on his decisions we cannot know, but it is plausible that they had little influence at all. Nothing in Rosser's long history of conflict suggests he weighed circumstances carefully before entering a fight. The standard practice in his Laurel Brigade was to attack the enemy on sight. In the eternal struggle between deliberation and action, Rosser lived devoted to the latter. With a fight in the offing, all other circumstances and conditions and consequences dwindled to insignificance. He would stand and fight.[18]

Rosser deployed his troops in a shallow, convex arc facing the base of the northern slope of Coffman's Hill. Munford held the left of the line. Keeping the 3rd Virginia in reserve, he sent his 2nd Virginia with the 1st Virginia down to where the Back Road crossed the creek to oppose the Federal advance. Most of Colonel Payne's tiny brigade of 300 men remained mounted higher up the slope in support of the artillery. The Laurel Brigade, under Col. Richard H. Dulany, about 600 strong, formed to Payne's right, and so held down the right flank of Rosser's whole position. The 12th Virginia Cavalry held the right, or east end, of Rosser's line amid the knolls just south of the Smoots saw mill, where a small road crossed Tom's Brook.[19]

As the largest of the three brigades, the Laurels would play a major role in Rosser's plans. Colonel Oliver R. Funsten, Sr., aided by Lt. Col. Mottram

---

18 Welsh, *Medical Histories,* 189; Rosser to wife, October 12, 1864, Papers, MSS 1171-g, Box 1; Daniel Allen Wilson to "My dear Col.," October 21, 1864, Beverley Randolph Wellford Papers, Section 112, Virginia Historical Society, Richmond, VA. In addition to praising Rosser for his physical toughness and tenacity, Wilson noted, "The cavalry is daily increasing in efficiency under his management and daring leadership."

19 Munford, "Annals." In his post-war memoir, Early set the strength of Rosser's brigade at 600 when it reported to him on October 5, but the number of men present for duty on October 9 may have been significantly smaller. Munford believed the Laurel Brigade lost substantial strength that week through desertion. Many of Rosser's men were from the Valley, and Munford suggested that when these men saw fire and smoke in the directions of their homes a large number of them took unofficial leaves of absence due to their anxiety for their families. Munford, "Reminiscences . . . No. 3," 135; M.D. Ball, "Rosser and His Critics," *Philadelphia Weekly Times,* July 12, 1884.

D. Ball, deployed the 11th Virginia and ordered the best-armed men to dismount and move forward on foot.[20] Among these dismounted riflemen was Colonel Ball's brother, Pvt. William Ball of Company I, 11th Virginia. The young Ball was two weeks shy of his 18th birthday, but he was an old veteran, having enlisted with his older brother in April 1861 when just 14 years old.[21] Colonel Funsten kept the remainder of the 11th Virginia mounted about 100 yards behind the riflemen. The 7th Virginia Cavalry deployed beside the 11th Cavalry. To the right of both regiments stood the 12th Virginia.[22] The fourth outfit in the brigade, holding the left of the brigade's position, was the 35th Battalion, also known as White's Battalion, or "the Comanches." On the morning of October 9, they numbered almost 200, and composed about a third of the entire brigade.[23] The regiments in the Laurel Brigade carried a variety of arms, including Sharps carbines, Henry repeaters, Burnside carbines, Colt revolvers and sabers.[24] Most of these weapons had been captured in earlier fights. Lieutenant Nicholas Dorsey, in the absence of more senior officers, commanded the Comanches that morning. At some point during the day Capt. William Dowdell returned to duty with the battalion and assumed command. The fight would open with about 40 of the better-armed Comanches in the creek bottom on foot as skirmishers.[25]

Rosser was blessed with fine artillery but not enough of it. The gun crews were experienced and the leadership was excellent. Like all Confederate artillery, it was handicapped by inferior ammunition and faced a constant struggle to replace worn-out horses. Captain Jimmie Thomson's two guns had arrived in the Valley only days earlier and had been marching

20 Ball, "Rosser and His Critics." The commander of the 7th Virginia, Col. Richard H. Dulany, commanded the entire brigade that day. See Divine *35th Battalion,* 60, 61, 100.

21 Richard L. Armstrong, *11th Virginia Cavalry* (Lynchburg, VA, 1989), 120.

22 Ball, "Rosser and His Critics"; McDonald, *Laurel Brigade,* 305; Myers, *The Comanches,* 338-39; Armstrong, *11th Virginia,* 120.

23 Myers, *The Comanches,* 337, 338.

24 Inspection Reports and Related Records Received by the Inspection Branch in the Confederate Adjutant and Inspector General's Office, M935, 8-J-39, National Archives, Washington, D.C.

25 Lieutenant E. J. Chiswell of Company B commanded these dismounted skirmishers. They deployed in a line a quarter mile long. Myers, *The Comanches,* 338-39. Colonel Elijah White, commander of the battalion, was absent recovering from a wound.

almost every day. Artillerymen Charles McVicar, one of Thomson's gunners, saw the battery's horses had been "in bad shape, almost worn out" when they had arrived in the Valley on October 3, and since then they had pulled the guns more than 70 miles. Thomson put two rifled guns on the face of Coffman's Hill just behind Munford's troopers and about a mile from the advancing Federal line. Captain Philip Johnston's battery of four pieces arrived and went into position near Thomson's two guns.

The deployment of Rosser's artillery might offer clues about his intentions. Massing his artillery near the center of the line committed Rosser's guns—just six precious pieces—to anti-battery fire against the enemy's guns. Rosser and artillery commander Major Breathed certainly understood such a deployment would necessarily concentrate the fire of the Federal batteries on the six Southern guns. Both men were known as exceptionally aggressive and willing fighters eager to close with the enemy. Neither would fight defensively by choice. If, however, they believed they were about to fight a defensive engagement, they might have considered keeping some of the cannon limbered up and ready to respond to threats on the flanks. Instead, their massing of the guns suggests, perhaps, they did not expect to remain on the hill long and therefore would not concern themselves with the flanks. Instead, they were using the guns to take the fight to Custer. In such a scenario, the Southern guns might begin the fight deployed en masse but would not necessarily remain so for long before being directed to join an offensive move. Such a plan would certainly be in character for both Rosser and Breathed. Regardless of what was in the minds of the officers, veteran gunner George Neese did not like the placement of the guns. "It is true the hill we were on was considerably higher and commanded the enemy's position," he explained, "but it was a mistake to put our guns in battery on the slope facing the enemy's battery and line." Firing from a position utterly devoid of cover, the Confederate guns would make excellent standing targets.[26]

Custer had given his long-time friend Colonel Pennington the honor of leading the division forward. The morning saw something of a reunion, for Custer, Pennington, and Rosser, and Wesley Merritt as well, had all been on friendly terms at West Point, though they were not all in the same class.

26 Neese, *Three Years*, 323. Thomson's two guns were commanded by Lt. John W. "Tuck" Carter. McVicar Diary.

Capt. Charles H. Peirce, 2nd U.S. Artillery, whose gunner's neutralized the Confederate artillery on Coffman's Hill.

U.S. Army History and Education Center

Battery commander Charles H. Peirce had served as an engineer sergeant at West Point for years, and he likely knew men on both sides of Tom's Brook from their days on the Hudson River. Pennington deployed his brigade in long lines extending away on both sides of the Back Road. Peirce's U.S. battery would follow Pennington, and Col. William Wells's brigade would stand as the reserve. The 5th New York Cavalry led Pennington's advance, and Custer was right with them, riding beside regimental color bearer Sgt. John Buckley. Likely, nearby rode the band members Custer habitually used to inspire his men with musical accompaniment while advancing into a fight.[27] Moving at an easy trot, the Federals pushed Munford's pickets back, and the long line crested a low ridge and took into view the brook and the surrounding terrain. Custer called a halt. With colors, guidons, and Custer's headquarters flag jumping in the stiff breeze, he sat in his saddle and studied the situation.

From the perspective of the Federals looking up at it, Coffman's Hill presented an imposing sight. A New York officer thought it a "commanding eminence." An Ohioan saw it as a "splendid commanding hill" that gave the Confederates "every advantage of position." Custer saw the enemy arrayed on the high, open slope with mounted troops and six artillery pieces visible. A wood stood on the eastern portion of the hill, but a large number of Confederates seemed to be deployed on the nearly treeless portion toward the west. Closer inspection revealed dismounted troops behind a makeshift breastwork made from pieces of fencing a little way up the hill and more riflemen on foot at the base of the hill along Tom's Brook behind fences, logs and walls. Lieutenant James Brown of the 8th New York believed the

27 Heitman, 1:780; Beaudry, *War Journal*, 178; Rodenbough, *18th Regiment*, 60.

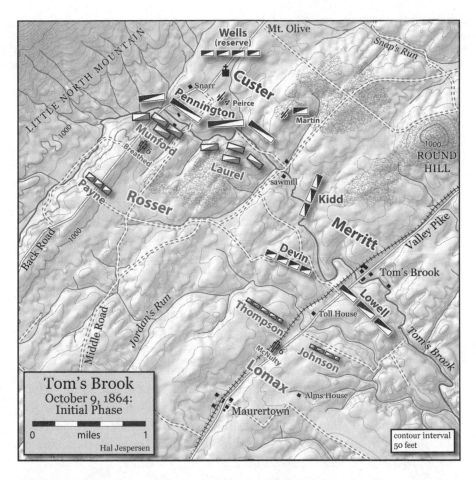

Tom's Brook
October 9, 1864:
Initial Phase

0   miles   1

Hal Jespersen

contour interval
50 feet

Confederates could see "every move we made" and thought, "I suppose they thought themselves secure upon that high hill." Even Custer thought the position "was well adapted to defense."[28]

But Custer was wrong, as was Rosser and all the other observers who were initially impressed by the sight of Coffman's Hill. They had all fallen victim to the "Myth of the Commanding Defensive Position." Though centuries of military history suggest the importance of high ground and "naturally strong" defensive positions, no such position has ever existed in a natural state. Those same centuries of history provide countless examples of high ground and "naturally strong" defensive positions that proved useless

28 Brown memoir; Hannaford memoir; *OR* 43, pt. 1, 520.

because they were impossible to defend. That October 9, 1864, at Tom's Brook would add another such example to the annals. Certainly a position can offer favorable conditions to the defenders, but a strong defense must include enough defenders to not merely take advantage of the ground's inherent strengths but, far more important, to compensate for its weaknesses. Every defensive position draws its strength from having the number of its defenders in the proper proportion to compensate for the position's weaknesses. Custer and Rosser both came under the initial spell cast by the looming slope of Coffman's Hill and both, at least initially, overvalued the strength of the hill as a defensive position. For Custer, the misjudgment was trifling, and he soon compensated for it. For Rosser, the error was momentous, and he never recovered. Simply because he did not have enough men to properly compensate for the hill's flaws as a defensive position, Rosser held a position with fatal weaknesses, as Custer would shortly prove.

A private in the 12th Virginia described this deployment stage of the fight as disorderly with the desultory popping of stray shots and "something like volleys from dismounted men in our front, answered by pistols and a few carbines, with a confusion of swerving horses." Events seemed to move slowly, without direction on either side. "It seemed to us a hap-hazard way of going into action," the soldier recalled, "the firing continued, I don't know how long, with little execution that we could see, and we were beginning to consider it a little monotonous." An officer in the 1st Vermont took advantage of this strange lull to examine the Confederate position, and he retained visual images even years later:

> The ground was favorable for a cavalry fight, the rail fences having long ago vanished from that thoroughfare of armies, and the ground being for the most part smooth and open. The hostile lines deployed along opposing crests, in plain view of each other, in the bright sunlight. . . . Rosser's line was on the higher ground of the two. His guns were posted on the rounded crests, and his skirmish line, dismounted, was behind a line of stone fences, near the base of the ridge.[29]

Custer noticed a cluster of horsemen on Coffman's Hill and gleefully recognized his old friend from West Point days. Custer's and Rosser's men had clashed twice in recent months, at Todd's Tavern in May and at

29 Ranson Reminiscence; Benedict, *Vermont*, 2:663.

Roving artist Alfred Waud sketched the dramatic moment when
Custer bowed to Rosser at Tom's Brook. *LOC*

Trevilian Station in June, but Sunday morning, October 9 was the first time
the two young generals had looked at each other across the chessboard of a
battlefield on which each would direct all the moves. Custer had been in the
habit of leaving messages for his Southern friends from West Point. As the
Federal cavalry moved through an area, Custer would scribble a teasing note
or a friendly jibe and leave it at a farmhouse, knowing the Confederate
cavalry would soon be coming by. In May, Custer had twice left such
messages for Rosser. After the fighting in the Wilderness he wrote that from
across the battlefield he had clearly seen Rosser exposing himself and had
tried to stop Federals from shooting at him. After chiding his friend for
recklessness, Custer added that he wished Rosser to survive so the next time
they met in battle he could give him a good thrashing and they could laugh
about it when the war was over.[30]

Now that the wished-for moment was at hand, Custer at once gratified
his taste for the theatrical by cantering forward alone, removing his
broad-brimmed hat and making a sweeping bow in Rosser's direction.

30 Ball, "Rosser and His Critics"; Ferguson, "Memoranda," 4.

Rosser returned the compliment, and the men of the ranks "sent up a deafening cheer." A Confederate officer who witnessed the exchange found it both touching and typical of the two friends, both of whom were ostentatiously brave. The officer thought of the *moraturi te salutant* of the Roman gladiators: "Those who are about to die salute you." Rosser said to an officer beside him, "Do you see that man in front with the long hair? Well, that's Custer, and we must bust him up to-day."[31]

With all questions of decorum satisfied, the two commanders set their troops to work. The Confederate batteries opened fire first, but had some difficulty finding the proper range because they were firing downhill. Pennington sent three regiments forward toward the brook—his own 3rd New Jersey held the center, and the 2nd Ohio spread out to the left, with Peirce's guns firing over their heads. The 5th New York, with some of the men deployed as skirmishers, stood on the right of Custer's line. The 18th Pennsylvania Cavalry initially stood in a hollow, behind the 5th New York, just west of the Back Road, and the 2nd New York Cavalry supported Captain Peirce's battery.[32]

Charles Peirce had been in the army since George Custer was six years old. He had joined the engineers as a private in 1846, quickly rose to sergeant and was recognized for his performances in the engagements at Contreras, Churubusco and Mexico City. After many years in the garrison at West Point, Peirce was promoted to lieutenant and switched to the 2nd U.S. Artillery. He spent much of the war on recruiting duty in Philadelphia before taking command of a battery in June 1864 and leading it throughout the summer and autumn in the Valley Campaign. On this morning at Tom's Brook, Peirce placed his battery on a hill east of the road and fired at a mass of led horses and dismounted skirmishers. The Federal battery fire was at

31 Rosser, "Annals," March 22, 1884; Ball, "Rosser and His Critics"; Custer, *Boots and Saddles,* 275. Rosser's comments that morning referring to Custer exist in different forms in different sources. No two sources present the comments in anything near identical form, but Rosser's aggressive intent is plain in all versions. The version quoted here, according to Mrs. Custer, was spoken by Rosser to her husband in one of their post-war meetings in Dakota Territory and then passed on to Mrs. Custer in a letter from her husband and thence into her book. See also Munford, "Annals."

32 Hannaford memoir; *OR* 43, pt. 1, 541. Custer reported the small 1st Connecticut Cavalry Battalion stood in reserve, but the battalion, or most of it, had been on detached duty since October 5 escorting a wagon train to Martinsburg, West Virginia. Ibid., 520; Robert B. Angelovich, *Riding for Uncle Samuel* (Grand Rapids, MI, 2014), 469-74.

first inaccurate, and though Custer would fault defective ammunition, the high winds likely contributed to the poor marksmanship. When the Confederate artillery made no direct reply against his guns, Peirce divided his battery into two sections of two guns each and moved one group to a second hill, behind the house of Joseph Snarr and close to where the 18th Pennsylvania stood just west of the Back Road. The two sections kept up a steady fire at a range of about 800 yards.[33]

Stung by Peirce's battery, the Confederate gunners now opened an accurate, plunging fire that impressed both Custer and Peirce. Lieutenant Edward Heaton, with two of Peirce's rifled guns, was able to find partial shelter from Confederate counter-battery fire. Lieutenant Samuel B. McIntire, with his two 12-pound smoothbores in an exposed position, was not so fortunate. One Confederate gun crew launched a magnificent shot though the stiff breeze, and the shell struck with lethal accuracy, exploding just six feet in front of McIntyre's right-most gun. Shards of hot metal tore through the cold air: One fragment shattered a wooden spoke of one of the gun's wheels, another fragment snapped in two the wooden sponge shaft held by a member of the gun's crew. Shrapnel ripped through Pvt. George Davis's leg, which was later amputated. Pvt. August Lent went down with fragments in both legs and Pvt. David Meeks, with wounds in both feet. Other fragments hit George Ball in the left hand and Sgt. Henry Garman in the left shoulder. Every man in the gun crew was hit by at least one piece of shrapnel from that single, well-aimed shell. Pvt. David Pomeroy was killed instantly.[34] Peirce's Regular Army batterymen were not to be outdone and replied in kind. George Neese, serving one of the Confederate guns, remembered he and his comrades were "fully exposed to a raking fire of their guns all the time and all over . . . their shell and shrapnel and solid shot raked and plowed up the sod all around our guns."[35]

Beneath the umbrella of shot and shell sailing from one side of the little valley to the other, the cavalrymen, whether mounted or on foot, searched

33 Heitman, 1:780; Guy Vernor Henry, *Military Record of Civilian Appointments in the United States Army* (New York, NY, 1869), 1:218-19; *OR* 43, pt. 1, 549.

34 Ibid., 521, 549-50; American Civil War Research Database, Duxbury, MA, Historical Data Systems, Inc. http://www.civilwardata.com/index.html.

35 Neese, *Three Years,* 323; Custer claimed Peirce's fire dismounted one of the Confederate guns. *OR* 43, pt. 1, 521.

and probed, looking for an opening.[36] Young Pvt. William Ball of the 11th Virginia recalled the skirmishing in the brook bottom: "We were in easy rifle range, and neither side advanced but stood our ground and kept up a brisk fire. We had a dozen or so men who had Winchester rifles, a deadly accurate gun, shooting sixteen bullets before reloading."[37] Rosser apparently made the first aggressive move by calling upon the 35th Battalion to charge on Custer's left.[38] The Federals parried the thrust. Custer, meanwhile, attempted to test the strength of an obvious point by sending the 18th Pennsylvania to strike where the Back Road crossed the brook, but the 3rd Virginia east of the road and the 1st and 2nd Virginia regiments on the west stymied the Pennsylvanians. Over on the Federal left, Pennington led a mounted charge that dispersed the skirmishers of the 35th Battalion and pushed back the dismounted troopers of the 11th Virginia. The balance of the Comanches charged to the rescue of its comrades. The riflemen of the 35th rallied with the men of the 11th Virginia and repelled Pennington's foray. In the ebb and flow, Payne's Brigade made three countercharges against the Federals.

Custer grew more active in seeking an advantage, and the fighting waxed furious at times as charge and countercharge through the bottomland by the brook kept the contest in balance. Nowhere were men falling in great numbers, so the status quo remained intact. The men in the mounted portion of the 7th Virginia continued to hold the center of the Laurel Brigade's line, supporting the dismounted sharpshooters of the 11th Virginia. The 12th Virginia still stood on the brigade's right. For some of the Southerners, holding their place in line was more than they could bear. Company B of the 12th Virginia, for example, was armed entirely with pistols and sabers, so it

36 McDonald, *Laurel Brigade,* 306.

37 William Selwyn Ball, *Reminiscences*, Virginia Historical Society, Richmond, Virginia; The Winchester Repeating Arms Co. did not exist until 1866. Gun maker Benjamin Henry had designed a lever-action repeater in the late 1850s, and the Henry rifle was sold by Henry's employer, the New Haven Arms Co. which later changed its name to Winchester. Captured Henry rifles were used by some Confederates at Tom's Brook, and it is to this weapon that Ball refers.

38 Rosser later recalled he had given the order to Col. Elijah White, but White had been absent since September 30th and subsequently treated in a Charlottesville hospital for fever. Divine, *35th Battalion,* 108; Rosser, "Annals," March 22, 1884. Finley Anderson, "Shenandoah. The Successful Operations of the Union Cavalry," *New York Herald*, October 14, 1864.

could not respond to the Federal thrusts. Captain George Baylor asked brigade commander Colonel Dulany for permission to move forward where he and his men could engage the Federals. As he had two days earlier at Mill Creek, Dulany refused to permit an aggressive movement. "Finding that our lives would be sacrificed without injury to the enemy," Baylor admitted, "I disobeyed orders and led a charge." The impetuosity of the 21 men of Company B could have had little effect on the Federal advances, however, and they very soon retraced their steps—fewer of them climbing the hill than had hurtled down it a few minutes earlier.[39]

The lead and iron flying through the cold autumn air struck several officers on the Confederate side of the brook: Lt. Col. Mottram Ball of the 11th Virginia and Rosser staff officer Lt. John Emmett both went down with ankle wounds; Lt. Isaac Walke, also a member of Rosser's staff and "a modest and retiring gentleman," was shot dead. A bullet crippled Colonel Dulany's left arm, and he passed command of the Laurel Brigade to Funsten. Funsten's son, Lt. Oliver R. Funsten, Jr., of the 11th Virginia, apparently working in the thick of the action, kept to the field even after his horse was three times wounded. Another bullet hit young Funsten in the thigh, cutting an artery, and finally forced him out of the fight. Captain John Calvin Shoup of the 7th Virginia was one of those men in Rosser's command who was native to the Valley. On Friday, two days earlier, the Federals had burned his family's barns in Timberville. On Sunday on the slopes above Tom's Brook, the Federals killed Shoup, who left his parents, wife and 14-month-old daughter, and joined in death his brother Jacob, who had been killed at Gettysburg.[40]

Custer conspicuously galloped back and forth across the field, his headquarters flag snapping close behind him. Custer tried hard to be noticed wherever he was, but on the battlefield his efforts to grab attention had a practical purpose. First, he tried to offer his men an example of apparent

39 Ball, "Rosser and his Critics"; Baylor, *Bull Run*, 252.

40 Ball, "Rosser and his Critics"; Robert E. L. Krick, *Staff Officers in Gray: a Biographical Register of the Staff Officers in the Army of Northern Virginia* (Chapel Hill, NC, 2003), 122, 294; Gray Jacket, "The Cavalry Fights in the Valley—The Fight of Sunday Last," *Richmond Sentinel*, October 15, 1864; McDonald, *Laurel Brigade,* 307; Christine M. Smith, "Biographies of Homan Correspondents," Rockingham County, VA, GenWeb Project, accessed May 26, 2014, http://www.rootsweb.ancestry.com/~varockin/Homan_bios.htm.

fearlessness and encourage them by exposing himself to the flying bullets and raining shrapnel. Second, like the commanders throughout history who chose to ride splendid chargers into battle, Custer was attracting the attention of the enemy, and if the Confederates were paying attention to the ostentatious officer in front, they might be less likely to pay attention elsewhere. Confederate Col. Munford later looked back on the fight and believed Custer perfectly fooled the Confederates with decoys to the front. Custer had to this point in the engagement used only one of his two brigades and had focused on probing, testing, and learning the strengths of the center and right portions of the enemy's position. When Custer was ready to broaden his explorations, he called upon his additional brigade and directed it toward the glen on Rosser's left. There Custer's horsemen would discover Rosser's great mistake.[41]

---

41 Brown memoir; Untitled typescript, Munford-Ellis Papers, Duke University, Box 17, folder "Writings: Civil War Mss. of Thos. T. Munford (Rosser-Munford Dispute) 4 of 4."

CHAPTER SEVEN

No More Flanks

"It was the Devil Take the Hindmost!"

Before Custer prepared to send men around the Confederate left, Merritt began his forward movement southward on the Valley Pike. One of Merritt's first directives sent troops to explore the undulating ground between the Back Road and the Valley Pike. The men of the 6th Michigan Cavalry moved briskly toward what they believed to be part of the Confederate line on the high ground south of Tom's Brook. With the crackling of combat resounding to their right, the blue-clad troopers crossed the brook, climbed the ridge, and looked for the expected enemy. As the minutes passed and the high ground that should have been occupied by Confederate soldiers was found to be empty, the Michiganders knew they had discovered something important. What they did not know was that neither Lomax to the east nor Rosser to the west had enough men to cover this area of several hundred yards between them, so it was wide open for the Federals to use as they wished. When the 6th Michigan found no enemy soldiers, Col. James Kidd led portions of the rest of the Michigan Brigade into the gap and onto the flank of Rosser's position.[1]

---

1 George W. Barbour diary, 1863-1865, Bentley Historical Library, University of Michigan. Kidd's "Michigan Brigade" included the 25th New York Cavalry. Early on the morning of October 9, two of the five regiments in the brigade were detached for special

Just 10 days earlier, the Michigan brigade had been Custer's command. He and his "Wolverines" had risen to fame together and the troopers loved their former commander as much as they loathed his transfer to another division. They had gone out of their way to mimic his affectations of dress, and each man now sported a red neckerchief like Custer's. One Michigan man believed Custer looked to his left that morning at Tom's Brook, saw the approach of troopers wearing scarlet neck-ties, and happily seized upon the arrival of his former brigade to launch a charge and break the stalemate below Coffman's Hill. In truth, Custer had begun planning for the decisive charge long before Kidd's men were in sight.[2]

Earlier, after Custer had decided to investigate the strength of Rosser's flank by extending his line westward, two scenarios presented themselves. First, Rosser might discover the movement, and, if he did so, he might be forced to abandon his position or to extend his own line to prevent the Federals from moving around his western flank. By attempting to protect more ground with his small force, Rosser would necessarily weaken his line elsewhere. Second, Rosser might not discover the extension to the west, and if he did not, then his left flank would be caught by surprise, turned, and the entire Confederate position rendered untenable. Either result would satisfy Custer. Though the tactic of using his ample reserves to extend his line was basic, Custer nevertheless was alert enough to recognize the opportunity and competently take advantage of it. Rosser did not discover Custer's movement until too late.

Custer began by strengthening his skirmish line. The 18th Pennsylvania Cavalry advanced to the brook on the 5th New York Cavalry's right and extended westward along the streambed and the base of Coffman's Hill. At the same time, Custer called up troops from Col. William Wells's brigade, which had so far stood in reserve. The 8th and the 22nd New York regiments moved behind the Pennsylvanians through woods and ravines north and west of the Snarr house and into the narrow glen below the western slope of Coffman's Hill. The two regiments together totaled only about 350 men, all under the command of Lt. Col. William H. Benjamin of the 8th New York.

---

duty: the 1st Michigan served on the Valley Pike in the early morning and later operated with Lowell's Reserve Brigade, and the 5th Michigan, which was detailed to support Martin's 6th New York Battery. *OR* 43, pt. 1, 448.

2   Grand Rapids *Daily Eagle*, July 8, 1876.

Maj. John Phillips and his troopers in the 18th Pennsylvania Cavalry played key roles in the drama that unfolded at Tom's Brook on October 8 and 9, 1864.
Virginia Magazine of History and Biography

After a short ride through the glen across the broken country, Benjamin brought his men onto flat ground under cover of the steep western face of Coffman's Hill. From his perspective, the rear of Munford's brigade lay just over the crest of the hill, and Benjamin hoped that the Confederates had been so occupied with Custer's energetic efforts along Munford's front at the northern base of the hill that they had not seen the column of New Yorkers slipping through the concealing country of the glen. Under the direction of one of Custer's staff officers, Benjamin put his force in three parallel columns, tails toward Little North Mountain and all eyes facing the western slope of Coffman's Hill.

At the same time, on the Back Road, Custer aimed to hold the Confederates' attention with a thrust. He ordered Maj. John Phillips of the 18th Pennsylvania Cavalry to tear down all the fences to the front and to deploy his regiment as mounted skirmishers. Custer formed the 1st Vermont and 1st New Hampshire cavalry regiments, both of Wells's brigade, in columns with the intention of sending them across the ford and up the hill on the Back Road. At about the same time, Custer sent word to Benjamin to advance his column in support of Phillips's Pennsylvanians. All the while, the fire of Federal Batteries was telling upon the Confederate gun crews in their exposed position. Overmatched by counter-battery fire and seeing the building pressure on their front, the Southern gunners limbered and withdrew to a new position to the rear, farther up Coffman's Hill—a position very near where Colonel Benjamin's flanking attack would soon appear. With the withdrawal of the Confederate guns and the approach of Kidd's Michiganders on the left, and with Benjamin's flanking column in position

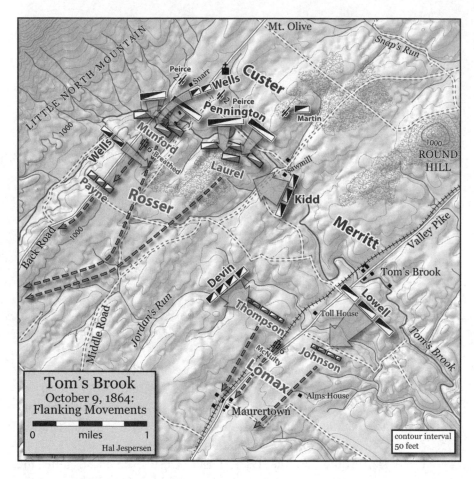

Tom's Brook
October 9, 1864:
Flanking Movements

0   miles   1
Hal Jespersen

contour interval
50 feet

on the right, Custer saw or sensed the moment for the final push had arrived. He unleashed the 1st New Hampshire and the 1st Vermont.[3]

In the glen, Benjamin saw portions of slope were too steep to be scaled by mounted troops, so he aimed his columns at the northern end of the byroad leading out of the glen to the crest of the hill. With all ready, the columns shot forward at the gallop.[4] Charging up the western face of

---

3   *OR* 43, pt. 1, 521; Rodenbough, *18th Regiment*, 60; Anderson, "Shenandoah."

4   *OR* 43, pt. 1, 543-544. Major Caleb Moore of the 8th New York Cavalry was detailed to lead the 22nd New York Cavalry, which was short of officers. Moore's men formed the right column, Maj. Albert L. Ford of the 8th New York the center column, and Maj. Edmund M. Pope, also of the 8th New York, the left column. Benjamin's report implies the 18th

Coffman's Hill, angling left toward Custer's main line, Benjamin's men crested the slope to see Thomson's two artillery pieces to their right athwart the Back Road. Some of the New Yorkers at the head of the column quickly wheeled and charged the guns.[5] To Benjamin's left, shouts of "we're flanked" raced through the ranks of Munford's troopers on the lower slope of Coffman's Hill and in the bottom along the brook. First one, then dozens, then scores of men in the 1st and 3rd Virginia cavalry regiments broke for the rear. Hard on their heels, in column of fours, the 1st Vermont troopers charged across the ford and directly up the road. As the head of this charging column topped the crest, it sustained a heavy shock from the canister of Thomson's guns. Behind the Vermonters, the rest of the Federal column threw down fences on the right of the road and shifted to the west, where they reformed and charged again, firing their Spencer carbines as they went in.[6]

Custer, personally carrying a flag and followed by his staff and his escort, rode in among the men of the 5th New York Cavalry in the bottom by the brook. Gathering men from the left-most companies of the 18th Pennsylvania Cavalry in with the New Yorkers, Custer led the mixed force forward in the hoofprints of the New Hampshiremen and Vermonters.[7]

Of the three Confederate brigades on Coffman's Hill, Munford's had been in the worst predicament. The unit was positioned on the Back Road with two regiments west of the road. When Custer's flanking column under Colonel Benjamin reached the Back Road near the top of the slope, the Federals were not just on the flank of Munford's brigade but in its rear. When the dreaded cries of "flanked!" came racing along the firing line from the left and rear, Munford realized he and his men did not have "a glimmering of a chance" to hold their position, but could still rapidly disengage and retire "without trouble, and with credit." Retiring in good order from a flanked position was not an easy maneuver under any circumstances, let alone when the only escape route was straight up the slope of a long, steep hill. Within moments the stampede had begun.

Pennsylvania Cavalry provided mounted skirmishers during the movement, but whether the Pennsylvanians participated in the movement up the slope is not clear.

5   *OR* 43, pt. 1, 544.

6   Cummings, "Six Months," 299.

7   Beaudry, *War Journal,* 176; *OR* 43, 1: 541; Anderson, "Shenandoah."

Under such circumstances, any of Munford's men fighting on foot, and there were many, were at an almost insurmountable disadvantage. Cavalry troops worked in teams of four, with three men fighting on the firing line on foot while the fourth man remained behind the line, but nearby, to hold the horses of his three comrades. A dismounted man's chances of escape depended entirely on the selflessness and reliability of the man minding his horse. If panicked horse holders fled, then the men on foot would be without mounts and unable to outrun the enemy cavalry. Even the mounted men of Munford's brigade faced the prospect of an uphill flight over ground already swarming with Custer's men. Munford's fugitives headed southward toward the Middle Road, angling diagonally across the face of the slope, away from the concentration of Federals on the Back Road.

Over on Rosser's right, the 11th and 12th Virginia regiments had been holding firm against Federal sallies and remained unaware of the chaos enveloping the Back Road. Major McDonald of the 11th Virginia Cavalry received an order to move his men to the left to support Munford's brigade. After spurring his horse into a gallop toward the Back Road, he saw that "it was filled with Yankees in heavy column." McDonald immediately wheeled his horse to retrace steps to inform his men the left had given way, but he would be too late.[8] The 11th and 12th Virginia regiments, were veteran outfits, so when a battalion of the 2nd Ohio Cavalry worked its way across the brook, around the Confederate right flank and rear, and began pouring in fire, the Virginians sensed events were moving toward a climax.[9] With the carbine bullets humming by in greater numbers, men of the 12th Virginia Cavalry prepared to receive a charge from the enemy, but no amount of time and activity could have prepared them for what was coming. "Before we could get ready for them," explained Pvt. Thomas Ranson, "their fire became too hot for endurance and our thin line broke." The Federals came from the flank and from the front, and they came almost at the same time. Ranson remembered chaos: "They were so close on us and so overwhelming in numbers that no other attempt was made to front them, and at some points the running fight degenerated into a stampede. It was every man for himself, every now and then a hand to hand business with the sabre, a good many

8   McDonald, *Reminiscences*, 115.

9   *OR* 43, pt. 1, 539.

prisoners taken, a good deal of the ludicrous mixed up with the tragedy, and a good many remarks made unfit to be repeated to ears polite."[10]

The charging Federals belonged to Colonel Kidd's brigade. They had arrived on the right of 12th Virginia Cavalry not long after Custer had moved forward on Rosser's left. Kidd saw that the enemy's line was "rather thin," so, without communicating with Custer, he had put his 6th and 7th Michigan and 25th New York regiments in line and immediately attacked with "great impetuosity." Two of Pennington's regiments, the 3rd New Jersey Cavalry and the bulk of the 2nd Ohio Cavalry, had found shelter from the fire of the Confederate artillery behind a slope north of the brook, but as Kidd's men arrived, the 2nd Ohio drew sabers and joined the charge upon the Laurel Brigade's right.[11]

From a hill high above Tom's Brook, the men of Capt. Joseph Martin's 6th New York Battery had been firing in enfilade on the Confederate guns and any bodies of Southern troops that exposed themselves.[12] Supporting the New York battery were the troopers of the 5th Michigan. The Wolverines sat on their mounts and enjoyed a splendid view of the action below. Just as Custer's long lines of mounted men had begun to surge forward, the Federal batteries stopped firing to avoid hitting friends, and as the smoke over the battlefield trailed away in the breeze, the men of the 5th Michigan stood in their stirrups, holding their breath for the result of the charge, watching. When the Southerners began to give way, the 5th regiment let out "a mighty cheer" and rushed forward to join with Custer's men.[13]

Lieutenant Colonel M. D. Ball of the 11th Virginia Cavalry had kept to the field despite an ankle wound, and later remembered looking behind him and seeing "the whole country to my left rear covered with the flying regiments of other brigades, the enemy pressing them close." These were mainly Munford's men, but Ball's men were joining in the flight. The slashing attack by Kidd and Pennington upon Rosser's right stove in the flank of the 12th Virginia Cavalry, which quickly fell back. The dismounted

---

10 Ranson Reminiscence.

11 Kidd, *Personal Recollections*, 401; Anderson, "Shenandoah"; *OR* 43, pt. 1, 465, 539.

12 *OR* 43, pt. 1, 447.

13 James Henry Avery, *Under Custer's Command*, Karla Jean Husby, comp., Eric Wittenberg, ed. (Washington, DC, 2000), 112.

skirmishers of White's Battalion and the 11th Virginia, who had stood in the bottom land by the brook and resisted all comers, now saw themselves flanked on both sides—by Kidd and the Ohioans on their right and Custer's thrust on the left. Among these dismounted Confederates, 17-year-old William Ball heard an officer yell, "Get back to your horses!" Ball and his comrades were not slow to obey, and the teenager remembered "a foot race for our horses." Amid the growing chaos, the 7th Virginia Cavalry, in the center of the Laurel Brigade's line, held firm to give the dismounted men in front an opportunity to get to their horses, but swarming Federals were disarming and capturing many of the foot-slow Laurels. Private Ball and his mates discovered the men detailed as horse holders for the troopers fighting on foot had fled, as had most of the horses. "But my faithful John," recalled Ball, "was one which had not, and don't you say I was not glad to see that horse! I was on his back in a moment and joined in the rush, men begging to be taken on behind and no attention paid them. It was devil take the hindmost!" Sergeant William Brent, who had been involved in the execution of prisoners a few days earlier, showed more compassion, at least briefly. Brent recalled that as he was turning his horse for the rear, he saw "a big stout fellow" who had stayed too long on the skirmish line and whose tongue was hanging out after a long run. Brent told him to climb up behind him and they would both make for the rear on Brent's horse. The big fellow was so heavy the horse objected by kicking and bucking, almost causing Brent to lose his seat. With the Federals coming on toward them, Brent decided that ridding himself of this man now was a matter of life and death, and compassion for a comrade quickly changed to ruthless self-preservation. He frankly admitted later he would have pulled out his pistol and shot his passenger if he had not needed both hands to manage the frantic horse. The murderous solution was not necessary, for Brent regained control of the frightened animal and both men and horse escaped up the hill. [14]

Less lucky was selfless Pvt. George Watson, who with his comrades of the 12th Virginia Cavalry had not been on the firing line but instead had been deployed mounted with the expectation of moving forward against the Federals. Suddenly came the unexpected order to fall back. As Watson reined his mount around, a spent ball struck his right arm. Moments later, his

---

14 Ball, "Rosser and his Critics"; Gray Jacket, "The Cavalry Fights"; Ball, *Reminiscences*; Myers, *The Comanches,* 339; William A. Brent memoir.

comrade, Onnie Higgins, crashed to the turf when a bullet wounded his horse and the animal fell, trapping Higgins. Watson and a friend dismounted and freed Higgins, who was able to scamper off on foot and find a hiding place. Having lost precious moments as Federals bore down on him, Watson was able to reach his horse, but the terrified beast jumped and reared so violently that Watson, with his wounded arm, could not mount him quickly. After he was finally in the saddle, Watson whirled his horse and started after his retreating comrades. Only then did he see the Federals arriving on the flank and firing as they came. Suddenly, his horse went down wounded, pitching Watson forward out of the saddle. Not badly hurt, he jumped over a fence and hid in short weeds, but before nightfall the Federals found him and added his name to the POW list.[15]

Farther up the hill, the Confederate artillery was again on the move. Artilleryman George Neese later claimed the fire from Peirce's battery "was too hot for us, and a large body of cavalry was advancing on our position on both flanks with but a few scattering cavalrymen on our side to oppose them." From their new firing position, Neese and his battery mates watched "blue horsemen swarm all over the hill we had just left." With Generals Payne and Rosser in the lead, a portion of Payne's brigade charged across the hill to protect the guns—but the effort came too late. The Federals came on from three directions and the gun crews could no longer fire fast enough to be effective. Breathed saw that the guns would be lost if they did not again withdraw. "The Yankee cavalry pressed us to the yielding point soon after we opened fire," Neese explained, "and our cavalry rendered us very little support, as they were scattered all over the hills and fields and preparing to make a dash to the rear, which they accomplished in fine style."[16]

From the crest of Coffman's Hill, the ground extends as a plateau southward for miles. Somewhere on the plateau near a belt of woods, Confederate officers began consolidating fugitives, including Thomson's artillery. A Federal shot had knocked a wheel off a Confederate gun carriage, and the gunners abandoned it they when they moved the remaining guns to another position. The flood of blue horsemen kept coming. Three horses fell

15 George W. Watson, *The Last Survivor: The Memoirs of George William Watson*, Brian S. Kesterson, ed. (Parsons, WV, 1993), 31-32.

16 Neese, *Three Years,* 323; McDonald, *Laurel Brigade,* 306-07; Ferguson, "Memoranda," frame 399; Anderson, "Shenandoah."

wounded or dead beneath Captain Thomson as he fought by his guns. Still, the Federals kept coming. George Neese and his comrades limbered up their guns for a final withdrawal then heard someone shout, "Boys, save yourselves!" Neese turned to see Federal cavalrymen charging from the left. "Five men of the Eighth New York Cavalry dashed on us with leveled pistols, and brought my gun to a halt with me on the limber chest, and in less than five minutes there were a thousand Yankee cavalrymen, with drawn sabers, around us." Neese stated his gun had fired 75 rounds that morning; they were the last shots he would fire in the war. Within days, he was on his way to Point Lookout Prison, where he would remain for the duration.[17]

Some witnesses saw courageous young officers trying to rally troops on the top of the hill. Lieutenant John Seibert of the 11th Virginia Cavalry inspired a small group to stand with him. Munford commended Capt. James Breckinridge of the 2nd Virginia Cavalry for establishing a stable rallying point near a wood lot on the plateau. A private of the 12th Virginia Cavalry thought the action there was "good and hot" for a short time: "The air was lively. My pistols were empty except for two shots which I sent as straight as my fool horse would let me." As the number of blue suits increased on the top of the hill, fewer Confederates tarried in their run for the rear. "On reaching the crest of the hill," admitted Private Ball, "we discovered a solid line of bluecoats leisurely coming after us. Without a word, as one man we turned and joined in the retreat, not madly but in a slow canter." Rosser's entire line on Coffman's Hill had collapsed. A trooper in Rosser's Laurel Brigade watched with mingled feelings of anger and shame as Custer's men captured Lt. Tuck Carter's two field pieces and added insult to injury by quickly turning the two guns about and firing upon the retreating Confederates.[18]

Amid the swarming troopers of the 18th Pennsylvania Cavalry, four aggressive veteran lieutenants looked beyond the broken and retiring

17 Benedict, *Vermont,* 2:662-64; "The Confederate Dead in Stonewall Cemetery, Winchester, VA. Memorial Services, June 6, 1894," *Southern Historical Society Papers,* 22:44; Hannaford memoir; Neese, *Three Years,* 323; Robert H. Moore, *Chew's Ashby, Shoemaker's Lynchburg and the Newtown Artillery* (Lynchburg, VA, 1995), 106.

18 Munford, "Reminiscences . . . No. 3," 136-7; Robert J. Driver, *2nd Virginia Cavalry* (Lynchburg, VA, 1995), 199; Ranson Reminiscence; Ball, *Reminiscences*; "A Story Corrected," Staunton *Spectator*, February 6, 1889, p. 3, col 4. See also Staunton *Spectator*, January 30, 1889, p. 3, col. 5.

Confederate troopers and artillerymen and saw the enemy's wagon train on the Back Road in the distance. The four officers called together what troopers they could and took off at a gallop. Swerving around the faltering Southern artillery teams and leaving the guns as easy pickings for the next wave of Federals, the Pennsylvanians plunged deeper into the Confederate rear, hurtling after the wagons. A cluster of Confederate cavalrymen stood in the corner of a woodlot firing upon the charging Pennsylvanians. One of the four lieutenants, John Winters, had emptied his revolver in the charge up the hill and drew his saber to charge at the men in the trees. Winters fell dead, but the Confederates withdrew and the Pennsylvanians swiftly overtook the wagon train.[19]

Almost all of the Confederates who recorded their impressions of the final minutes on Coffman's Hill wrote of chaos and panic. Typical was the account of Maj. Edward McDonald, who found himself hemmed in by Federal columns east and west and was forced to flee for a mile by galloping through a field of standing corn. As the turmoil increased, the growing fear fed upon itself and became contagious for man and beast. A private never forgot the terror that gripped his mount: "My horse was clean crazy, but I was willing as he was to get out of it. I am frank to admit we were about equally demoralized."

Rosser, however, perceived events differently. He later declared that even after the attack on his left flank he organized an orderly withdrawal of one brigade at a time, which succeeded "very well." Rosser likely did believe he had matters well in hand. He was on a battlefield, his natural element, so even as his lines collapsed and his guns were captured and his troopers streamed past him toward the rear, Rosser retained his confidence in himself. One of the privates streaming by in retreat never forgot seeing Rosser sitting placidly on his handsome dappled horse amid the blooming disaster on top of Coffman's Hill. The soldier thought, "He was as cool and nonchalant as if nothing had happened out of the ordinary."[20]

Rosser's account stands in stark contrast to the majority of the testimony. Staff officer James Ferguson, who kept an official diary at

19 Rodenbough, *18th Regiment*, 111-12; *OR* 43, pt. 1, 541.

20 McDonald, *Reminiscences,* 115; Rosser, "Annals," March 22, 1884. M. D. Ball, one of Rosser's strongest supporters, offered a similar portrayal of events. Ball, "Rosser and his Critics"; Ranson Reminiscence.

Rosser's headquarters, saw nothing resembling the orderly withdrawal asserted by the general. Written on the day of the battle, Ferguson's account relates a scene of pandemonium as panic took hold of even veteran troopers, and Rosser's men abandoned the artillery, the caissons, the limbers, the wagons, the ambulances, the wounded, and the slow of foot, to flee in "wild confusion" across the fields to the south.[21]

21 Ferguson, "Memoranda," frame 399.

CHAPTER EIGHT

Merritt Opens the Turnpike

"A General Smash-up of the Entire Confederate Line."

Well before General Rosser's disaster on Coffman's Hill had fully evolved, General Lomax, just two miles to the east, presided over a bad situation that held every promise of worsening rapidly. Like Rosser, Lomax would that morning go through the same process of surprise and then alarm when he realized the Federals had turned the tables and would attack. Unlike Rosser, Lomax had little reason to hope his depleted and partially demoralized command could at least put up a good fight in a pitched battle. Lomax had with him only the remains of two small brigades and one broken-down battery, a total of about 800 men. So wretched were the arms, mounts, leaders, and reputations of his troops that Lomax would have been hard pressed to identify the chief weakness of his command.

Over the past three days, Lomax had dutifully obeyed Jubal Early's orders to harass and pursue the Federals, but he had accomplished little. On the night of the 8th, Rosser had sent a message to Lomax to say he would advance again at dawn.[1] After declaring that he had driven the Federals hard

---

1 Rosser also appears to have written to Early, who was still at New Market. Jed Hotchkiss, Early's topographical engineer, recorded in his journal on the night on October 8, 1864, that headquarters received word that Rosser's division was in camp on Tom's Brook and had skirmished successfully during the day. *OR* 43, pt. 1, 578.

Gen. Bradley T. Johnson's brigade
had been reduced by casualties,
disease, and desertion to perhaps
350 men at Tom's Brook.
Miller's *Photographic History of the Civil War*

that day, Rosser apparently expressed confidence, but Lomax did not share it. In his encampment between Woodstock and Maurertown, Lomax conferred with his senior subordinate, brigade commander Bradley Johnson, and shared the essential information in Rosser's dispatch. Lomax made clear to Johnson that he felt compelled to again go on the offensive in the morning, especially given Rosser's determination to push on after the Federals. According to a staff officer present, both Lomax and Johnson expressed misgivings about pushing on too vigorously. Both men well understood the sorry condition of their troops, and Lomax plainly expressed his lack of confidence about what the morning might bring.[2]

Lomax, like Rosser and some of their subordinates, later expressed displeasure over Early's orders that had sent them 25 miles ahead of the army and the nearest assistance. The officers implied Early should have closed the distance by moving the army north from New Market. From a tactical viewpoint—and both Lomax and Rosser were necessarily focused on their tactical situation—their concern over those 25 miles between them and their support is understandable. One man in Rosser's division, who went

2 Booth, *Reminiscences*, 152. Local lore holds that at least part of Lomax's division camped at the Shenandoah County Alms house near Maurertown on the night of October 8. No primary source specifically mentioning the Alms House has been found. The National Park Service Study, *Civil War Sites in the Shenandoah Valley of Virginia*, repeats the assertion that Lomax camped at the Alms House, but provides no contemporary source. Garland Hudgins, a resident of Maurertown and a reliable source for local historical information, served as an advisor to the creators of the NPS study.

by *nom de plume* "Gray Jacket," implied criticism of the army commander in a letter to a Richmond newspaper: "Gen. Early stopped, with his infantry, near New Market . . . *why* I do not know."[3]

The explanation is not complex. Unlike his two cavalry commanders, Early was primarily focused on the strategic situation, not the smaller tactical picture. Early's goal was to again engage the main body of Sheridan's army as soon as favorable conditions could be found to do so. To accomplish that goal, he wished to prepare his infantry, but he also required information about Sheridan's movements. Because part of the function of cavalry was to gather information, Early sent his mounted troops to follow and observe and harass the enemy and to report what they learned.[4] Geography and his strategic assignment convinced Early to remain at New Market, which was as close as he could move to Sheridan's army while retaining ready access to the passes through the Blue Ridge Mountains at New Market Gap and Thornton Gap. Focused on defeating or detaining the Federal army, Early struggled to discover what was in Sheridan's mind. On the afternoon of October 9, Early mused in a letter to Lee:

> the question now is, what he intends doing—whether he will move across the [Blue] Ridge, send a part of his force to Grant, or content himself with protecting the Baltimore and Ohio [rail]road. If he moves across the Ridge I will move directly across from this place [New Market] to meet him, and I think I can defeat his infantry and thwart his movements on the east of the mountains.[5]

The best roads for such a movement across the Blue Ridge were in the southern end of the Valley, beginning with Rockfish Gap on the south followed by Brown's Gap, Swift Run Gap, and Thornton Gap in the central valley east of New Market. These roads gave Early a direct path to the Virginia Central Railroad and the most direct route to Richmond and Petersburg. If Early were to advance north of New Market, he would be moving farther from the roads to Richmond, but, more important, he would

---

3 Gray Jacket, "The Cavalry Fights."

4 Bryan Grimes and Pulaski Cowper, Gary W. Gallagher, ed., *Extracts of Letters of Major-General Bryan Grimes, to his Wife: Written While in Active Service in the Army of Northern Virginia, Together with Some Personal Recollections of the War* (Wilmington, NC, 1986), 73.

5 *OR* 43, pt. 1, 559-60.

be moving away from the gaps most favorable for any movement and concentration to a point east of the Blue Ridge. His best option north of New Market for crossing the Blue Ridge would be at Chester Gap at Front Royal, 30 miles to the north, which remained in Federal hands and which Sheridan himself might use in any eastward movement. As Sheridan moved northward, the geography of the Valley limited Early's options until he gained more information. Thus Lomax found himself 25 miles ahead of Early's army and alone with his responsibilities—except for his 800 soldiers, who were too few and too unsteady to be of great comfort.

Lomax's division moved northward at first light on October 9. Like Rosser, Lomax had, on this fourth morning of his pursuit of the Federals, little reason to expect a full scale attack by the Federal cavalry. October 9 seemed likely to be just another day in which Lomax tried to follow through with Early's injunctions to keep the pressure on Sheridan. Videttes led Lomax's column through thick morning fog, but they had not gone far before shots rang out in the gray mist up ahead. Already the Southerners had reached the enemy picket line. "Without hesitation," recalled a staff officer, Lomax's leading regiments charged and forced the Federals pickets to scamper back toward Tom's Brook.[6]

As recently as 1852, the settlement known as Tom's Brook, consisting of just four domiciles, one of which was a stagecoach tavern, had been little more than a way station on the turnpike.[7] By 1864, the community could not have been significantly more than a hamlet. The few buildings were clustered near where the pike crossed the brook itself at the bottom of a vale between high ground that rose up on both the north and south ends of the settlement. From the stream, the ground rose steadily to the south for half a mile to the crest of a ridge. The Valley Turnpike Company operated a Toll House on this ridge. Continuing southward along the pike, the ground dipped sharply from the Toll House ridge, crossed Jordan's Run, and then rose again to a second ridge, upon which stood the Shenandoah County Alms House. On these two ridges along the Valley Pike, Lomax would fight. The first, or the Toll House ridge, between Tom's Brook and Jordan's Run, offered a commanding view of the pike as it stretched northward arrow-

6   Booth, *Reminiscences*, 152.

7   Wayland, *The Valley Turnpike*, 25.

straight for more than a mile and a quarter down into the hamlet and then up the ridge on the far (north) end of town toward Round Hill. This position offered a fine field of fire for Lomax's artillery and was therefore the better of the two ridges for Lomax's purposes. The second rise, the Alms House ridge on the south side of Jordan's Run, offered the better view of the pike southward through Maurertown and toward Woodstock. Federal officers almost certainly had pickets on one or both of these ridges on the morning of October 9, and it was these pickets Lomax's advance struck and drove off in the morning fog. Whether Lomax advanced immediately to or beyond the Toll House ridge and established his line there is uncertain, but the morning's fight would ebb and flow over both of the ridges above Jordan's Run.[8]

The ground was familiar to Lomax and his men. Bradley Johnson's men had been over this ground the evening before. Lomax carefully deployed his men, placing the Valley Pike in the middle of his line, deploying Johnson's men to the east, and Col. William Thompson's brigade on the west. John McNulty's guns went into battery in the center of the line athwart the pike.[9]

Lomax had reached the moment of decision. Having deployed for battle, he now had to choose whether to fight offensively, defensively, or not at all. He knew the enemy ahead of him was more numerous, was better equipped and fed, and was, therefore, man-for-man, horse-for-horse and regiment-for-regiment, far stronger. He knew his command was in no condition to oppose Wesley Merritt's division. Lomax also knew Rosser was advancing on his left down the Back Road, and any decision he made would affect the safety of Rosser's command. By Lomax's own admission, he had "no arms to resist a charge mounted, not a saber or pistol being in the command." Yet invite a charge is precisely what the Confederate commander determined to do. Lomax decided he must hold his high ground and accept battle from the Federals.[10]

The Federal plan for the morning was to advance on both the Back Road and the Valley Pike and gradually concentrate on the Back Road, where the

---

8 Neither ridge appears to have been christened, but the two buildings that stand upon them serve as useful references. Though "Jordan's" is the accepted modern spelling of the run between the ridges, some war-era maps show the stream as "Jordon's."

9 *OR* 43, pt. 1, 612; A Soldier, "The Cavalry"; Hoge, *A Journal*.

10 *OR* 43, pt. 1, 612-13.

Col. Charles R. Lowell was widely respected for his calm under fire.
LOC

enemy had been most aggressive most recently.[11] To oppose Lomax's 800 men and one battery along the Valley Pike, Merritt fielded a division of about about 3,000 experienced, well-armed, well-led veterans. Colonel Charles Lowell's Reserve Brigade, forming the division's left, moved southward on the pike. Devin's brigade, in the center, moved southward across country west of the Valley Pike to seize the high ground south of Tom's Brook. Kidd's Michiganders moved on the division's right with orders to focus on the enemy's flank toward the Back Road. Neither Torbert nor Merritt seem to have expected Lowell to find anything on the pike, for, as Merritt explained in his report, Lowell was to move his men southward through the village and on to the high ridge—the Toll House ridge—just south of the brook. Then, having secured the high ground, Lowell was to turn westward toward the Back Road, where his men had skirmished with the aggressive Confederate force the previous evening. Merritt's entire division could then move along the Toll House ridge and concentrate on the flank of whatever enemy force might be discovered opposing Custer.[12]

Early on that cold, damp morning near Tom's Brook, Colonel Lowell looked at his watch, saw it was 7:00 a.m., and decided he had time to write a

---

11 Because his men had skirmished with the enemy the evening before, Torbert, of course, knew of Rosser's presence opposite Custer on the Back Road. He also knew Lomax had been on the Valley Pike the night before, but the evening reconnaissance revealed the Confederates were not much north of Woodstock.

12 *OR* 43, pt. 1, 460, 447, 483.

letter home. Lowell, according to one Federal staff officer, "was known as one of the very bravest men in the whole army. He was a fatalist and believed one must die when his time came and no possible precaution could alter the fact." Lowell was a Harvard graduate, first in his class 10 years earlier, and had no military experience before joining the U.S. Regular Army at the beginning of the war, but Sheridan eventually placed Lowell in command of the brigade of Regular Army troops, a startling act of confidence and approbation. That morning Lowell wrote home that he expected another cavalry fight that day, but his letter betrayed no concern. Instead, he expressed annoyance about not having enough water to wash his face. Soon came the popping of gunfire as Federal pickets encountered Lomax's videttes in the early morning fog and returned with word of the Southerners' advance. Lowell moved forward with three U.S. Regular cavalry regiments and the respected 2nd Massachusetts Cavalry. Lowell learned almost immediately the program for October 9 was not to go as expected.[13]

When his brigade reached the place where the turnpike crossed the brook, Lowell sent out an advance guard. A Confederate officer thought the fog was of some advantage to the Lomax's men because it obscured the insignificance of their numbers from the Federals. If that was the case, the advantage disappeared along with the dissipating mists, exposing the Confederate line on the high ground.[14] The greater portion of Lowell's command had until then remained in column on the Valley Pike—in traveling, not fighting, formation. After discovering the enemy's presence on the ridge, Lowell ordered out a skirmish line to more fully explore what lay ahead. The Confederates did not await such investigation. The Southern battery opened fire from the pike, and Colonel Thompson's brigade, deployed west of the pike, charged with a yell.[15] Most of the Federal column

---

13 Sanford, *Fighting Rebels,* 273; Edward Waldo Emerson, *Life and Letters of Charles Russell Lowell* (Port Washington, NY, 1971), 58-9.

14 Booth, *Reminiscences,* 153.

15 *OR* 43, pt. 1, 491; W. W. Goldsborough, *The Maryland Line in the Confederate Army, 1861-1865* (Baltimore, MD, 1900), 292. In the absence of abundant evidence, historians have speculated about Lomax's initial deployment. Though Lomax's report states Johnson's brigade stood west of the Valley Pike later in the afternoon, the source relied upon here, a first-hand account by a participant in Jackson's (Thompson's) brigade, who, regrettably, did not identify himself, gives evidence that at the beginning of the fight Lomax

was too far back in the road to be affected by surprise, especially since the Confederates did not press their advantage. After the briefest of thrusts, the Confederates fell back and regrouped.

In the meantime, Lt. Frank E. Taylor's guns, 1st U.S. Artillery, attached to Thomas Devin's brigade, went into battery on high hills west of the pike. Lowell deployed his brigade to force a passage of Jordan's Run and the ridge beyond.[16] With the 2nd Massachusetts in the lead, Lowell advanced to the dismounted picket line himself. The chaplain of the regiment recalled that the men "crouched behind trees, rocks, and fences, or anything that promised shelter. But the Colonel rode fearlessly along the line, and, though he was thus a conspicuous target for the enemy's musketry, he seemed not to mind." Lowell, in fact, had in many engagements established a reputation for coolly remaining a mounted target. A week or so earlier, an officer of the 1st Rhode Island Cavalry watched Lowell in a skirmish. While the rest of Lowell's men withdrew rapidly under fire, Lowell calmly rode his horse at a walk, the last man to fall back, "Confederate bullets were whistling about him, and frequent puffs of dust in the road showed where they struck right and left." The surgeon of the 2nd Massachusetts fretted that Lowell routinely "exposed himself mercilessly." At Tom's Brook, he saw Lowell ride calmly to a fence where two skirmishers crouched to protect themselves. As enemy bullets zipped by, Lowell spoke to the men and ordered them to advance. "I dared not look at him," recalled the surgeon, "for I *knew* he would fall, yet he came back steadily and all right, his horse always wounded or killed, and himself never. . . but how, God alone knew." Lowell's habit of riding along the skirmish lines and close to the action proved deadly to his mounts. His staff kept count of the horses killed and wounded under their colonel, and when his roan fell dead on the evening of the October 8 during the skirmish on the Back Road, the equine casualty figure reached an even dozen in just a two-month period. On the morning of the 9th, Lowell was just about out of horses of his own and rode a horse borrowed from a sergeant who had been wounded the previous evening.[17]

---

had deployed Johnson's brigade east of the road and Jackson's brigade, commanded by Thompson, west of the Valley Pike. A Soldier, "The Cavalry."

16 *OR* 43, pt. 1, 491.

17 Charles A. Humphreys, *Field, Camp, Hospital and Prison in the Civil War, 1863-1865* (Freeport, NY, 1971), 164; George N. Bliss, *Cavalry Service with General Sheridan and Life*

Thomas Devin's brigade of New Yorkers performed superior service throughout October 9, 1864.

LOC

Opposite Colonel Lowell's skirmishers, Bradley Johnson's brigade, east of the Valley Pike, moved forward early in the fight and advanced in line of battle against light resistance for several hundred yards, but withdrew when it advanced too far ahead of Thompson's regiments west of the pike.[18] Lomax resorted to deception to disguise his weakness. Because the rifles carried by many of his men were useless on horseback, he dismounted many of the men and sent them forward to fight as infantry along a tree line. He told his officers they must move the men about frequently and rapidly through the woods to fire from many different locations. At the same time, following standard procedures, Lomax kept a portion of his force mounted to respond to Federal movements. Lomax's overmatched troopers fought with determination. A captain of the 1st U.S. Cavalry described this early part of the engagement as "a pretty sharp fight." Captain George Sanford, of Torbert's staff, saw the Confederates obstinately hold their ground for about two hours. Lowell's men advanced repeatedly, "but in each case counter charges by the enemy would regain any ground captured." Sanford believed Lowell's brigade "was quite unable to drive the enemy from their position."[19]

---

in Libby Prison (Providence, RI, 1884), 23; Emerson, *Life and Letters,* 61, 58-9; Henry E. Alvord, "A New England Boy in the Civil War," Caroline B. Sherman, ed., in *The New England Quarterly*, vol. 5, no. 2 (April 1932), 332.

18 Hoge, *A Journal.*

19 A Soldier, "The Cavalry"; Charles H. Veil memoir; Sanford, *Fighting Rebels*, 283.

On Lowell's right, "Uncle Tommy" Devin's brigade advanced west of the Valley Pike and gained the Toll House ridge without opposition and well clear of Lomax's left flank. Colonel Devin's brigade had been whittled down to less than its full strength, with most or all of the 4th New York and 17th Pennsylvania regiments absent from the battle line on detached duty. Devin's regiments faced eastward toward the Confederate flank and without undue delay moved forward to assist Lowell.[20] As Devin's men advanced, they came upon Southerners, presumably some of Colonel Thompson's men, on the edge of a patch of woods. Devin dismounted two squadrons of the 1st New York Dragoons and sent them forward as skirmishers. At the same time Devin received a gift in the arrival of the 5th U.S. Cavalry, which belonged to Lowell's brigade but had been on detached duty at Merritt's headquarters. Having ridden to the sound of the guns, the Regulars had arrived at the right place and time, and Devin sent them forward to support the New York Dragoons. As the New Yorkers made contact, one trooper took a moment to appreciate the scene. With the long line of battle extending away from him on both sides, he thought, "It was a magnificent place for a cavalry fight, smooth ground and free from fences. Both sides deployed in full view of each other, the skirmishers opening with their carbines."[21]

Lomax undoubtedly knew that despite the advantages the high ground gave him to his front, his position was untenable. Neither of his flanks was anchored on anything like a formidable feature of the terrain, and, with only 800 men, the Confederates were a match only for the fewer than 600 men of Lowell's brigade.[22] As soon as Devin turned eastward on the Confederate flank, Lomax had little hope of standing. Probably not long before Devin had gained his flank, Lomax received word from Rosser. At some point during the rising chaos on Coffman's Hill, Rosser had written a hasty dispatch to Lomax to inform him he was withdrawing. Receipt of this news, Lomax recalled later, prompted him to begin what he characterized as an orderly withdrawal.[23]

---

20 *OR* 43, pt. 1, 48.

21 Ibid., 483, 447, 492; Bowen, *Three Years of Active Service*, 247.

22 *OR* 43, pt. 1, 445.

23 E. B. Goggin to Gen. Lomax, "Last Days of the Confederacy," 1867, Chicago Historical Society; *OR* 43, pt. 1, 612.

Colonel Lowell, however, had already decided the time had come to break Lomax's line. The 1st U. S. Cavalry, in column of fours, would lead the charge, supported by the 2nd Massachusetts. Artilleryman Lt. Edward Williston, who had posted two guns of his battery far forward and been lashing the Confederate skirmishers with canister, loosed one final discharge and then ceased firing as the Regulars and the Bay Staters hurtled forward bellowing cheers. A Confederate staff officer thought the Yankees came on in such strength that "the very ground seemed to spew forth cavalry."[24]

As his cavalry supports pulled out, Confederate battery commander McNulty tried to sacrifice one of his cannon to allow the rest of the battery to escape. A hasty blast of canister from the martyred gun had no effect on the charging column, but Lt. Moses Harris of the 1st U. S. Cavalry saw that even as he and his men roared up the pike the gun crew worked frantically to reload and fire one more round point blank. Just before the gunner could pull his lanyard, the Regulars were on him. "Nobody thinks of pausing to secure trophies," Harris recalled, "our only thought is to press on so that there shall be no possibility of their disorganized forces halting to reform." Cursing Confederate officers entreated their men to stand firm, but the Federals were too much to withstand, and Lomax's Valley Cavalrymen broke and ran. A little more than two hours of maneuvering, charging and counter charging had resulted very suddenly in what Sheridan called, "a general smash-up of the entire Confederate line."[25]

The engagement at Tom's Brook was over, and what would become known as "the Woodstock Races" had begun.

24 "Moses Harris, "With the Reserve Brigade, Paper 2," *Journal of the United States Cavalry Association*, 3(1890):245; "Recollections of George W. Towle;" Booth, *Reminiscences*, 154.

25 Moses Harris, "With the Reserve Brigade, Paper 2," 245; Frank M. Flinn, *Campaigning With Banks in Louisiana, '63 and '64, and With Sheridan in the Shenandoah Valley in '64 and '65* (Boston, MA, 1889), 206; Gray Jacket, "The Cavalry Fights;" Sheridan, *Memoirs* 2:58.

CHAPTER NINE

The Woodstock Races

"The Endurance of Horseflesh."

O̶n̶c̶e̶ the Confederates abandoned Coffman's Hill and headed southward, Rosser's officers struggled to restore order. Hundreds of disorganized cavalrymen rode briskly across the landscape, and they either regained their composure and rallied at defensive positions or they did not. Amid the chaos, Rosser and his officers knew only that too few of their men chose to rally. As Munford succinctly put it, after the fight left Coffman's Hill, "It became more a contest of speed than valor."[1]

Much of Rosser's division fled southwestward on the Back Road, but some fugitives took a side road just in the rear of Coffman's Hill and escaped almost due southward on the Middle Road toward Woodstock.[2] The Federals pressed both groups. After a wild, every-man-for-himself stampede of two miles, many of the Confederate troopers regained their self-control, and officers regrouped them at Pugh's Run, a small stream flowing across the Back Road about three miles from Coffman's Hill. Munford's brigade still retained some continuity, and he placed his four regiments in two lines

---

1 Munford, "Annals."

2 Ferguson's notation that Munford's brigade "crossed over to the back road lower down" suggests that Munford's Brigade retained some continuity during the flight and that it had used the Middle Road as an escape route before moving to the Back Road at Columbia Furnace. Ferguson, "Memoranda," frame 399.

of two regiments each. The Federals appeared in such numbers that Rosser realized resistance was futile and said, "We can't do it." The withdrawal continued.[3]

Rosser portrayed the retreat along the Back Road as a fighting withdrawal. He said he had selected a position where he intended to collect his various commands and make a stand. He did not identify the position, but his account of events does not fit with the small shreds of evidence of what transpired at Pugh's Run. At this unnamed position, Rosser ordered the 1st Virginia regiment to establish a defensive position behind a stone wall selected as the rallying point. "Failing to find this regiment in the position it was ordered to take," Rosser admitted, "I failed to check the enemy at this point and my command was badly broken up and driven in confusion for about two miles." Rosser claimed he again rallied his men and launched an attack, but found "my force was too feeble to make much impression on him and I withdrew about three miles farther and took position at Columbia Furnace, from which the enemy made no effort to dislodge me."[4] Rosser declared the incident at the stone wall resulted from the "misbehavior" of the colonel of the 1st Virginia, whom, out of courtesy, he did not name. The identity of "the misbehaving colonel" was no secret within the army, however. Rosser relieved Col. Richard Welby Carter on the night of October 9, and he relieved Maj. Henry Carrington of the 3rd Virginia as well. Rosser planned to court martial both men for cowardice.[5]

---

3 Munford, "Annals."

4 Rosser, "Annals," March 22, 1884. When writing his recollections in 1883 or early 1884, Rosser almost certainly did so without the aid of accurate maps. He did not possess a keen sense of the distances between points on the Back Road. The distance between Coffman's Hill and Columbia Furnace is 12 miles, not the 8 miles he seems to estimate. More significant is that Rosser's recollection is at odds with Ferguson's journal entry made on October 9, which states division headquarters were at Joseph Helsey's at Cabin Point (a.k.a. Cabin Hill, modern Conicville), some four miles farther south of Columbia Furnace (16 miles from Coffman's Hill). Ferguson, "Memoranda," frame 399. Topographer Jed Hotchkiss states in his report that when Rosser and his refugees arrived at Stony Creek at Columbia Furnace, they turned on the Federals and "checked them, and captured their trains and 8 pieces of artillery." No other source, including Rosser himself, makes such a claim or supports such a claim. Because Hotchkiss was not present with Rosser's command on October 9, he received his information second hand, and his assertion is almost certainly egregiously wrong. OR 43, pt. 1, 1030.

5 Carter and Carrington Compiled Service Records; Ferguson, "Memoranda," frame 399. Carter and Carrington had spent many months in Northern prisoner of war camps—Carter at

* * *

On the Valley Pike, Lomax's withdrawal began under Sheridan's own eyes. The army commander, watching from the summit of Round Hill, could see the movements of the troops below, and after Devin's men gained Lomax's flank and Lowell's Regulars surged southward on the Pike, the engagement on Jordan's Run ended quite suddenly.[6] Lieutenant McNulty and most of his Marylanders managed to escape with five guns, leaving one sacrificial piece behind in the faint hope of delaying the charging Federals. The abandoned cannon got off only one ineffectual round before the 1st U. S. Cavalry scattered the gunners and captured the piece fully loaded with a parting shot never fired.[7] As Lomax's line began to melt away, all of Devin's men, many of whom had been fighting on foot, went to saddle and were off in pursuit. Devin himself rode with the 9th New York, and ordered the bugler to sound "forward" and "gallop." Captain Newell Cheney of the 9th New York recalled advancing at a rapid gait past the camps occupied the previous night by the Confederates, where breakfasts were still cooking. Soon Cheney and his men were overtaking wagons and ambulances and slow-moving Confederate troopers.[8] "The success of the day," in the words of Merritt, "was now merely a question of the endurance of horseflesh."[9]

Immediately in the rear of Lomax's abandoned position and extending south of Maurertown, the open country along the Valley Pike offered few places to hide or reform. There the fleeing Confederates were most vulnerable, and there they asked their horses for speed. On the hills north of

---

Camp Chase, Ohio, and Carrington at Johnson's Island, Ohio, and Point Lookout, Maryland—and a reluctance to experience another northern winter in confinement likely played a role in their conduct. Rosser also brought charges against Col. Reuben Boston of the 5th Virginia Cavalry after Tom's Brook, but a court acquitted Boston. According to a newspaper account, one of the specious charges against him was he failed to rally his men and allowed himself to be cut off from them. Boston proved at the trial that he had remained on the field "after those who had preferred the charges had left." *Daily Dispatch* (Richmond, VA), November 23, 1864, p. 1, col. 6. See Rosser to wife October 15, 1864, Rosser Papers, 1171-c, Box 1 and untitled typescript, Munford-Ellis Papers, Box 17, folder "Writings: Civil War Mss. of Thos. T. Munford (Rosser-Munford Dispute) 4 of 4."

6   Sheridan, *Memoirs*, 2:57-8.

7   "Recollections of George W. Towle;" Harris, "With the Reserve Brigade, Paper 2," 245.

8   Cheney, *History of the Ninth Regiment*, 227.

9   *OR* 43, pt. 1, 447.

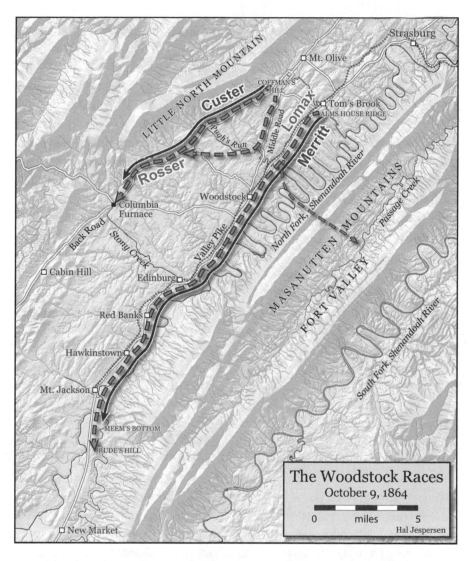

The Woodstock Races
October 9, 1864

0   miles   5

Hal Jespersen

Woodstock, where they had skirmished with the Federals the previous afternoon, Lomax and his officers rallied enough men to make a stand. "General Lomax was everywhere on the field," recalled an admiring trooper of Thompson's brigade, "animating and cheering his men in the hour of defeat . . . ." This position might well have been on the high ground south of Pugh's Run. After crossing the stream, Federals moving south would find the Valley Pike rose 120 feet in half a mile to the plateau north of Woodstock. Through the years many horsemen on this much travelled highway had likely lingered at the crest to allow their horses a blow. On this day, however, the Federals scarcely paused to examine the position before spurring into a charge. The 1st United States thundered up the Pike, followed by the 5th U.S. The 2nd Massachusetts had been broken into squadrons and drove forward on Lomax's flanks, both of which were "in the air." Sergeant John Hoge of the 8th Virginia Cavalry saw his captain, Thomas B. Harman, fall dead and lamented that he could not move the body because "the enemy were so close that we had to leave him."[10] Having come fewer than three miles from their initial position, the Confederates saw no option but flight, and as Sergeant Hoge put it, "then commenced one of our noted stampedes. Our men all scattered—some went by the road and others went to the mountains." Hoge fled across the North Fork of the Shenandoah River and scaled the ridges of the Massanutten Mountains, from which he remembered he had "a fine view" of the Federals charging after his comrades on the Valley Pike. "The enemy's resistance became very feeble," thought Merritt, "and presently his retreat became a rout."[11]

While Lomax's men headed southward from Woodstock on the Valley Pike, Captain John J. Shoemaker's respected veteran battery of Confederate horse artillery moved northward away from Mt. Jackson on the same road. Fate had kept Shoemaker's men out of the emotional and eventful days of The Burning. After fighting in the battle of Third Winchester and the days of skirmishing near Waynesboro, the worn-down battery had been ordered east across the Blue Ridge mountains to rest and refit for a couple of weeks. Though the battery had received "fresh" horses shortly before it returned to the Valley on October 5, an arduous trek over the Blue Ridge apparently wore these replacements down as well. For want of fit horses, Shoemaker had kept his cannoneers near New Market when Lomax's men had followed the Federals northward. After drawing fresher animals on the morning of the 9th, Shoemaker and his men proceeded northward on the Valley Pike.

In this part of the Valley, the North Fork of the Shenandoah River gains in size and strength. As it grows in breadth, the river begins to meander in long, graceful loops—like the letter "S" repeated over and over in a series with each "S" forming part of those before and after it. Before noon, north of Hawkinstown, Shoemaker came upon a large park of wagons halted in one

---

10 Hoge, *Journal*.

11 A Soldier, "The Cavalry"; Hoge, *A Journal*; Jack L. Dickinson, *8th Virginia Cavalry* (Lynchburg, VA, 1986), 88; *OR* 43, pt. 1, 491-92, 447.

On the afternoon of October 8, Lomax's men drove Merritt's rearguard northward on the Valley Pike past Woodstock's 1794 stone courthouse. The next day, the roles were reversed in "the Woodstock Races" as the Federals again charged past the local landmark, this time headed south in pursuit of the fleeing Confederates. The building was still in use in 2016. Wayland's *Stonewall Jackson's Way*

of the broad, grassy loops in the river east of the road. Stonewall Jackson had rested his men in this area near the large estate known as "Red Banks," and Shoemaker, like many other commanders, recognized it as a good place to rest and water horses.

During the morning, Shoemaker's men had heard artillery fire to the north but now noticed the firing had stopped. A courier, who had been sent ahead by Shoemaker for instructions from Lomax, suddenly reappeared at the gallop. He brought news of the rout of Lomax, but almost immediately Shoemaker would see the evidence for himself. One of Shoemaker's men, Lewis Nunnelee, recorded in his diary an amazing sight: A grand disorganized rush of "several hundred" Confederate cavalrymen pounding southward on the Pike, moving at such a high rate of speed that Nunnelee quipped it looked like "the whole Yankee army with Abe Lincoln in the lead" was after them." The teamsters of the wagon train, who two minutes earlier had been enjoying a quiet Sunday morning by the river while their animals grazed, frantically hitched up and joined the stampede southward. Shoemaker at once put his guns in firing position near the pike, hoping to serve as a rallying point should more of Lomax's fugitives appear.[12]

In a very few minutes, the artillerists saw a mob of riders approaching at a gallop. Shoemaker hailed them, but their speed and evident panic made clear these men had no interest rallying. "They didn't pay the slightest attention to us," a shocked Shoemaker recalled, "but kept on going faster than ever, if it were possible." Among Shoemaker's men shock quickly gave way to indignation. They knew the reputation of the Valley Cavalry, and here they saw for themselves the proof. "Neither Munford's, Rosser's or Wickham's brigades, who were on the backroad, would have deserted us that way," Shoemaker declared. One of the artillerymen began shouting, "Run, damn you, run: the Yankees are right behind you!" and the rest of the gunners jeered and laughed at the cowards.[13]

Shoemaker then faced a dilemma dreaded by every artillerymen. Two fundamental rules for artillery officers held that they should not try to fight alone and that they could not outrun cavalry. Shoemaker had to choose which fundamental rule to break. If he immediately wheeled his guns around and withdrew, he would likely only be postponing the inevitable moment when the Federal cavalry encircled them. If he stood and fought, he might kill and maim some of the enemy, but his guns would still likely be surrounded and captured. "Imagine, if you can, our predicament," Shoemaker pondered, "a battery of artillery alone and unsupported eighteen miles in front of our army and a victorious enemy approaching, and not a chance for us to escape. The situation was intense, but impossible to describe or be forgotten." Shoemaker addressed his band of 90-odd men and told them he would not blame any man who headed to the rear. None did, and all rallied their spirits with three ferocious cheers.[14]

12 Janet B. Hewett, Noah Andre Trudeau, Bryce A. Suderow, eds. *Supplement to the Official Records of the Union and Confederate Armies*, Part I, vol. 7, serial no. 7 (Wilmington, NC, 1997), 614-15; John J. Shoemaker, *Shoemaker's Battery, Stuart Horse Artillery, Pelham's Battalion, Afterwards Commanded by Col. R.P. Chew, Army of Northern Virginia* (Gaithersburg, MD, 1980), 85-6; Robert J. Trout, *Memoirs of the Stuart Horse Artillery Battalion* (Knoxville, TN, 2008), 105-06.

13 Shoemaker, *Shoemaker's Battery*, 84-5.

14 Ibid., 85-6.

Expecting a Federal charge at any moment, Shoemaker's Virginians attempted to forestall the inevitable with a slow, methodical fire that sent one round hurtling down the Pike at intervals of half a minute, "as regular as clockwork." When the Federals did not immediately appear, Shoemaker and his officers decided to sacrifice one gun and its crew to ensure the escape of the rest of the battery. After a few minutes, when still the Federals did not come on, Shoemaker, who had remained behind with the sacrificial piece, withdrew under the protection of a second gun planted some distance to the rear, and the second gun soon did the same under the whooshing shells of a third. The undulating terrain offered plenty of knolls from which Shoemaker's successive withdrawal tactic would allow his guns to fire, and the battery retired one piece at a time, at high speed, for eight miles to Meem's Bottom, where Early and a body of infantry offered them protection. The skillfully managed fighting retreat had allowed Shoemaker to reach safety with all of his guns, but his battery horses, fresh that morning, were once again completely broken down.[15]

*   *   *

To the north, Devin's men trotted passed Woodstock using byroads and driving a gaggle of Lomax's fugitives across Narrow Passage Creek. Lowell's men came upon Lt. McNulty's battery just south of Woodstock. After the rigors of the morning and a run of perhaps four miles, some horses among both the pursuer and the pursued were reaching the limits of their strength. The mounts of Lowell's brigade were so worn down that some staggered as they walked, and only the best-mounted men could pursue beyond Woodstock. Likewise, some of the Confederate battery horses, which Lomax declared were in "miserable condition" to begin with, finally gave out. McNulty's artillerymen unlimbered their guns and tried to hold off the pursuers, but as soon as Federals on jaded horses faltered, Federals on fresher mounts appeared to take their place and the Northerners took two of the Confederate guns. A few miles later, north of Edinburg, Lowell's men took two more. A story reported by a New York correspondent told of one of Merritt's cavalrymen pursuing two fleeing Confederates, and believing he could not capture both, went after the one in the "brighter" uniform in the

---

15 Shoemaker, *Shoemaker's Battery,* 87-8.

hope he would catch a high-ranking officer. He overtook the natty officer, who proved to be a mere captain of artillery, and learned from him that the dingily dressed man he had chosen not to pursue was General Lomax.[16] The Federals did manage to capture Lomax, but he later escaped by knocking one of his captors to the ground and joining in a Federal charge upon his own men. He later joked he was the bravest among the Yankees "for he charged right into the rebels."[17]

Aside from Lomax's escape, little else went right for the Southerners. One Federal claimed that citizens in Woodstock, after watching the ignoble Confederate retreat, became so imbued with "the spirit of the chase" that they actually cheered the pursuing Yankees dashing through the streets. Colonel Devin led the 6th and 9th New York regiments on a four-mile canter to near Hawkinstown, where they found what remained of McNulty's battery struggling along southward. The Confederates again unlimbered the guns, loaded them with canister and prepared to fight to the last. Even so, cavalrymen who were supposed to be protecting the guns continued to fly by, riding over or around McNulty's increasingly few and desperate men. Though ready to discharge canister into the enemy, McNulty held his fire because many of the fleeing troopers were between him and the Federals. A staff officer heard McNulty shout, "Captain, if you will only get your runaway cavalrymen out of the road I will let into them." But no one could do anything to bring order to the chaos. McNulty had already been flanked on the west, and he saw the road before him packed with "the confused rabble of our flying people and pursuing federals in one general melee."[18] McNulty told his men to run for it and save themselves, abandoning one gun in the hope of saving the other. The 9th New York added the field piece, and a few more wagons, caissons, forges, and ambulances to the trophies of the day. Determined to have McNulty's last cannon, Devin split his command to pursue on two roads and pushed on into Mt. Jackson. The Confederates maintained a large hospital in the town, and Devin heard from the surgeons there that they had watched in astonishment as the Southern cavalrymen

16 "The Late Operations in the Valley," Richmond *Dispatch*, October 15, 1864, p. 1, col. 4.

17 "Recollections of George W. Towle"; *OR* 43, pt. 1, 613, 447; A Soldier, "The Cavalry"; Jed Hotchkiss, *Virginia*, 628-30. Hotchkiss states Lomax was captured twice and escaped twice, but no other found account verifies the statement.

18 Harris, "With the Reserve Brigade, Paper 2," 245; Booth, *Reminiscences*, 154.

Artist James Taylor's panoramic sketch portrays some of Lomax's men (right of center) before the Confederate hospital in Mt. Jackson making one last effort to resist the onslaught of Devin's New Yorkers thundering up the Valley Pike.

The Soldier in Our Civil War

flew by at a rapid gait and in evident terror. The men of the 6th New York thundered through Mt. Jackson, past the charred wreckage of the depot they and their comrades had burned two days earlier, but found they were too late to snap up the Marylanders' last cannon. With all of Shoemaker's battery and the more fortunate of Lomax's fugitives, McNulty and his men had crossed to the south side of the Shenandoah River. Merritt dismissively wrote that the enemy could be seen flying in disorder across Meem's Bottom, and "where they stopped the terror-stricken wretches could scarcely tell themselves, I cannot."[19]

The marathon was over. A resident later claimed the thunderous rumbling created by hundreds of horses pounding up the Valley Pike that day had been audible miles away.[20] Colonel Devin estimated the chase had covered nearly 20 miles, eight of that at a gallop, and many of his horses had broken down. The colonel ordered rest. The Federals found themselves with an embarrassment of riches in Mt. Jackson, including abandoned caissons and a park of thirty-one wagons loaded with ordnance and quartermaster's

19 *OR* 43, pt. 1, 448, 484, 483. The various accounts of the capture of McNulty's guns defy reconciliation. The sources agree only that the Federals took five of six cannon; where they were captured cannot be determined. Topographer Jed Hotchkiss, writing in his journal at Early's headquarters, stated cavalrymen "came rushing back" into New Market about 4 p.m. Ibid., 578.

20 Wayland, *The Valley Turnpike*, 27.

stores. New Yorkers, piled fence rails and set fire to all of the vehicles and supplies. Near evening Devin's men began the long ride back to Woodstock, accompanied by the pyrotechnics and booming percussion of exploding artillery shells roasting in ammunition boxes.[21]

In returning from their long chase of the enemy, the 1st New York Dragoons were in high spirits. Having vanquished the Southern cavalry, they found themselves in a mood to harass the civilians who had taunted them a day earlier. As they passed through the dark streets of Edinburg and Woodstock, they began to howl and jeer and, according to the regimental historian,

> Bedlam was let loose. The men tried to out do each other in hideous and demoniacal yells, screechings, and cat-yawls. They bleated, bellowed, cackled, and crowed, while the buglers and [the] band produced unearthly discords by tooting each instrument in a different key, and the drummers beating out of time. The hubbub was contagious, spreading to other regiments, until the inhabitants must have imagined themselves in a veritable pandemonium.

Thus did the victors in the "Woodstock Races" proceed ingloriously through the charred landscape and chastened people of the Shenandoah.[22]

---

21 *OR* 43, pt. 1, 483-84; Cheney, *History of the Ninth Regiment,* 228. The men and horses who turned northward with Devin at Mt. Jackson and retraced their steps to Woodstock, where they went into camp, covered approximately 35 miles in the course of the day. Merritt praised the "soldierly qualities" of the troopers in his division for taking such excellent care of their mounts that "their horses, with but few exceptions, endured a run of nearly twenty miles and were found the next day in condition for a reasonable march." *OR* 43, pt. 1, 447.

22 Bowen, *Three Years of Active Service,* 248.

CHAPTER TEN

Exhilaration and Despair

"The World May Fault Me, but Gen. Lee Cannot."

— Chicago *Tribune*, August 26, 1892

October 10 dawned very cold with heavy frost and ice, but Brig. Gen. George Armstrong Custer, United States Volunteers, was warmly dressed. Sporting his usual bright-red necktie and broad-brimmed hat, Custer wore the embroidered uniform coat of a Confederate brigadier general of cavalry, a fact he found immensely amusing. The gleeful Custer shared the joke with the men of his Third Cavalry Division by cantering ostentatiously through their camps clad in the gray coat; the men, too, saw high comedy in the charade. The slim Custer purposely cut an absurd figure, with drooping sleeves and lapels tucked nearly under his armpits, but the veteran troopers understood the more subtle humor of the performance as well. They had themselves captured Custer's costume the day before—the coat formerly belonged to Thomas L. Rosser, whose headquarters wagon had been abandoned as the Southerners took flight. Custer could not resist the temptation to bait his friend and rival and sent a note through the lines asking Rosser to have the tailor cut the tails of the replacement coat a bit shorter so next time Custer could enjoy a better fit. Rosser grumbled in a letter to his wife that Custer was "impudent."[1]

---

1 Ferguson, "Memoranda," frame 399; Rodenbough, *18th Regiment*, 60; Custer, *The Custer Story,* 122; Custer, *Boots and Saddles,* 275; Elizabeth Bacon Custer, *The Civil War Memories of Elizabeth Bacon Custer*, Arlene Reynolds, ed. (Austin, TX, 1994); Rosser to

Beyond its clownish braggadocio, Custer's farce held symbolism. For much of the war, the Confederacy's horse soldiers in the Eastern Theater had been routinely superior to the North's mounted arm. Having learned well from their early defeats and embarrassments, the Federals had gained ground and produced a mounted arm superior in equipment, logistics, organization, tactics, and leadership. The Northerners had attained parity on some cavalry battlefields in 1863, but the Southerners had remained formidable opponents. On October 9, 1864, the Union horsemen decisively asserted their dominance. Thanks to the coincidence of technology, enlightened leadership, and suitable terrain in the Shenandoah Valley, Federal cavalrymen fought with great effectiveness while mounted or dismounted. Merritt's and Custer's men at Tom's Brook represented the highest state of development of this "hybrid cavalryman." Thomas D. Ranson, a veteran Confederate cavalryman who had been taken prisoner at Tom's Brook, reflected upon his long-time adversaries and willingly gave credit where it was due. While many former Confederates ascribed the Federal triumphs to overwhelming numbers and superior firepower, Ranson thought his adversaries had also grown in ability, leadership, and discipline. He admitted that "the cavalry we used to despise had gotten to be a working machine. They had learned in the school of adversity."[2] The reversal of roles was complete. At Tom's Brook, the Federal cavalry assumed figuratively what Custer donned literally—the mantle of mounted supremacy previously owned by the Confederates.

A paucity of records makes it difficult to determine with accuracy the casualties and captures on October 9, 1864. The protracted marching and skirmishing of the days previous to the engagement made enumeration of the men present for duty difficult even for officers, and the long running fight made it impossible for Confederate leaders to distinguish among their killed, wounded, and captured. Rosser, understandably reluctant to chronicle the extent of the disaster, made no report, nor did he call for one from Colonel Munford nor, apparently, from any of his subordinates.[3] *The Official*

---

wife, October 15, 1864, Rosser Papers, Acc. 1171-g, Box 1. As late as 1873, Rosser's coat was still in the Custer home in Monroe, Michigan. After her husband's death, Mrs. Custer donated the coat to the U.S.M.A. museum, where it remains.

2   Ranson Reminsencence.

3   Munford, "Reminiscences . . . No. 3," 134.

Rosser's uniform coat, captured by Custer's men at Tom's Brook, remained a conversation piece in the Custer household for decades. Mrs. Custer donated the coat to the U.S. Military Academy.

West Point Museum Collections, United States Military Academy

Records of the Union and Confederate Armies published after the war include not a single report from any officer in Rosser's command regarding the events of October 9, 1864. Of the two division commanders, five brigade commanders, and 24 commanders of a regiment, battery, or battalion, exactly one report by a Confederate officer regarding the action at Tom's Brook appears in the *Official Records*, and that scrap of testimony came from Lunsford Lomax, who devoted to the affair a single paragraph. Lomax admitted his material losses but did not enumerate them or suggest a figure for his losses in men or animals.[4]

The victorious Federals, on the other hand, were eager to detail the occurrences of the day. Sheridan informally estimated the number of prisoners at 330. The meticulous Merritt reported the capture of 43 wagons full of ordnance, quartermaster's stores, and rifles as well as three ambulances, five pieces of artillery with limbers (all of McNulty's guns but one), caissons, forges, mules, horses, sets of harness, and more than 50

---

4 Captain Booth recalled that musters on the morning of October 10 revealed that "our losses in men and horses were not great." Booth, *Reminiscences*, 155.

prisoners.[5] Custer had taken six pieces of artillery, the headquarters wagons of Rosser and Munford, the division's wagon trains, 106 prisoners, and General Rosser's coat and pet squirrel.[6] The 1st Vermont Cavalry reported recapturing some of the sheep and cattle they had lost two days earlier at Mill Creek. Somewhere near Woodstock, Pvt. Edward Hanford of the 2nd U.S. Cavalry took possession of the colors of one of the fleeing Confederate outfits and thus became the only man to receive the Medal of Honor for actions during the day.[7] All the prizes came at a low price: Torbert simply stated, "My losses in this engagement will not exceed 60 killed and

5   *OR* 43, pt. 1, 31, 448. Lieutenant Colonel Casper Crowninshield of the 2nd Massachusetts Cavalry reported that the Reserve Brigade captured one battle-flag, four pieces of artillery, four caissons, two forges, two ambulances, seven wagons, and 50 prisoners and lost only seven wounded in the entire brigade (the 2nd U.S. cavalry remained behind in support of a section of artillery and did not participate in the pursuit). *OR* 43, pt. 1, 491-92. For additional enumerations that vary slightly regarding the captures by Merritt's division, see reports published in the New York *Herald* on October 14 and 17, 1864. The claim of 52 prisoners does not agree with evidence from Confederate rosters and other sources.

6   *OR* 43, pt. 1, 521, 103; "Sheridan's Army," *The Evening Telegraph* (Philadelphia, PA), October 17, 1864, Third Edition, p. 1, col. 4; Custer, *The Custer Story*, 123. Reverend Denison, the regimental historian of the 1st Rhode Island Cavalry, declared that the six guns taken from Rosser by Custer's men at Tom's Brook were, ironically, the same pieces that had been captured from the Third Cavalry Division during a raid at Ream's Station, south of Petersburg, in the summer of 1864. Correspondent Finley Anderson states that only two of the recaptured guns had been lost at Ream's Station. In a dispatch to Grant, Sheridan stated, "Some of the artillery captured was new and never had been fired before. The pieces were marked, Tredegar Works." Frederic Denison, *Sabres and Spurs: The First Regiment Rhode Island Cavalry in the Civil War, 1861-1865* (Central Falls, RI, 1876), 410; Anderson, "Shenandoah"; *OR* 43, pt. 2, 327.

7   Charles Farr Diary, USAHEC. The identity of the Confederate unit that lost its flag to Hanford remains a mystery. His Medal of Honor citation reads "the 32nd Battalion Virginia Cavalry," but that battalion no longer existed. The 32nd Battalion Virginia Cavalry had been merged months earlier with the 42nd Battalion Virginia Cavalry and then absorbed into a new regiment designated the 24th Virginia Cavalry, and that regiment was serving in Gen. Wade Hampton's cavalry in eastern Virginia on October 9, 1864, 100 miles or more from Woodstock. It is possible that whoever recorded the identity of Hanford's flag made a clerical error. The 34th, 35th, and 36th battalions Virginia Cavalry all belonged to brigades engaged at Tom's Brook, and the 34th and 36th served in Lomax's division and were therefore likely to have retreated through, and perhaps lost a flag at, Woodstock. Understandably, no member of any of the Confederate cavalry battalions present came forward to clear up the mystery by admitting to the embarrassment of losing its colors. *OR* 43, pt. 1, 550; Lee A. Wallace, Jr., *A Guide to Virginia Military Organizations 1861-1865* (Lynchburg, VA, 1986), 65.

After the Valley Campaign, Sheridan (far left) posed with some of his more
prominent officers (l to r): Chief of Staff James Forsyth, Wesley Merritt,
Thomas Devin, and George Custer. LOC

wounded, which is astonishing when compared with the results." Sheridan
later officially reported nine men killed and 48 wounded for a total of 57.[8]

Incomplete records suggest most of the Federal casualties came in
Custer's division. Peirce's battery had one gun damaged and lost in addition
to losing the whole gun crew killed or wounded. The 1st New Hampshire
and 1st Vermont regiments led the regimental casualty lists. At least six of
the Hampshiremen went down wounded, and one more man was missing
and assumed taken prisoner. The 1st Vermont Cavalry lost at least
seven—two killed and five wounded. That these two New England
regiments together lost more men than any other two Federal outfits suggests

8   *OR* 43, pt. 1, 327, 431, 60.

the strength of the resistance they met as they charged together up the slope of Coffman's Hill during Custer's climactic assault. Vermonter Albert Drury described the fighting as "desperate," and some of his comrades thought the charge worthy of special note in the regiment's long record of service.[9] Likewise, most of the Confederate casualties fell in Rosser's division, with the most severe losses coming in Munford's brigade. Of the nearly 200 documented casualties in Rosser's command, nearly half belonged to Munford.[10]

In addition to the many other trophies taken that day, Custer captured in prose both the ineffectiveness of the Confederate fugitives and the arrogance of their powerful pursuers. With evident joy, he wrote, "Vainly did the most gallant of this affrighted herd endeavor to rally a few supports around their standards and stay the advance of their eager and exulting pursuers, who, in one overwhelming current, were bearing down everything before them." In a letter home, Colonel Lowell belittled the contest with Lomax's men as a mere "brush," and suggested it did not even rise to the level of a "fight." Torbert, who certainly realized that the victory by his men had saved his job, gloated with delight in his report. "There could hardly have been a more complete victory and rout," he crowed. "The cavalry totally covered themselves with glory, and added to their long list of victories the most brilliant one of them all and the most decisive the country has ever witnessed." Merritt concluded that "Never has there been, in the history of this war, a more complete victory than this of Tom's Creek." Sheridan sent word of the victory to General Grant, praising his cavalry and making no effort to hide his contempt for the enemy. After mocking Rosser as the "Savior of the Valley," Sheridan wrote with the air of a man swatting a fly, "I deemed it best to make this delay of one day here and settle this new cavalry general."[11]

The results of Tom's Brook were significant. "The fact is," Jubal Early wrote to Robert E. Lee on the day of the fight at Tom's Brook, "that the enemy's cavalry is so much superior to ours, both in numbers and

9   Albert Drury, *The Better Part of Valor: Albert Drury and His 1st Vermont Cavalry in the Civil War's Eastern Campaign* (privately printed, 1995), 91; Charles R. Farr Diary, USAHEC.

10 See Appendix B for further information on casualties.

11 *OR*, 43, pt. 1, 521, 431, 448, and ibid., pt. 2, 327; Emerson, *Life and Letters*, 59.

equipment, and the country is so favorable to the operations of cavalry, that it is impossible for ours to compete with his."[12] The costly defeat at Tom's Brook accelerated the steady decline of the Confederate cavalry, and, in Early's words, "crippled us smartly."[13] Early's cavalry would never again approach parity with its Federal counterparts in the Shenandoah Valley. Ten days after Tom's Brook, the Federals nearly destroyed Early's army at the Battle of Cedar Creek, where the Confederate horsemen struggled to achieve any effectiveness while the Federal cavalry captured 45 pieces of artillery.[14] The morale and spirit of the Federal cavalry had never been higher than in October 1864. On October 10, the day after the fight, Custer reveled in the supremacy, and in the glow of his success shared his joy with his wife:

> Darling little one, Yesterday, the 9th, was a glorious day for your Boy. He signalized his accession to his new command by a brilliant victory. I attacked Genl. Rosser's Division of 3 Brigades with my Division of 2, and gained the most glorious victory. I drove Rosser in confusion 10 miles, captured 6 cannon, all his advance trains, ambulance train, all Genls. Rosser's, Lomax's & Wickham's headquarters wagons containing all their baggage, private & official papers. . . .Genl. Torbert has sent me a note beginning "God bless you—."[15]

*   *   *

12 *OR* 43, pt. 1, 612; A Soldier, "The Cavalry." Merritt remarked that the extent of the victory was due in no small part to the training and discipline by which his men had kept their animals in such good condition that despite the active service of the first week of October they were still able to chase a beaten enemy 15 to 20 miles, or more, at rapid gait. *OR* 43, pt. 1, 447, 559.

13 Early to Rosser, May 10, 1866, Rosser Papers, 1171-a, Box 1.

14 *OR* 43, pt. 1, 435.

15 Custer, *The Custer Story*, 122. Captain Sanford, of Torbert's staff, relates an anecdote that has proved popular among Custer admirers. According to Sanford, during the engagement at Coffman's Hill, he informed Custer that five Confederate cannon had been captured by the First Cavalry Division in the fighting on the Valley Pike and that Custer immediately boasted, "All right, hold on a minute and I'll show you six." Sanford declares Custer then launched the attack that captured all six of Rosser's guns. If Sanford spoke as he claims, then he misled Custer. Lomax's fifth and final Confederate gun would not be captured until later in the day when the pursuit had extended many miles south of Tom's Brook, long after the fight at Coffman's Hill had ended. It is possible that either Sanford deliberately goaded Custer with a misrepresentation or, more likely, he misremembered the sequence of events. Sanford, *Fighting Rebels*, 284.

Despite the stampedes from Tom's Brook and the general rout, the Confederates could point with pride to many acts of courage and even heroism: Captain Shoemaker's 90 stout-hearted men who rejected a blame-free offer to retreat and chose to risk capture by standing their ground and resisting the enemy; Lieutenant McNulty and his men, who fought their broken down battery to the last gun; Captain Thomson, who stuck by his guns on Coffman's Hill after three horses fell beneath him; General Lomax, who repeatedly rallied troops during the withdrawal, hindering the Federal advance at close quarters until he was captured and escaped, possibly twice. Even near the end of the retreat, when all seemed almost lost, some Confederates remained willing to sacrifice themselves. Artillery Captain John C. Carpenter watched in dismay as the fugitive cavalrymen began arriving at Meem's Bottom. Although his battery was not engaged, Captain Carpenter understood the cavalry had abandoned other batteries someplace to the north. Carpenter followed the old military proverb and "rode toward the sound of the guns" to find the endangered batteries to help save them. His conspicuous courage earned him the praise of superiors, who honored him by bringing his actions to the attention of General R. E. Lee. Carpenter paid with the loss of an arm.[16]

The incidents of individual bravery did little to alleviate the Confederates' sense of shame. What one New Yorker blithely characterized as "a lively and entertaining Sunday morning ride," was a humiliation for those Confederate cavalrymen and artillerymen chased from the field. "It was a new sensation, to be pursued by Yankee Cavalry," quipped a sardonic Virginian, "and I felt we were all disgraced.[17] General Lomax, in his disorganized and cheerless camp near New Market, asked staff officer Captain Booth if pickets had been placed around the camp. Booth, thinking Lomax projected "deep sorrow and mortification," told the general no pickets had been posted because "there was no organized command."[18] A Southern gunner recalled the anger he and his comrades felt at the loss of their guns and the stinging mockery in the laughter of other soldiers. The men of his battery talked of schemes to make independent raids to recapture

16 *OR* 42, pt. 1, 864.

17 Cheney, *History of the Ninth Regiment,* 228; Ranson Reminsencence.

18 Booth, *Reminiscences,* 155.

their cannon.[19] Few in Early's army spared any compassion for the cavalry. An infantryman from North Carolina wrote his parents, "I do wish that the Yankees would capture all the cavalry. . . . They never will fight so I think it useless to have them in the army eating rations from the Government."[20] An artilleryman lamented, "Sunday at Rude's Hill we met the first stampede I ever saw—Our forces have disgraced themselves. . . . I was never so mortified in my life."[21] A staff officer thought Lomax's cavalrymen, "not worth the powder necessary to shoot them down. They do not want to fight and run away from the enemy as soon as they can. The best thing to do with these people, would be to get them down from their horses and to put them into the infantry. May the devil get all these fellows." According to an officer at Early's headquarters, after Tom's Brook, Lomax took steps to punish misconduct in his division by arresting 30 officers.[22]

The gloom in Rosser's camps south of Columbia Furnace was as deep. The Federals had captured almost everything on wheels and much else besides. With his typical bravado, Custer would declare that during the fight that morning Rosser's Confederates had been "deficient in confidence, courage and a just cause." By evening, it seemed as though Rosser's men were deficient in everything else. One Confederate noted they could not even find the small comfort of a clean shirt. Artillery commander James Breathed, subdued after the loss of all six of the guns with which he had started the day, and of seven caissons, dozens of horses with harness and chests of ammunition, and at least 35 men who were captured along with the guns, seemed stunned as he frequently repeated, "No guns for me."[23] Rosser, at the dawn of the day, might have had reason to feel he had made progress

---

19 Lewis Brady, "Notice of Chew's Battery," *Southern Historical Society Papers,* 16 (1888), 214-15.

20 Samuel P. Collier to parents, October 11, 1864, Samuel P. Collier Papers, P.C.416, North Carolina State Archives, Raleigh, North Carolina.

21 McVicar Diary.

22 Oscar Hinrichs and Richard Brady Williams, *Stonewall's Prussian Mapmaker: The Journals of Captain Oscar Hinrichs* (Chapel Hill, NC, 2014), 193; Thomas H. Carter, *Gunner in Lee's Army: The Civil War Letters of Thomas Henry Carter,* Graham T. Dozier, ed. (Chapel Hill, NC, 2014), 263.

23 *OR* 43, pt. 1, 522; Munford, "Reminiscences . . . No. 3," 138; Untitled typescript, Munford-Ellis Papers, Box 17, folder "Writings: Civil War Mss. of Thos. T. Munford (Rosser-Munford Dispute) 4 of 4."

toward earning the flattering title "Savior of the Valley." By sundown, the boastful *nom de guerre* could not have been pleasing to his ears. When his staff officers brought him the accounting of the day's losses, the division commander learned the extent of the disaster: all of the artillery, all of the division and brigade headquarters wagons, the entire forward wagon train of the division, including 14 wagons full of ordnance and 56,000 rounds of carbine ammunition, 16 ambulances—10 of which had been filled with wounded—and 89 precious serviceable horses and mules, all gone.[24] Most significant in the camps that night was the absence of almost 200 men. Rosser had lost about 14 percent of the soldiers he had taken to Coffman's Hill that morning—one-seventh of his entire command. More than half of them were bound for Northern prisons, principally Point Lookout, Maryland. There they would endure, as one of them later wrote, "Eight months of slow starvation and poisonous water and suffering nights. . . . Men died and were carted out by the score."[25] Tom's Brook had been a whipping of unsparing and unprecedented thoroughness, the effects of which would linger.

On the afternoon of the 9th, Rosser notified Early of the defeat. Three days later, and again on the 15th, Rosser sought to unburden himself in letters to his wife. He wrote, no doubt, with a heavy heart, but he gave no hint of remorse or guilt. Instead, he saw himself as a victim and blamed others. Because Early had ordered him to push on aggressively and strike at Sheridan if possible, Rosser held Early responsible: "Early is the only person that can be censured for the Cav'y disaster," he declared. "I have all his orders, and they were urging me on all the while, telling me to press on + get in Sheridan's rear and capture his trains, +c." In Rosser's mind, Early's decision to remain at New Market while sending his cavalry far ahead in pursuit of the enemy also made him culpable. "I was thirty miles from support," Rosser told his wife with some exaggeration, "and there was no remedy for my losses!" Rosser also blamed some of the troops: "part of my commd is greatly demoralized but I hope to cause them to do their duty in future. My Brig. is in fine spirits and behaved well in the fight and if the other Brigs. should act again as they did in the late fight I will not command them

24 "Sheridan's Army," *The Evening Telegraph*; Anderson, "Shenandoah."

25 Ranson Reminsencence.

longer." And he blamed some of his officers: "although the troops behaved badly I think the difficulty was with the officers and they will not do so again."[26] Rosser apparently did not consider the possibility that "the difficulty" was he had erred in choosing to fight. Conditioned by long habit, the career-minded Rosser fretted about what damage the "disaster" might do to his future, and he feared censure: "I fought my best until whipped! The world may fault me, but Gen. Lee cannot."[27]

At the same time, Rosser displayed a desire to control information about the engagement. After reiterating "Early is the responsible man" and admitting he had "come near to being destroyed with the entire command," Rosser told his wife he did not trust Early and worried about how that general would report the event to R. E. Lee. Rosser planned to write a report, presumably faulting Early, and then send it outside of the chain of command directly to Lee instead of his immediate superior as he was required to do. Later, after Early did not censure him for the Tom's Brook defeat, Rosser decided the less said about the disaster the better, and he made no report at all. Because he never submitted a report—and did not require subordinates to file reports—Rosser prevented details of the affair from becoming public. As a result, the extent of the whipping was not widely understood until years later.[28]

26 Rosser to wife, October 12 and 15, 1864, Rosser Papers, Acc. 1171-g, Box 1.

27 Rosser to wife, October 12, 1864, Rosser Papers, Acc. 1171-g, Box 1. In unpublished notes among his personal papers, Munford asserted that he wrote reports of his brigade's actions during the autumn operations and that in them he "reflected upon Rosser's shameless management and loss of 11 pieces of artillery and all his wagons + prisoners, which could have been avoided." In these notes, Munford also implies that he sent these reports not to Rosser, as adherence to the chain of command required, but directly to Early's headquarters. Munford asserts that in late January 1865, Rosser visited Early's headquarters and retrieved Munford's reports and "kept them." In support of this claim, Munford cites the published extract of the journal of topographer Jed Hotchkiss, who served at Early's headquarters and who met there with Rosser on January 27, 1865. See I 46, pt. 1, 513 for the relevant passage of Hotchkiss's journal, which reads: "Rosser came and gave details of Beverly affair at night, and got from Munford actions of his brigade during campaign." The meaning of the passage is ambiguous, and Munford offers no clarification. Because Hotchkiss was at the time gathering information about past operations of the units in Early's army and translating that information into maps, the journal passage might also be read as meaning that Hotchkiss himself "got from" Munford details about the actions of Munford's brigade. Untitled memoranda, Munford-Ellis Papers, Box 17, folder "Miscellany: Civil War Notes Folder 2 of 2."

28 Rosser to wife, October 15, 1864, Rosser Papers, Acc. 1171-g, Box 1.

Rosser's efforts to control the public perception of the defeat may have gone deeper. Just a few days after the battle, a man in Rosser's command, plainly one of the general's admirers, sought to place on the public record a version of events very favorable to Rosser and implying criticism of Jubal Early. The writer, the aforementioned Gray Jacket, sent a letter to the Richmond *Sentinel* newspaper. From Gray Jacket's perspective, the defeat had not been an embarrassing rout but rather an honorable struggle. In an article published six days after the fight, Gray Jacket sought to refute rumors of a chaotic retreat, stating categorically: "Did we run?—We did not." After adamantly declaring, "There has been no stampede of Rosser's cavalry," Gray Jacket maligned those who said otherwise as "cowardly dogs" and "despicable wretches." Although no known evidence demonstrates that Rosser had anything to do with the article, the correspondent spoke of Rosser in heroic terms and employed many of the same extenuations Rosser would later use in his own defense: "Far in advance of his friends, 16 miles from our infantry, unsupported by other cavalry, the enemy's infantry close at hand and all his cavalry moving against him, the heart of Rosser abated not a jot of its faith or its boldness. But there was no stampede." Gray Jacket also dismissed as insignificant the loss of the six pieces of artillery, an argument that Rosser also would make. "True, we were defeated," admitted Gray Jacket, "but except for the loss of the artillery, the advantage would have been with us; and beaten or not, we lost not honor nor our old glory."[29]

*   *   *

Though Rosser admitted to his wife he had been "whipped" at Tom's Brook, he did not connect his decision to fight on Coffman's Hill with that whipping. The kind of fighting Rosser had managed so well over the previous three days—hit and run attacks repeated at every advantageous opportunity—was entirely different from the kind of fight he accepted at Tom's Brook. The lightning, slashing strikes on the rear guard of a retreating column perfectly suited the capabilities of his small, mobile, and aggressive command, but that same small command was not suited to fight a general engagement in which the two foes faced each other, deployed troops and artillery, and then exchanged blows. When the enemy turned to face him on

29 Gray Jacket, "The Cavalry Fights in the Valley."

the morning of October 9, Rosser lost part of the advantage of mobility. When Rosser tied his defense to the terrain at Coffman's Hill, he sacrificed more mobility. Rosser's fatal error was attempting to cover too much ground with too few men. As a veteran cavalry commander, Rosser undoubtedly understood tactics. At Coffman's Hill, he could call upon the experience of dozens of fights, small and large. That experience did not include controlling three brigades in a general engagement against a numerically superior opponent. In that sense, Rosser was a novice at Tom's Brook. His inexperience should have given him pause. Instead, Rosser accepted the challenge Custer brought him, and his conduct of the fight reflected his inexperience.

For any cavalry commander the stiffest challenge was a general engagement against opposing cavalry on an open field. Because of the speed with which mounted troops moved, a single mistake by a commander could be punished immediately, leading with stunning speed to disaster.[30] In cavalry-versus-cavalry encounters, accepted wisdom decreed that a commander should embrace a few general rules to avoid defeat: He should keep ample reserves, should not fight from a defensive posture, and should strongly guard his flanks. At Tom's Brook, the ground and the relative sizes of the two forces engaged combined to make it almost impossible for Rosser to adhere to these rules.[31]

First, because cavalry battles so often evolved into a series of charges and counter charges and thus became tests of endurance, cavalry officers were taught that the commander who retains the last reserve of fresh troops retains the advantage in the fight. History has demonstrated that an ample reserve "generally turns the fortune of the day."[32] Even after designating Payne's tiny brigade as a reserve, Rosser simply did not have enough men to maintain a strong front line along a broad front and a significant reserve against a force the size of Custer's.

---

30 L. E. Nolan, *Cavalry: Its History and Tactics* (Columbia, SC, 1864), 130. For insight on cavalry tactics and the general rules governing conventional practices of mid-nineteenth century mounted troops in combat, see Nolan's discussion on pages 129-45.

31 George T. Denison, *Modern Cavalry: Its Organisation, Armament, and Employment in War, With an Appendix, Containing Letters From Generals Fitzhugh Lee, Stephen D. Lee and T. L. Rosser, of the Confederate States Cavalry; And Col. Jenyns' System of Non-Pivot Drill in Use in the 13th Hussars* (London, 1868), 145-50.

32 Nolan, *Cavalry*, 133; Denison, *Modern Cavalry*, 143.

Second, the imposing face of Coffman's Hill may have deluded Rosser into believing it a strong position upon which to mount a defense. Whatever his reasoning, Rosser chose to deploy his troops defensively—mounted troops in ranks behind dismounted riflemen—and he began the fight in this defensive posture. Cavalry, far more than infantry and artillery, was ill suited to defense, especially against opposing mounted troops. Throughout history, cavalry succeeded best against other cavalry when used offensively, thus the truism "That cavalry that awaits the shock of opposing horsemen will always be overthrown."[33] Some evidence suggests Rosser might have intended to attack from the hill rather than to fight defensively on the hill. If Rosser intended to find a weak spot and strike it forcefully enough to drive the enemy back, he failed to find such a weakness quickly enough. The engagement then became a series of probes in which both sides maintained the status quo with an effective defense. In such a static situation, the commanders were tempting fate by "awaiting the shock" of the charge that eventually would come. The advantage would go to the contender who first found the key to the enemy's position, and at Tom's Brook, as in most cavalry engagements, the man who found the key was the commander who possessed more troopers. Rosser did not have enough men to hold his line defensively and thoroughly explore the enemy's line for weaknesses. Custer did.

Inevitably, the contest became a question of flanks. One writer on cavalry tactics succinctly stated the wisdom of centuries when he explained, "Cavalry attacked in flank, while engaged in front, must give way."[34] Whatever explanation Rosser might have offered for his defeat at Tom's Brook, the inescapable fact is that the position he chose to fight upon was flanked on both ends of his line. This fact leads to the inescapable conclusion that Rosser's flanks were inadequately protected. Furthermore, Rosser's flanks were vulnerable for the same reason that his reserve was inadequate and that he was unable to mount an effective offense from Coffman's Hill: Rosser did not have enough men to successfully fight the kind of engagement he attempted to wage.

33 Ibid., 145.

34 Ibid., 150.

Major James Ferguson, the official recorder of events at Rosser's headquarters, attributed "the misfortunes of the day" on October 9, 1864, to four causes: injudicious orders from Early, rashness on the part of General Rosser, misbehavior of two officers in the 1st and 3rd Virginia cavalry regiments, and Rosser's Laurel Brigade being too far away to offer any support at the point where the Federals broke through the line along Back Road.[35] Certainly all of these causes contributed to the events of the day, but to what degree did each contribute? The distance of more than a century and a half complicates the modern observer's efforts to arrive at a reasonable judgment. When declaring Early's orders "injudicious," was Major Ferguson referring to the document Early wrote on October 7, or to other orders that have not come to light? Likewise, it is unquestionably true that the "misbehavior" of the two officers, specifically Col. Richard Welby Carter of the 1st Virginia Cavalry and Maj. Henry Carrington of the 3rd Virginia Cavalry, produced negative results. But Early's orders only controlled events before the fight began on Coffman's Hill, and the "misbehavior" of the two officers occurred after the fight on the hill had been lost. Neither of these two factors could have played as large a role in the defeat as the two other causes identified by Ferguson—Rosser's rashness and the misplacement of the Laurel Brigade. These two causes are, in fact, interrelated. The Laurel Brigade stood too far away to offer aid during the breakthrough and collapse along the Back Road because Rosser had rashly decided to defend too much ground. Rosser's rashness remains the essential fact of the day.

Rashness, taking action without due consideration of possible consequences, led to all manner of military and political disasters between 1861 and 1865. Rashness was the great error for soldiers and politicians alike. It was worse than mere thoughtlessness and just one step short of recklessness. It lost battles and ruined careers. Abraham Lincoln repeatedly warned his generals to beware of it. Sheridan explicitly advised against it, as did Jeb Stuart.[36] In July 1863, Stuart regretted that too many of his cavalry officers were still ineffective. Again and again he had tried to correct what he called "defects in the mode of fighting" by his subordinates, and he

---

35 Ferguson, "Memoranda," frame 399.

36 *OR* 23, pt. 2, 369; *OR* 25, pt. 2, 4; *OR* 43, pt. 1, 505.

eventually issued "General Orders No. 26, Cavalry Tactics," specific instructions for cavalry officers to follow in combat. Stuart addressed both technical matters, such as troop placement and the conduct of advances and charges, and he addressed matters of morale and philosophy. He preached vigor and aggressiveness, but also emphasized the importance of discretion. He wished cavalry commanders to be able to restrain aggressive impulses long enough for them to see the larger picture. Heedless aggression was not an asset to a cavalry commander. In fact, Stuart declared, "rashness is a crime," and he urged his officers to understand that "boldness is not incompatible with caution, nay, is often the quintessence of prudence."[37]

"Rashness" was a word especially common in the language of cavalrymen because of the nature of their work. In a business in which seizing the moment was of supreme importance, cavalrymen had to recognize an opportunity and commit to a course of action instantly and then follow through with boldness and vigor. As Stuart wrote, "to falter is to fail," so there was little time for sober second thoughts. However, because rashness is almost by definition an excess of the spirit of dash, the tension between the two concepts creates a conundrum: How much dash is rash? To win a victory, those aggressive, impulsive, brave spirits with dash must aggressively and impulsively and bravely test limits in every situation, and thereby risk rashness. Some cannot see the invisible line and rein in their dash short of rashness. Therefore, this "dash-rash" conundrum is especially dangerous because one can only know what is rash after the fact—after having experienced the sting of embarrassment and defeat. Recognizing the line and staying on the right side of it was a skill Stuart wished all of his commanders to develop. Many of them did.

Long after the war, Colonel Munford maintained Rosser was simply "pig-headed" on Coffman's Hill, and he declared without equivocation, "To make the fight at Tom's Brook was against all the rules of discretion and judgment, and the whole responsibility belongs to Rosser."[38] Munford's is a biased opinion. He disliked Rosser, who had publicly insulted him by promoting a junior man to general over Munford's head. After the war, Munford criticized Rosser freely, sometimes using mockery and sarcasm.

37 *OR* 27, pt. 3, 1,054-55.

38 Munford to Jed Hotchkiss, October 12, 1897, Hotchkiss Papers, roll 49, frame 240; Munford, "Reminiscences . . . Paper No. 3," 135.

But in this narrow instance regarding events on Coffman's Hill, Munford's bias does not make his judgment of Rosser's decision at Tom's Brook less valid. Finding his command in a dangerous situation in which he would for the first time have to control three brigades on a battlefield, Rosser ignored too many disadvantageous realities and made an ill-considered decision that forced him to violate too many basic tactical principles. Rosser never offered a reasonable explanation for deciding to fight at Tom's Brook. The only excuse he ever gave was that Early's orders forced him to fight at Tom's Brook—a statement refuted by evidence and denied by Early.

When Rosser informed the army commander of the results at Tom's Brook, the curmudgeon Early, not known as a fount of sympathy, took a page from Robert E. Lee's principles of leadership and generously commiserated with Rosser while encouraging him to boldly meet the next challenge. "General," Early wrote, "Your notes have been received. I am sorry for the reverse of yesterday, but I know the enemy's great superiority in numbers + equipment. But we must not be dispirited, but reorganize and try again." In his next sentence, Early left the past behind and moved on to the present and the future by briefing Rosser on the strategic situation, thereby treating Rosser as an important member of his team rather than as the author of a disaster. Done was done. Early was careful, however, to explicitly caution his overaggressive subordinate that in his next assignment, Rosser must not provoke the enemy cavalry into a general engagement. Early's explicit warning came two days too late.[39]

39 Early to Rosser, October 10, 1864, Rosser Papers, Acc. 1171-a, Box 1.

CHAPTER ELEVEN

General Rosser's Long Fight

"There is Usually a Great Deal of Discord in Gen. Rosser's Wake."

*S*ix months to the day after the fight at Tom's Brook, Robert E. Lee surrendered his army to U. S. Grant at Appomattox Court House. During those six months, Rosser continued to aggressively seek out encounters with the enemy, and he again found success in raids against enemy outposts and in small unit actions. In the second week of April 1865, however, with the Army of Northern Virginia nearly surrounded at Appomattox and in Lee's view unable to continue resistance, the commanding general decided to end the struggle. Rosser, predictably, disagreed.

As Rosser told the story, on April 8 he had seen riders under flags of truce pass through the lines at Appomattox, and he surmised Lee and Grant were exchanging communications. He said he felt filled with "the dread suspicion that the grand old Army of Virginia was about to be surrendered." Not all of the officers in the army agreed with Lee that the time had come to lay down arms, and Rosser stood prominent among the dissenters. He later argued that if the men of the army had been consulted they would have replied, "We can die, but we cannot surrender." Rosser conferred with Maj. Gen. John B. Gordon, who, according to Rosser, also wished to continue the fight. Rosser urged Gordon to dissuade General Lee and proposed a night attack on Grant's wagon trains. After Gordon rode off to see Lee, Rosser spent the night of April 8 conversing in the parlor of Wilmer McLean's house in Appomattox Court House. Rosser explained he had been friendly with McLean four years earlier when stationed near the farmer's home in Manassas, Virginia.

About 2:00 a.m. on April 9, generals Fitz Lee and Gordon entered McLean's home and informed Rosser that the army commander had decided he would either surrender or disperse the army the next day. According to Rosser, he stood up and replied, "General Lee would not surrender me in the morning," and he left to make preparations for an attack. After sunrise, Rosser and Gordon attacked in concert, and Rosser managed to break through the encircling Federals. He kept going, leaving the rest of Lee's army to its fate. Forty years after Appomattox, Rosser declared that "without hesitation or doubt" the proudest moment of his life was leading the successful charge to open the Lynchburg Road on April 9, 1865, which permitted him to leave "that fatal field in triumph, refusing to surrender either myself or my command to the enemy."[1]

The episode is not historically significant, but Rosser's selection of his action that day as one of the supreme moments of his life reveals much about him. There at Appomattox, while his peers, comrades, and brothers in arms communed in conceding a bitter defeat, Thomas L. Rosser refused to concede anything. He did not believe in concessions or in defeats. Others might quit or bow to reason or to pragmatism, but Thomas L. Rosser would not be among them. As he had shown time and again throughout his life, Rosser believed in his power to control events and his destiny. He believed no victory lost until he admitted it was gone, and no fight ended until he declared it over. Victory was always possible as long as he refused to admit defeat. And so, Rosser never relinquished his belief that he could somehow undo what had happened at Tom's Brook.

*   *   *

In 1866, Jubal Early wrote his *A Memoir of the Last Year of the War for Independence in the Confederate States of America*. It was the first military

<hr>

1   Thomas L. Rosser, "Annals of the War: Rosser and His Men," Philadelphia *Weekly Times*, April 5, 1884; "Capture of the Lynchburg Road," Unidentified clipping in Rosser Scrapbook 1877, 98; Chris M. Calkins, *The Battles of Appomattox and Appomattox Court House April 8-9, 1865* (Lynchburg, VA, 1987), 123-24.

memoir written by any general officer who had served in the war. Forty-six years later, Early's second memoir appeared in print after the general's death. Between the two Early books rose a flood tide of titles in what became a genre unique in American literature: the Civil War reminiscence. In 1874 came Gen. Joseph E. Johnston's memoir, and in the 1880s came books by Gen. John B. Hood, Grant, George B. McClellan, Sheridan, and William T. Sherman. Some, like Grant, wrote to generate income for their families. Others, like Early in particular, wrote to place facts on the record and to, in a common phrase, establish "the truth of history." Many others wrote to secure their legacies as men who had held important positions during the greatest trial in the history of the United States. Some wrote to settle old scores by damaging the reputations of longstanding enemies.

None of the principal actors in the drama at Tom's Brook left a complete memoir. Custer died in battle in 1876 before he had the opportunity to complete his recollections, installments of which had been published in *The Galaxy* magazine. Torbert, Merritt, and Lomax took their unshared memories with them to their graves. Munford published a series of articles in journals and newspapers but left nothing of book length. Rosser attempted at least three times to record his memoirs of the war, but he, like Munford, could never produce a book-length chronicle, and he succeeded in publishing only articles and letters in newspapers.

Newspapers and magazines were the two great media for veterans wishing to share their memories and views. Magazines or journals like *The Century*, *The Galaxy*, *Southern Bivouac*, *Confederate Veteran*, and *The Southern Historical Society Papers* thrived during the postwar decades by giving veterans the opportunity to place themselves on the historical record. Many newspapers, including the Richmond *Dispatch*, the Philadelphia *Weekly Times*, and *The National Tribune* also printed recollections. Almost every newspaper in the country, however, would provide space for prominent former soldiers to express their views in the form of a letter to the editor. The editorial page thus became the great postwar battleground on which old soldiers grappled for control of the historical record, and few combatants were as well armed for success on this new field of strife as was Thomas L. Rosser. He had held high rank, he held strong opinions, he wrote well and persuasively, and he would fight ruthlessly for his reputation.

By the early 1880s, Rosser enjoyed wealth and power. He had emerged from the war a pauper, like countless others in the South, and after trying law school and an abortive business venture, Rosser went west and labored to

Many observers noted Rosser's impressive physical stature and soldierly
bearing, which are evident in this portrait made in 1866, the
year he marked his 30th birthday.

Rosser Papers, Albert and Shirley Small Special Collections,

University of Virginia

build his future by building railroads. In his version of the story, he began as an axeman, but his education and leadership attributes soon earned him the position of chief engineer for the Northern Pacific Railroad. He would later fill the same position for the Canadian Pacific Railroad. Because Rosser helped select the routes of the railroads, he could use privileged knowledge to purchase land at low prices and resell it at much higher prices after the route of the railroad became general knowledge. Rosser acquired valuable property in Minneapolis, Minnesota, where he lived before buying and relocating to a home near Charlottesville, Virginia, so his son could attend the university there.[2] By the time he reached his late forties, Rosser had, through diligent industry and ability, built a comfortable life for himself and his family. With his financial present and future seemingly stable, he looked for other fields of conquest and began to devote himself to public affairs and politics. Knowing that war veterans dominated politics—North and South, local and national—Rosser took advantage of his status as a former Confederate general.

The savvy Rosser understood the power of publicity. Years earlier when seeking promotion to general, Rosser wrote to his wife about having favorable articles about him placed in newspapers.[3] Beginning in the early 1880s and continuing almost until his death in 1910, Rosser labored, especially in the press, to define his legacy as one of the South's leading military men. One of his early efforts involved placing in the public record a version of the events of October 9, 1864. Rosser saw Tom's Brook as a blemish on his military career. Custer told his wife that Rosser had admitted to him "the worst whipping he had during the war was the one I gave him the 9th of October," and Rosser had also admitted to his own wife that he had been "whipped" at Tom's Brook. But outside of the circle of intimate friends and family, Rosser would never accept responsibility for the defeat on Coffman's Hill. More than any other Confederate, Rosser brooded on the defeat and nurtured resentment. As the 20th anniversary of the engagement drew near, Rosser launched a new attack in an effort to turn Tom's Brook into a victory.

2 Ken Storie, "General Rosser's Legacy," *Manitoba History*, Manitoba Historical Society, No. 56 (October 2007); Thomas, "Under Indictment," 211-12.

3 Rosser to wife, October 5, 1863, Acc. 1171-c, Box 1, folder 1863.

Rosser wrote a rambling war recollection of about 13,000 words for the Philadelphia *Weekly Times*. The controversial article incited strident rebuttals from former comrades, and Rosser's version of Tom's Brook stirred the most rancor. Rosser's representation of events leaves no doubt his purpose in writing about Tom's Brook after 19 years was the same as it had been when he wrote to his wife just after the battle. As he had blamed others privately 1864, he would do so publically in 1884. In his article for the Philadelphia newspaper, Rosser unequivocally assigned principal responsibility to Jubal Early.

Rosser had begun blaming Early the moment he had left Coffman's Hill. Not only did Rosser fault Early in his private letters, but he did so to subordinates as well. Major Edward McDonald, who had long served under Rosser and greatly admired him, was so shocked by Rosser's antipathy toward Early that he felt compelled to publish his version of an incident that occurred 10 days after Tom's Brook during the Battle of Cedar Creek. According to McDonald, Early ordered Rosser to move his division of 1,200 men to a position guarding the left flank of the army. After reaching the assigned position, Rosser withdrew from it and permitted his men to unsaddle and feed their horses. That afternoon, a Federal counterattack drove southward toward where Rosser was supposed to be. On picket with men from his 11th Virginia Cavalry, McDonald recognized the danger to the flank of Early's army and rode rearward to urge Rosser to meet the threat. According to McDonald, Rosser refused. "He said that he was not going to take his men back there," McDonald related, and "that Early had made him lose nearly all of his artillery a few days before at Tom's Brook; and that he did not intend to risk any more of it." If McDonald's version of events is correct, Rosser was so motivated by spite and other personal concerns that he would willingly fail to fulfill his part in the army commander's plans and risk the defeat of the army that day. McDonald's admiration for Rosser suffered a blow at Cedar Creek, and he believed Rosser's actions contributed to the rout that nearly demolished Early's army.[4]

In his article in the Philadelphia *Weekly Times*, Rosser claimed Early issued orders that had forced him to fight at Tom's Brook against Rosser's better judgment. After emphasizing that the Federals greatly outnumbered

---

4   Edward H. McDonald, "Generals Early and Rosser at Cedar Creek," *Southern Bivouac*, Louisville, KY, 1884, vol. 11, no. 12 (August 1884), 536.

him, Rosser claimed Early explicitly ordered him to continue pushing northward beyond the Federals to Winchester. "I could see no particular reason why I should go on to Winchester," he wrote, "yet my instructions were perfectly clear, and that point had been repeatedly fixed upon by General Early as my objective point, and regardless of Sheridan's position I had to go to Winchester."[5] Regarding the decision to fight on Coffman's Hill on the morning of the 9th, Rosser again portrayed himself as having been without any choice: "under my instructions I would not have dared to retreat and as fight was the only thing I could do I proceeded to prepare for battle."

To support these claims, Rosser presented an order he said he received from Early on the morning of October 7. The order, as printed in Rosser's article, reads:

Harrisonburg, Va., September 6th, 1864

General Rosser, commanding cavalry on Back Road:
Press on and get into the rear (front) of the enemy and destroy his trains, for he is running out of the valley. Yours truly,

J. A. Early
Lieutenant General

It is difficult to see why Rosser believed these six lines would support his contention that Early ordered him to Winchester. Nowhere is Winchester mentioned. In addition, the date is obviously incorrect. To have any meaning, the order should be dated "October 6" rather than a month earlier. Written in Rosser's handwriting, the original manuscript of the article survives in Rosser's papers and shows that the date in the manuscript was changed; Rosser originally wrote "September 7," in his manuscript but overwrote the "7" with the numeral "6." Why did Rosser make the revision? Did he make an error in transcription? Did he misread the text he was copying? Was the original order misdated? If the writer of the original order saw and corrected his error in the day of the month, why did he not notice the more egregious error in the name of the month? These questions lead to the

5   Rosser, "Annals," March 22, 1884. Rosser embellished his statement by declaring that Winchester was "thirty miles in the Federal rear," when the distance was actually closer to 19 miles.

most important question: Where is this original document? A thorough search of the papers left to posterity by Rosser and his family has failed to produce the original order. Certainly it is possible that this puzzling document existed, or even still exists, but two facts cast doubt on the authenticity of the order or on Rosser's recollection of it: Researchers have not found the original in Rosser's papers and, more important, Jubal Early stated he never wrote the order. Together, these circumstances raise valid questions about the veracity of Rosser's evidence and, by extension, his claims.

Rosser might have cited an unquestionably legitimate document—an order signed by Early and dated October 7—which does survive in Rosser's collected papers. Though reproduced earlier in this work, the order's pertinence justifies reproduction:

New Market 7 p.m.
October 7th 1864

General
Your courier did not reach me until sunrise this morning, + I immediately wrote to you to follow the enemy + endeavor to do all the damage you could. I thought I wrote you full instructions by Mr. Calloway on yesterday. I wish you to continue the pursuit + harass the enemy as much as possible. Lomax is following down The Pike having passed this place at 10 o'clock this morning. It is possible that Sheridan may cross the mountains to the East side + go to the Rappahannock or he may go to send a part of his force to Washington to be shipped to Grant. I wish to ascertain what he intends + I shall remain here tomorrow, to get the information, so that I may move across the mountains myself if necessary. You must continue on + go as far as Winchester—if you can. Lomax has sent a brigade down the Luray Valley. If you find a chance to strike a blow do so, without waiting instructions.

Respectfully,
J.A. Early
Lt. General[6]

Like the missing and mysterious "September 6" document, this existing order does little to support Rosser's claims of rigid constraint by Early. In

6   Early to Rosser, October 7, 1864, Rosser Papers, Acc. 1171-a, Box 1.

fact, this irrefutably authentic manuscript directly counters Rosser's claims by showing that Early allowed Rosser much discretion. The conditional phrases "as much as possible," "If you can," and "If you find," leave to Rosser all judgments of what was possible and likely to produce good results. Early wrote that Rosser should go to Winchester only "if" in his judgment he could do so to advantage. We cannot be sure how many orders Early sent Rosser in the three days of pursuit during The Burning, but neither the October 7 order nor the questionable "September 6" document supports Rosser's statement that Early had peremptorily ordered him to Winchester. Likewise, the October 7 order, because it allows Rosser so much freedom of decision, refutes Rosser's statement that Early forced him to fight at Tom's Brook. Early nowhere *requires* Rosser to fight at all let alone engage in a pitched battle with a more powerful Federal division. The phantom document Rosser cites to support his two claims supports neither claim, and the document Rosser *does not* cite refutes both. Ultimately, Rosser's contentions are untenable for lack of evidence.

Circumstantial evidence likewise opposes Rosser's allegations. In his version of Tom's Brook, Rosser casts himself as a man of moderation and judgment who sees the errors of his recklessly aggressive superior officer yet, as a dutiful subordinate, has no choice but to obey. "I fully appreciated the perils of my situation," he wrote, "but determined to obey General Early's order at the hazard of losing my command, for he allowed me no direction in the matter."[7] Rosser's passive, almost fearful expressions—"at the hazard of losing my command" and "I would not have dared"—are so unlike the language and tone in the rest of his wartime letters and postwar writings they ring as false notes. Throughout his unfinished memoirs, Rosser portrays himself as a bold, assertive, aggressive man of principle who would always act upon his own best judgment regardless of consequences. Rosser's two portraits of himself are irreconcilable: Was he the combative, cocksure young man who impetuously turned his back and walked out on the secretary of war rather than accept an appointment he disliked? Was he the principled subordinate who repeatedly disobeyed direct orders from the chief of cavalry? Was he the adamant warrior who refused to surrender at Appomattox? Or was he the timid man who so feared Jubal Early he would

7   Rosser, "Annals," March 22, 1884.

disregard his own instincts and lead his command into what he believed was certain defeat rather than exercise his own judgment?

Rosser's second attempt to avoid blame for the defeat was even more ignoble than his unsubstantiated charges against Early. In his article, Rosser blamed Col. Richard W. Carter for the tactical defeat and the loss of all the artillery and wagons. Rosser claimed the "misbehavior of one of the colonels in Munford's brigade" caused him to lose "a strong position in the rear" at which he intended to make a stand. The position Rosser wished to hold included a stone wall, behind which Carter was to place his regiment. Rosser declared, "The regiment commanded by this colonel was one of the best in the service and if it had been ably commanded on this occasion I believe I should not have lost my artillery." His argument is that, despite the recklessness and folly of Early, Rosser still was managing the unwanted engagement well until one of his subordinates lost his nerve, disobeyed an order, and thereby brought on the catastrophe.

Again, as in his case against Early, Rosser never offered evidence that Carter's misbehavior led directly to the loss of the guns or of the engagement. Instead, Rosser's article employs a rhetorical trick—a *non sequitur* in which it is implied that since a court-martial board found Carter guilty of cowardice, then Carter's cowardice made him responsible for the disaster. In fact, the two issues are not necessarily connected. The court was asked to rule only on the first issue—whether Carter had fled the field. The court martial board found him guilty of misbehavior in the face of the enemy and of neglect of duty. The sentence read simply: "Col. Carter will cease to be an officer of the Confederate States army from this date." The verdict does not hold Carter responsible for the disastrous results on Coffman's Hill. Yet, Rosser in his article, without offering specific evidence, connected the disaster with the cowardice and implied the one resulted from the other.[8]

Evidence suggests Carter's action, had nothing to do with the loss of the position Rosser chose to fight upon. Colonel Munford's version of events implies the incident occurred after the retreat from Coffman's Hill and the

---

8   Robert K. Krick, "The Coward Who Rode With J. E. B. Stuart," in *The Smoothbore Volley that Doomed the Confederacy: The Death of Stonewall Jackson and Other Chapters on the Army of Northern Virginia* (Baton Rouge, LA, 2002), 172-84. Major Henry Carrington of the 3rd Virginia avoided court-martial by resigning. It comes as no surprise that Carter thought Rosser an "unprincipled villain." Vogtsberger, *The Dulanys,* 260.

loss of artillery.[9] Rosser states explicitly his division had already been driven from Coffman's Hill before Colonel Carter's "misbehavior."[10] Munford thought Carter's flight meant little in determining the result of the fight. To Rosser's claim that the abandonment of the stone wall led to disaster, Munford sarcastically replied, "that wall should have been two miles long and very high to have availed him much at that stage of the fight."[11] Carter's actions might well have been unconscionable, and he might well have hindered Rosser's and Munford's efforts to rally on the Back Road, but by Rosser's own testimony, the "misbehavior" occurred at a secondary rallying point and did not contribute to the loss of Coffman's Hill and the stampede that followed. By linking Carter's incontestable "misbehavior" to the defeat, however, Rosser avoided closer scrutiny of his decision to stand on the weak Coffman's Hill position and his subsequent unsuccessful conduct of the fight there. In Carter, Rosser found a convenient scapegoat whose cowardly behavior served as a red herring drawing attention from other facts inconvenient to Rosser.

In addition to shifting the blame for the results at Tom's Brook onto other shoulders, Rosser also wished to portray his own role in the fight in the best light possible. Because neither Rosser nor Lomax required their subordinates to write reports after the fight, few details about the engagement existed in the public record. Two incontrovertible facts did exist, however: The Confederates had lost 11 cannon, and they had retreated from the battlefield. Rosser presented these facts as evidence not of a defeat but of a triumph.

On any Civil War battlefield, cannon were trophies. To take them was to win glory and to lose them was to suffer failure and shame. The Confederate expressions of humiliation after Tom's Brook focused on the loss of the artillery. Rosser, however, presented the loss of his artillery at Tom's Brook as proof of his fighting spirit:

> In this engagement I lost my battery of artillery, but I did not much regret it, for I sold it for an excellent price. It was captured while pouring canister into the enemy, and for

9 Munford, "Annals"; Munford, "Reminiscences . . . No. 3," 136-37.

10 Rosser, "Annals," March 22, 1884.

11 Untitled typescript, Munford-Ellis Papers, Box 17, folder "Writings: Civil War Mss. of Thos. T. Munford (Rosser-Munford Dispute) 4 of 4."

the sake of performing such service one can afford to throw away artillery. Many a battle was lost in this war by timid generals who were afraid of losing their artillery and consequently did not expose it to capture. I believe in pushing artillery to the front and using it freely, and if you lose it console yourself with the thought that you could well afford to. And if it was captured fighting you can rest assured that its captors paid dearly for it.[12]

Few officers of high rank in R. E. Lee's army, or men in the government in Richmond, would have agreed in 1864 that the Confederacy "could well afford" to lose more of its dwindling supply of artillery. With his blustering dismissal of the loss of his guns as trivial, Rosser turned orthodox opinion on its head and painted himself as a bold commander and a battlefield visionary unafraid of flouting convention. Yet, his generalized argument is only applicable to the story of Tom's Brook if the enemy actually "paid dearly" in taking Rosser's guns there. Data on Federal casualties on Coffman's Hill do not support Rosser's portrayal of his artillery slaughtering charging Yankees at close range. Custer's entire division sustained only about 44 casualties in the fight, and many of those men were wounded during the prolonged skirmishing along the brook before the climactic charges that captured the artillery. Even if all of the casualties in the eight regiments principally involved in the movement on the guns were wounded by short-range ammunition—an almost impossible scenario—Rosser's guns would have inflicted fewer than 25 casualties by canister fire. Furthermore, Rosser does not mention the loss of the 35 Confederate artilleryman captured with their pieces and sent to prison for the remainder of the war. If the Federals achieved a net gain of at least six guns and 10 soldiers, it would seem Rosser rather than the Federals "paid dearly" in the exchange.[13]

Rosser also attempted to alter any perception the loss of the field resulted from the behavior of his men. "My loss in killed and wounded in this battle was heavy," he wrote, "but I lost few prisoners." Because Rosser had not required his officers to file reports after the battle, official information about his casualties existed only in little-known sources in government files. The

12 Ibid.

13 See Appendix B for casualty figures. The eight regiments referred to are the 1st New Hampshire, 1st Vermont, 3rd New Jersey, 2nd, 5th, 8th, and 22nd New York, and 18th Pennsylvania.

Former artilleryman George M. Neese, posing near his home in New Market in the 1890s, was one of more than 100 men captured from Rosser's command at Tom's Brook. Neese remained a captive at Point Lookout Prison until June 1865.
Fritzi Orebaugh

obscurity of the evidence available in 1884 permitted Rosser to portray the fight any way he wished without fear of contradiction by any casualty figures in the public record. Years of work by historians, however, show conclusively Rosser's statement that he "lost few prisoners" is untrue. Audits of the raw data contained in the compiled service records of soldiers in the Confederate regiments and batteries on Coffman's Hill suggest Rosser lost a great many prisoners. Confederate service records reveal at least 162 documented casualties in Rosser's cavalry division that day, and about 47% of those men were taken prisoner. If the losses in the two artillery units fighting with Rosser are included, the number of documented casualties increases to 197, and 55% of those men were captured. As in other instances, available evidence does not support Rosser's carelessly asserted version of events.

By denigrating the loss of the six artillery pieces and inaccurately representing the casualty figures, Rosser attempted to portray the engagement as a desperate struggle against long odds in which his men steadfastly refused to surrender and fell at their posts while he willingly sacrificed his artillery as it effectively slaughtered the enemy in a gallant, but hopeless, fight. Evidence contradicts this portrayal of events on each point. The fight on Coffman's Hill was not the triumph of courage, fighting ability, and leadership Rosser claimed, but an unnecessary, poorly managed, humiliating misadventure in recklessness.

Rosser ended his version of the story of Tom's Brook by stating he had "chided" Jubal Early "for pressing me on the heels of a force so far superior to my own in numbers and equipment, while he remained twenty-five miles in the rear with his infantry, and he replied comforting me with assurances of his confidence, and related how much worse his other cavalry division had suffered than mine had." Again, Rosser's version is unsupported by evidence. Early did write to Rosser on the day after the battle, and Rosser preserved the note in his papers. In that note, Early did try to console the young general, but Rosser misrepresents the note when he claims Early included disparaging or invidious remarks about Lomax's division.[14] As to Rosser's claim that he had "chided" his commander for getting him into difficulty, Early declared it "a myth, a figment of the brain."[15]

*   *   *

Rosser's version of the story of Tom's Brook provoked immediate and strong reactions from Early and Munford, both of whom accused Rosser of deceit. Early had parted from Rosser in 1865 with no animosity. The next year, Rosser had written to Early, apparently in a spirit of friendship, to ask a favor. Early replied with a cordial letter in which he chatted amiably about

14 Rosser, "Annals," March 22, 1884; Early to Rosser October 10, 1864, Rosser Papers, Acc. 1171-g, Box 1.

15 "Relating to the Annals."

his health and his future and signed the letter "my best regards."[16] After the publication of Rosser's article in 1884, however, the two men would become fierce enemies and would parade their contempt for one another for all to see in the press. Newspaper editors, then as now, loved controversy, and the poison-pen letters from Early and Rosser were reprinted widely. Early read Rosser's article in a Virginia paper and responded immediately.

After denigrating Rosser's article as "bombastic egotism," "absurdity," and "romanticism," Early recalled Rosser's braggadocio of 19 years earlier:

> His ridiculous vaporing when he came to the Valley in the fall of 1864 in claiming he and his 'Laurel Brigade' came as the 'saviors of the Valley,' and were going to show the rest of my command how to fight, excited no little amusement at the time and is well remembered, but I never suspected him of being capable of the folly of which he has now been guilty.

Early condemned Rosser's article as full of "monstrous misrepresentations" and rebutted Rosser's statements one by one. He flatly rejected his assertions that he had been ordered to Winchester. These claims, Early declared, were "without any foundation in fact." The mysterious "September 6" document, Early proclaimed, "is either an illusion of memory or the perversion of the purport of one I may have written, if he has such in possession."[17] Early then accurately reiterated for his readers what he had written to Rosser on October 7, 1864, and to Robert E. Lee on October 9: Rosser and Lomax "were ordered to pursue the enemy, to harass him and ascertain his purposes."[18] Early also addressed the fate of disgraced Col. Richard Carter, and suggested Rosser's account "leads me to suspect that a great injustice may have been done to that colonel." Early, like Rosser a proud and combative man, closed out his public letter with a barbed pen:

> It is a great pity that Gen. Rosser has so far forgotten himself as to have written the articles for the Philadelphia Times, and his folly in doing so will be deeply regretted by many of his old comrades. He furnishes another lamentable instance of a Confederate

16 Early to Rosser, May 10, 1866, Rosser Papers, Acc. 1171-a, Box 1.

17 "Relating to the Annals."

18 *The State* (Richmond, VA), April 28, 1884, and excerpted in the Philadelphia *Weekly Times*, 17 May 1884; see also Philadelphia *Weekly Times*, June 14, 1884; *OR* 43, pt. 1, 559.

officer who has undertaken to build up a fictitious reputation for himself on the ruins
of that of others, his being the worst instance of the kind I have yet seen.[19]

Thomas Munford penned two articles in response to Rosser's piece, one a sarcastic refutation to the Philadelphia *Weekly Times* and the other a more serious and measured commentary in the *Southern Historical Society Papers*. In the Philadelphia paper, Munford praised Rosser's gallantry and energy "in a high degree," but accused him of criticizing "most ungenerously and unjustly his superiors in rank, making others bear his own blunders." Munford minced no words in putting the blame where he thought it belonged: "The Tom's Brook fight was the heaviest disaster that the cavalry of the Army of Northern Virginia ever sustained. It was wholly unnecessary and was the result of utter ignorance on Rosser's part." In a private letter to former Confederate colleague Jed Hotchkiss, Munford openly conceded Rosser's virtues ("a gallant fellow, full of dash") but condemned him as an "ambitious and unscrupulous" man who "never hesitated to resort to any means to accomplish his end."[20]

By the summer of 1884, Rosser, Early, and Munford had each had his say, and if the matter had ended there, history might have heard no more of Tom's Brook. But the three men were not done. The Second Battle of Tom's Brook would continue, and history would gain further sordid examples of proud men vying to elevate themselves by mauling one another with venomous public prose. Rosser felt provoked by the thrusts from Early and Munford. Just as at Tom's Brook, Rosser had been hit on both flanks, as it were, and, as he had at Coffman's Hill, and everywhere else for that matter, he refused to back down from a challenge and went on the attack.

Rosser's response was both caustic and dismissive. Rather than challenging Early's statements, Rosser attempted to undermine his opponent's credibility through *ad hominem* attacks. He characterized Early as "an old man" prone to "invective and evasive criticisms" who "only goes into the papers to vaunt his own glory." Rosser sought to deflect examination of his own actions and statements by making Early the focus of attention rather than himself. He avoided specifics and offered only generalities. "All

19 *The State* (Richmond, VA), April 28, 1884.

20 Munford, "Annals"; Munford, "Reminiscences . . . No. 3," 13:135; Munford to Jed Hotchkiss, October 12, 1897, Hotchkiss Papers, roll 49, frame 240.

I wished to do was to give the truth to history and show that the disasters in the valley were not due to the want of patriotism and courage on the part of the men," wrote Rosser, "but to the mistakes or to the incompetency of the commanding general." Rosser offered an ironic and patronizing lament for for his criticisms:

> General Early is an old man and I deeply regret having wounded his over-sensitive nature. I used the most delicate and silken lash at my command and would have spared General Early even that if I could have done so in justice to truth; but although very delicate and plied with a forbearing hand, the sting which it inflicted and under which he winces is convincing proof of its merit, its truth and its justice.[21]

To only one of Early's points did Rosser give specific notice: the existence of the mysterious "September 6" document. Rejecting Early's contention that the order was imaginary, Rosser stated, "As soon as I have leisure I shall publish the proof of my assertions in reference to the orders which General Early claims he did not send me, but which, I now repeat, I did receive."[22] Rosser never published such proof. His assertions, therefore, rest not on physical evidence, but upon his claim of the existence of physical evidence. Rosser likened Early's objections to those "a shrewd lawyer" might use in defending "a bad case." The absence of hard evidence, however, makes Rosser's case the weaker of the two. Early's contentions are supported by existing evidence, including his October 7 orders.

The two generals continued to spar in public letters. Early responded with a long, lawyerly, systematic dissection of Rosser's statements and focused again on Rosser's treatment of "the misbehaving colonel." "I have now a strong conviction that he was made a scapegoat for another," Early asserted, "and if any remedy for the injustice done him now existed it should be granted him." Early noted that after the army stripped the colonel of his rank and dismissed him in shame, Carter reenlisted in the same regiment as a private. "As the only reparation which I now have it in my power to make him, I give this public expression of my conviction that injustice was done him, and ask his old comrades to receive and treat him as one entitled to their

---

21 "General Rosser's Rejoinder," Philadelphia *Weekly Times*, June 7, 1884.

22 Ibid.

esteem and companionship in every respect."[23] Rosser countered by further insulting Early:

> I have only the kindest feeling for you and all the officers and men of the Confederate armies who did their duty in the service of their country to the best of their ability, whether it was much or little. Incompetency is not a crime and that you failed in the Valley was not due to your neglect or carelessness, for I know you were assiduous; but God did not make you a general, and it was General R. E. Lee's overestimate of you; or in other words, I may say it was General R. E Lee's mistake in trusting so important command as that you had to you before you had been more fully tried.[24]

Rosser soon turned his attention to Munford, who in his articles had labeled Rosser's version of events "not verifiable history." Rosser angrily fired back that Munford's account "was evidently written, not in the interest of history, nor for the love of truth, for it is neither history nor truth—it was written for the purpose of misrepresenting and maligning me." As he had in answering Early's criticisms, Rosser defended his story only by attacking his critic. After noting Munford had never been promoted to general, Rosser impugned Munford's courage: "Col. Munford was not promoted because he was not a man of sufficient coolness and judgment to command troops in battle, and nothing shows this more plainly than his own account of his nervous agitation when he says at Tom's Brook he advised me to retreat without giving battle." Rosser then turned specifically to Munford's account of events on Coffman's Hill:

> On page 136, he says: "The enemy are moving up to attack us and we can't hold this position against such odds." "A courier dashed up and said Capt. Strother says they are very near him." The fact of the business really was, that Col. Munford was whipped before a shot was fired, and with such a man in command of a brigade, although the brigade was one of the best, I am not surprised that I failed to hold the enemy in check. We were there to fight not to run, yet the only statement Col. Mundford [sic] makes in his article, which I am fully prepared to believe is on page 137—'I saw no possible

23 Early to *The State* (Richmond, VA), May 24, 1884.

24 Rosser to Early through *The State* (Richmond, VA), June 10, 1884.

chance now but to move out and that at a run—a quick run.' Yes, he did run like a wolf before a prairie fire.[25]

In this letter, Rosser contradicts his own earlier statements. In the Philadelphia *Weekly Times*, he stated he had grave misgivings about fighting on the morning of October 9 because he realized his little division could do little against the powerful Federal division, and that he fought only because Early forced him to do so. In that formulation of events, Rosser offered essentially the same arguments as Munford—that they could not hold their position against such great odds. After reading Munford's critical account, however, Rosser presented the situation differently and painted himself not as ruefully accepting an unwanted engagement, but as willingly accepting the fight. He fulminates against Munford's timidity and thunders, "We were there to fight not to run."[26]

In the newspaper war with Early and Munford, Rosser had sympathetic allies. Mottram Ball, wounded at Tom's Brook while commanding the 11th Virginia Cavalry, worked in 1884 as U. S. district attorney in Alaska. Ever a staunch supporter of Rosser, he backed his friend by writing a remarkably long, carefully constructed article filling five full columns in the Philadelphia *Weekly Times*. Ball declared Munford and Early were "utterly unjust" in their treatment of Rosser. He used a defense attorney's tactic of attempting to portray the victims of Rosser's attacks as the guilty parties. Early and Munford had written in reaction to what they perceived to be Rosser's untrue and unfounded attacks, but Ball reversed the roles and accused Munford and Early of assailing the "guiltless" Rosser. Like Rosser, Ball attempted to downplay the negative results of the fight, making statements that could not be independently verified and would eventually be disproved by evidence. "We lost a battery of artillery, some ordnance wagons and a few prisoners," he admitted. "The enemy's killed and wounded I have no doubt considerably outnumbered ours." Rosser's

25 Thomas L. Rosser to *The State* (Richmond, VA), Unidentified clipping [January 1885] in Rosser Scrapbook 1877, 40. Colonel Asher W. Harman, who served in the 11th Virginia cavalry of Rosser's Laurel Brigade, also had disparaging words for Munford's postwar writings: "My experience with Col. Munford is that his pen was more powerful than his sword." A. W. Harman to Jed Hotchkiss, March 15, 1886, Jedediah Hotchkiss Papers, Washington, DC, roll 39, frame 424.

26 See Rosser, "Annals," March 22, 1884.

division lost almost 200 men, half of them taken prisoner. Custer lost fewer than 50 men.[27]

In his defense of his former commander, Ball undermined his argument by unwittingly agreeing with Rosser's critics. The admiring Ball, who had been with Rosser on many battlefields, declared that whether meeting an enemy in the field or writing an essay for publication, Rosser always went ahead boldly. "General Rosser," explained Ball, "writes pretty much as he fought, *currente calamo*, with a smile and a gay toss of the head, a cheery word for the hesitating, a compliment to the successful, a hearty laugh at his own, an enemy's or a comrade's discomfiture."[28] Rosser's critics would certainly have agreed with Ball's characterization. It was this very offhandedness and lack of reflection before acting or speaking that caused Rosser most of the difficulty he had encountered in life. Rosser's passionate impulsiveness, his disdain of caution or discretion, his tendency to crash ahead unthinkingly were the very faults Munford claimed were responsible for the disaster at Tom's Brook.

*   *   *

Early, Rosser, and Munford had plenty of company in the fratricidal backbiting so common in the postwar era. While the controversies sold newspapers, some readers found the public disputes among former Confederates repulsive. A Valley newspaper editorial by an anonymous Virginian lamented the ugliness of it all. The writer praised Robert E. Lee, who chose to write nothing after the war and who engaged in nothing that might lead to discord. Among other Confederates, however, "The guns were soon turned against each other, and from President Davis down to General Rosser . . . we have had nothing but crimination and recrimination." The generals seemed to be worst of all as they "engaged in the boyish luxury of throwing dirt and mud at each other, seemingly to make notoriety in peace because sensible of their failure to make reputation in war."[29]

27 Ball, "Rosser and His Critics." See also Ball to Rosser, January 7, 1885, Rosser Papers, 1171-g, Box 2, folder 1880-1885. See Appendix B for casualty figures.

28 Ball, "Rosser and his Critics." The Latin term *currente calamo*, can be translated as acting in an offhand way without careful consideration. Adeleye, *World Dictionary*, 90.

29 "Rosser, Early, Sheridan," *Shenandoah Herald*. July 1, 1887.

Rosser's record of public quarrels would grow, and the cumulative effect of his many disputes would be self-destructive. The more Rosser engaged in controversy the more opportunities he gave his foes to attack him, and the events of October 9, 1864, remained a tender spot. As is usual in such public squabbling, facts meant little. It did not matter whether Rosser's opponents had their facts straight, just as it did not matter whether Rosser had his facts in order. In the rough-and-tumble public skirmishes, details were insignificant and truth mattered less than perception. In the matter of the fight at Tom's Brook, the fact that stood largest in the public mind was Rosser had been in command when the Confederate cavalry had taken its worst whipping and had run like hell. Rosser became the public face of the Confederate embarrassment, and he would never hear the end of Tom's Brook as long as he dealt in criminations and recriminations. If Rosser did not realize that truth by his fiftieth birthday in 1886, he would receive a lesson soon thereafter at the hands of that master of hard lessons, Philip H. Sheridan.

In the spring of 1887, Rosser thoughtlessly gave Sheridan the opportunity to tell the story of Tom's Brook on a national stage. Rosser heard rumors that Sheridan would visit the Shenandoah Valley. About that time, according to news reports, Rosser had "a congressional bee in his bonnet." Some theorized Rosser saw the prospect of a visit from Sheridan as a way to dust off his mantel as "The Savior of the Valley" and score political points with voters of the Seventh Congressional District, which included portions of the Valley. Whatever his motive, Rosser composed a letter condemning Sheridan for his coarse insensitivity in returning to the Valley and arranged for the letter to be printed in the Winchester *Times*, one of the principal newspapers in the Seventh District. "I had hoped that our beautiful valley should never again be desecrated by his footprints," Rosser wrote. He continued:

Cold, cruel and brutal must be the character of this soldier, who fondly cherishes memories of the wild, wanton waste and desolation which his barbarous torch spread through the Valley, laying in ashes the beautiful and happy homes of innocent women, young and helpless children and aged men, and who over these ruins boasted that now a crow cannot fly over this valley without carrying its rations.[30]

30 Rosser Scrapbook 1877, 42.

Newspapers from Baltimore to Sacramento reprinted or excerpted the letter, and hullabaloo followed. One paper decried Rosser's flings at Sheridan as being "in the worst possible taste," and declared that if everyone were to express such hostility "the country would not be worth living in."[31] Union veterans in Illinois passed a resolution rebuking Rosser for aspersing the character of Sheridan's men and calling upon Union veterans everywhere "to rebuke in the most positive terms this arrogance of a defeated rebel, who, with much unblushing pretense, assumes the role of a conqueror." As the reaction grew, so too did the story. More papers carried news of the controversy, and more Union veterans took the opportunity to tell tales of the Woodstock Races, and editors began printing witticisms about how if Rosser were to make as good a run for Congress as he did when Sheridan was chasing him up the Valley, he would win for sure.[32]

Inevitably, newspapermen sought out Sheridan to ask him about Rosser's letter, and the aging Union hero had his sharp tongue ready to provoke laughter at Rosser's expense. "Rosser has not forgotten the whaling I gave him in the valley," Sheridan said, "and I am not surprised that he loses his temper when he recalls it. . . . It was a regular frolic for our boys. Custer got Rosser's uniform, and occasionally wore it for the amusement of his command." Sheridan repeated a quip that had been retold in many forms since Tom's Brook:

> This incident was doubly humiliating to Rosser because he was hailed as the 'Savior of the valley.' His men wore small laurel twigs in their hats as an indication of their purpose to clean us out. Sometime after this, when Rosser again appeared in that vicinity, I understand the people advised him to substitute pumpkin vines for laurel, that plant being well known for running qualities.[33]

Sheridan's words, as Rosser's had, appeared in newspapers across the land. Even Mrs. Rosser saved clippings of the articles for her scrapbook. The

31 Bismarck *Tribune*, May 13 1887, p. 4, col. 2.

32 "Gen. Rosser Denounces Gen. Sheridan," New Ulm *Review* (MN), May 11, 1887; Sacramento *Daily Record-Union*, May 7, 1887; "His Name is Dennis," Salt Lake *Herald*, May 7, 1887, p.1, col. 4; St. Paul *Globe*, May 11, 1887.

33 Most of the writers who have repeated the witticism generally credit Jubal Early as the author, but that attribution might be mythical. See the Staunton *Spectator*, January 30, 1889, p. 3, col. 5, and February 6, 1998, p. 3, col 4.

whole affair appeared even more ridiculous after the revelation that Sheridan had not planned to visit the Valley because, unbeknownst to Rosser, he had already done so and been received graciously by residents. When Rosser visited Woodstock about the time of his attack on Sheridan, a newspaperman reported that his reception was cordial and respectful, but "it was no more so than the greeting Sheridan had received a few years earlier."[34]

Giving Rosser a good pasting in the press did not satisfy Sheridan. A year later he published his memoirs, and, not one to let concerns about veracity prevent him from adding insult to injury, Sheridan took the opportunity to heap humiliation upon Rosser by claiming "the citizens of the valley, intensely disgusted with the boasting and swaggering that had characterized the arrival of the 'Laurel Brigade' in that section, baptized the action (known to us as Tom's Brook) the 'Woodstock Races,' and never tired of poking fun at General Rosser about his precipitate and inglorious flight."[35]

After reading Sheridan's remarks, a newspaper editor in Pennsylvania suggested even Rosser would have to "agree with the rest of the world, that he was a darned fool for attempting to stir up ancient strife."[36] Readers who had never heard of Tom's Brook or of Rosser learned the story and connected the man with the "inglorious flight." The public associated Rosser with Tom's Brook more than ever. Sheridan had won again.

Rosser tried to salvage something from his mismanaged assault on Sheridan by attacking in a different direction. In doing so he landed in the newspapers again and endured still more public abuse. Rosser claimed in the press that his letter about Sheridan had been "misunderstood." He had meant no disrespect to Northern soldiers, he explained, but he believed it would be indecent of Sheridan to visit the region where he had sown so much misery. To illustrate his point, Rosser, according to a newspaper account, made an analogy between Sheridan and Jubal Early. "I would say the same thing," he wrote, "if Confederate Gen. Jubal Early should visit Chambersburg [Pennsylvania] the town he had burned wantonly. Early ought to have been

---

34 "Rosser, Early, Sheridan," *Shenandoah Herald*, July 1, 1887; "A Shenandoah County Fair," ibid., October 21, 1887.

35 "Sheridan on Rosser," New Ulm *Review* (MN), May 11, 1887; Sheridan *Memoirs*, 2:59. See also Chicago *Tribune* March 9, 1889, p. 4, col. 3.

36 Somerset *Herald* (PA), May 11, 1887, p. 2, col. 2.

Rosser had gained substantial wealth by the time he sat for a portrait in 1887,
but he had lost none of his compulsive combativeness.

Rosser Papers, Albert and Shirley Small Special Collections,

University of Virginia

hung for the act, and the citizens would be justified in tarring and feathering him if he came."[37]

Predictably, the phrase "Early ought to have been hung" appeared in newspapers across the continent and sparked another volley of verbiage from Early. Referring to "the somewhat notorious Gen. Thomas L. Rosser," who had already demonstrated "his utter disregard for the truth," Early proclaimed, "Having previously figured extensively as a falsifier of history, he has recently appeared in another role—that of a consummate ass, and it must be confessed that he has proved himself an adept in that character." In a well-conceived bit of grim ironic humor, Early took Rosser's reference to hanging and turned it back upon him: Early compared Rosser to Judas Iscariot, implying the best thing Rosser could do would be to follow the fallen apostle's example and hang himself. In response, Rosser claimed that just as he had been misunderstood in his attack on Sheridan, he had been misquoted in his remarks about Early.[38]

Rosser continued to find battles to fight in the public press, in lectures, political speeches, and during public meetings. Though the Reconstruction era had ended, the 1880s were years of bitter sectional strife as Northern Republicans condemned Southern Democrats for crimes against Republican voters in the South, most of whom were black. Governor Joseph Foraker of Ohio, for example, declared Southerners were actively perpetuating political warfare and "by fraud, by violence, by murder, by assassination, by bull-whips and shot-guns, the white leaguers and kuklux clans, by agencies of the most unscrupulous and diabolical character, by horrible barbarities" were denying freemen their right to vote. According to Foraker, Jefferson Davis, still a hero in the Old Confederacy, represented only "human slavery, the degradation of labor, the treason of secession and rebellion, the horrors and infamies of Libby and Andersonville."[39]

---

37 "Gen. Rosser Explains," Alexandria *Gazette and Virginia Advertiser* (VA), June 15, 1887.

38 Early to *The State* (Richmond, VA), undated clipping in Hotchkiss Papers, roll 58, frame 436. Early dated the letter June 18, 1887; "Gen. Rosser and Gen. Early," Staunton *Spectator* (VA), June 29, 1887.

39 "Vote Down Sectionalism," Richmond *Dispatch*, October 24, 1885, p. 2; Everett Walters, *Joseph Benson Foraker: An Uncompromising Republican* (Columbus, OH, 1948), 43.

Rosser did not, and perhaps could not, allow such attacks to go unanswered, and he responded in kind. He engaged so often in wars of words that editors across the country labeled him an extremist, an "incendiary" and a "Rampant Rebel."[40] His style of debate was to make blunt, brutal, confrontational statements designed to insult, demean, or humiliate his opponent. According to Rosser, Early was "old" and "incompetent"; Sheridan was "rubbish"; Foraker was "bigmouthed." The general who captured Atlanta was "poor, old, soured, decrepit, politically disappointed, blood-thirsty Sherman." Federal soldiers had been "hirelings," "conscripts," "bounty jumpers," "substitutes," and "vandals." The famous Confederate raider Col. John Mosby aptly described Rosser's impetuous, bludgeoning style in these literary assaults as fighting "with a tomahawk & butcher knife"[41]

At age 55 in 1892, Rosser ran for Congress, but he could not displace the incumbent, Charles T. O'Ferrall. A year later, Rosser sought the Democratic nomination for Governor of Virginia. Again, O'Ferrall stood in his way by also seeking the nomination. From local precinct meetings all the way to the party convention in Richmond, Rosser and his allies fought furiously against O'Ferrall. At a meeting in Rosser's home county of Albemarle, the general himself passionately led the offensive. Observers thought "at several stages in the proceedings in the court house it looked like a fight was imminent, and considerable incendiary language was used." During the nominating convention in Richmond, Rosser and an O'Ferrall man exchanged heated words during an open committee session and nearly exchanged blows before being separated. Rosser lost the nomination. He responded angrily with a public letter in the press reviling O'Ferrall and the "machine politics" that had defeated him. One editor, stunned by the severity of the bitter letter, lamented that Rosser had written his "assault" on the Democratic Party "without thought of consequences and not after calm reflection." Rosser denounced the party so vehemently that supporters feared he would leave the

---

40 "Rampant Rebel," Belmont *Chronicle* (OH), June 13, 1889.

41 For examples of Rosser's creative descriptions of foes, see his public letters to Early and Munford cited earlier, and his introduction and speeches in Thomas L. Rosser, *Addresses of General T. L. Rosser at the Seventh Annual Reunion of the Association of the Maryland Line, Academy of Music, Baltimore, MD. February 22, 1889 and on Memorial Day, Staunton, Va., June 8, 1889* (New York, NY, 1889); John S. Mosby, *Take Sides with the Truth*, Peter A Brown, ed. (Lexington, KY, 2007), 28.

WE record with genuine scientific interest the fact that General Thomas Launcelot Rosser, the great Virginia spouting geyser, is in perfect erupting form again. At Richmond, on Wednesday, he sent into the air a word stream 220 ft. long and 2 inches broad. and so hot that it fried in its own adjectives. Gen. Rosser has taken the contract for heating the State House next winter. His next exhibition will be with Eagle No. 6 Volunteer Fire Co. of Alexandria. It will be a contest of wind against water. General Rosser's friends are confident that he will win the prize—a silver-gilt spanner.—The New York Sun.

Why not enter Gen. Rosser in the oratorical contest proposed by the Sun between Greenhalge and O'Ferrall, the outcome of which is awaited with such impatience by the civilized world?

Rosser's long and controversial speeches earned him a national reputation for bloviation and gave critics opportunities for laughter at his expense. This item from the New York *Sun* (which errs in Rosser's middle name) was reprinted in the Winchester *Times*, June 6, 1894.

---

party altogether and "give comfort and assistance to the enemy," meaning the opposing People's Party. The impetuous Rosser did precisely that. He switched his allegiance to the populists and campaigned for them against O'Ferrall and the Democrats. His defection damaged his political future in Virginia, not only by alienating powerful Democrats, but by revealing himself as too volatile to succeed as a candidate in any party. A Virginia newspaper declared Democrats would be glad to see Rosser go. "General

Rosser's position has been too oscillating in the past to inspire confidence in his future movements," the editor concluded. "In his effort to court public favor or notoriety it is claimed that he has been obliged to assume too many roles and disguises."[42]

After the dimming of his prospects for elective office, Rosser continued to write public letters and speak at public ceremonies. Though he actively sought publicity, he could not control the nature of the renown that came to him. He could not alter the past, and though he had tried to establish "the truth of history" by casting responsibility for Tom's Brook onto others, his efforts had the opposite effect. As time passed, his name became ever more firmly connected with the most widely remembered defeat in the history of the Confederate cavalry. He could not escape Tom's Brook. In 1898, when, in preparation for the war with Spain, President William McKinley gave Rosser a commission as a brigadier general in the U. S. Army, a newspaper offered its readers a biographical synopsis of the new brigadier's life. The journalist wrote not of one of Rosser's military successes but of Tom's Brook, "in which Rosser's command was terribly whipped, and then chased over a large and very rough portion of Virginia."[43] In a speech, Rosser argued that Northerners and Southerners were "different creatures," making the broad generalization that "The Southern people are Saxon—the Northern People are Celt." An amused member of the audience was somehow reminded of Tom's Brook, and quipped, "General Thomas L. Rosser has a holy horror of the Celt. He has a recollection of a mellow autumn day in 1864 when a Celt, named Sheridan, at the head of a column of Union Soldiers, sent him 'whirling up the valley.' No wonder he hates Celts."[44] A former Federal soldier revisited the Valley in his old age and sent an account to a newspaper with a national circulation. He made a point of stopping at Tom's Brook and recalled how in the Woodstock Races the Federals had chased Rosser's men. The writer did not mention Lomax and his men, nor Jubal Early, nor any other Confederate. He associated Rosser's name with the Confederate debacle. The races ended after the 26-mile chase,

42 *The Daily Progress* (Charlottesville, VA), August 7, 1893, p. 1, col. 4; August 19, 1893. p. 1, col. 3; August 28, 1893, p. 2, col. 1; Thomas, "Under Indictment," 223; "General Rosser's Position," Roanoke *Times* (VA), October 5, 1883.

43 "Thomas L. Rosser," *National Tribune* (Washington, DC), June 30, 1898, p. 5.

44 "A Rampant Rebel," Belmont *Chronicle* (OH) June 13, 1889.

wrote the old Yankee, "with the exception that Rosser has been explaining ever since."[45] Even when the press mentioned Rosser favorably, a reference to Tom's Brook lurked not far away. The Chicago *Tribune* noted Rosser's great success as a railroad builder after the war and told a story of Rosser pushing a survey crew over a proposed route. When Rosser asked good naturedly if any of the men had ever covered more ground more quickly, one of the crew allegedly replied, "Yes, when I was with Custer, chasing you and old Jubal Early in the Shenandoah Valley."[46] Tom's Brook had become an indelible part of Rosser's public identity.

Rosser never backed away from his claims of innocence for Tom's Brook. It would be easier to credit Rosser's postwar claims if he had not acquired a reputation for insincerity. Back in July 1884, for example, Rosser attended a reunion of Minnesota veterans. Northerners and Southerners were still working at an uneasy reconciliation and according to a newspaper account Rosser entered wholly into the spirit of brotherly love. He offered a toast: "The Blue and the Gray—brothers equally brave, divided by war, but reunited in peace henceforth and forever," and then made a speech, praising the young men of Minnesota as "a band of patriots" who went forth to save the life of their nation. "And where was I?" Rosser asked rhetorically,

> With all my might I was there striking at that nation that they were endeavoring to serve, and the sublimity of this occasion to call me to this feast and tell me that my sins were forgiven! That I am one of them. [Cheers and prolonged applause.] I know it. I feel it. A demon can destroy, a savage can avenge, but he who is akin to a god alone can forgive.[47]

Less than five years later in Maryland and Virginia to audiences of former Confederates, Rosser delivered speeches so full of hostility and invective that they made news across the continent. At Confederate Memorial Day ceremonies in Staunton, Virginia, Rosser belittled Northern soldiers as mercenaries and the Northern people as greedy, unprincipled

---

45 J. E. Hott, "Through the Valley: Events Recalled by a Trip Through Shenandoah," *National* Tribune (DC), September 15, 1898, 10-11.

46 "Sidelights on Science and Scientists in Everyday Language," Chicago *Tribune*, January 25, 1914, sec. 8, p. 7, col. 2.

47 Clipping from the *Pioneer Press* (MN), July 23, 1884, in Rosser, Scrapbook 1877, 31.

seekers of wealth. Southern soldiers, he said, fought for the rights of states and the integrity of homes, for virtue, and for patriotism, while the Northern men had only a desire for "pelf, plunder and pay."[48] At a Confederate reunion in Baltimore, Rosser declared himself tired of "insincere reunions and 'blue and gray' love feasts" and vehemently denounced the North for its "malicious sectional hatred, and a morbid, irrational, puritanical, fanaticism, which cemented them in a holy union for an unholy and unchristian crusade against us."[49] That same year, he pondered, "The question now is, how does an honest, patriotic and manly Southern man feel today? Can he stand over the ruins of the past, the humiliations of the present and the threats of the future, before God and man and proclaim: 'I know no North—I know no South?'"[50] Yet in Boston, Massachusetts, in 1903, Rosser told an audience "I know no North, no South, no East, no West, but thank God for being an American. . . . The man from the South who says he wished the South had won is a fool. I thank God that the South did not win."[51] After one of Rosser's vehement denunciations of Northern soldiers in 1889, an editor in Minnesota observed, "Gen. Rosser seems to have a decided Dr. Jekyll and Mr. Hyde talent. When he lived in Minneapolis he was never accustomed to hiss his hatred of the North through his teeth."[52]

A few years after Rosser abandoned the Democrats and became a Populist, he very publically became a Republican and received a government job. A critic at a political meeting said to Rosser, "Why, sir, if I had made as many sudden political changes as you have, I should expect to find the seat of my pants twisted around in front of me!"[53] Some of Rosser's reversals seem ludicrous. In 1884, he had declared Jubal Early was "vain" and "incompetent," but three years later Rosser claimed his "first criticisms of Early were in an entirely friendly spirit."[54] After calling Sheridan "cold,

---

48 "A Rampant Rebel," Belmont *Chronicle,* June 13, 1889; Rosser, *Addresses*, 11.

49 Ibid., 24.

50 Ibid., 4-5.

51 "The Hooker Statue," *The National Tribune* (DC), July 2, 1903.

52 St. Paul *Daily Globe*, June 14, 1889, p. 3, col 1.

53 "Rosser and Massey," Staunton *Spectator and Vindicator* (VA), September 7, 1900.

54 "Gen. Rosser and Gen. Early," Staunton *Spectator and Vindicator* (VA) June 29, 1997; unsourced newspaper clipping, Hotchkiss Papers, reel 58, frame 439.

cruel and brutal," Rosser claimed these words had been misunderstood. Upon Sheridan's death, Rosser said in Minnesota, "I had no personal feeling in that controversy with Gen. Sheridan, and now that he is dead I have only the kindest thoughts of him." Four months later in Virginia, Rosser called Sheridan, "rubbish."[55]

In 1878, A. D. Payne, who had been a cavalryman under Rosser, warned a friend, former general Fitz John Porter, "Beware of Gen'l Rosser. Rosser has a motive in every thing he does, and has no scruples as to the mode of attaining his objects, he is in other words a Dugald Dolgetty, he is at any one's service who will give his price."[56] Rosser had the right to change his mind, but many thought he did so too easily and too often, and his actions struck some as mere opportunism. In his adoption of public "roles and disguises" he eventually came to look like a charlatan. After Rosser's death, a wag accurately observed, "He was by turns a Republican and a Democrat, and an extremist on whichever side he took."[57]

*   *   *

Despite his contentious nature, Rosser inspired admiration and affection among many who knew him. A surveyor who worked for Rosser on the Canadian Pacific Railroad in the 1880s described him as "a most lovable man." Clinton Gallaher, who rode with Rosser as a courier during the war and knew him for decades, declared, "I have loved no man more than I loved General Rosser. God Bless him and his!" Many mourned on March 30, 1910, when Richmond's *Times Dispatch* announced on its front page the death of Thomas L. Rosser. He had suffered a stroke five years earlier almost to the day. Respiratory and pulmonary symptoms came upon him suddenly about 10 days before his death, and his condition declined rapidly. He died at

55 St. Paul *Daily Globe*, February 24, 1889, p. 1, col. 2; Staunton *Spectator and Vindicator* (VA), June 12, 1889, p. 3, col. 3.

56 A. D. Payne to Fitz John Porter, May 11, 1878. Fitz John Porter Papers, Library of Congress, Washington, DC, microfilm roll 6, frame 312. Dugald Dalgetty, a character in Sir Walter Scott's novel *A Legend of Montrose*, is a mercenary soldier whose guiding principle is self-interest. Payne served as a captain in the 4th Virginia Cavalry.

57 "Some Newspaper Pen Portraits of Men Known in Minneapolis," St. Paul *Daily Globe*, February 24, 1889; "Senile Gen. Rosser," Staunton *Spectator and Vindicator* (VA), July 3, 1903; Death of Gen. T. L. Rosser, *National Tribune* (DC), April 14, 1910, p. 4, col. 5.

his home, "Rugby," near Charlottesville. A headline writer, with unintended irony, declared, "His End Was Peaceful."[58]

Rosser was many things, but he was not a man of peace. As an aggressive, assertive man of enterprise, he intended to have his own way and determine his own destiny, which is why his version of events at Tom's Brook is not credible. After the disaster, he painted himself as a passive, obedient figure who followed orders against his better judgment because he feared the wrath of his commander. Such a self-portrayal beggars belief, for Rosser's entire life and all of his published words are a reproach to everything submissive and passive. Nothing in Rosser's history suggests he would decide to back down from a face-to-face challenge on a battlefield, especially when facing his friend and rival Custer. And so Rosser decided to fight, and that decision began a chain of events that would continue for years. He deployed his troops and fought until driven from the field. And the jubilant boasting of Custer and the Federals worsened the humiliation. And Rosser refused to accept defeat and continued the fight by trying to prove he was not to blame for the debacle. And the more prominent and controversial Rosser made himself after the war the more opportunity he gave his foes to tell the comical story of "the Woodstock Races"—the day the Confederates ran away as they never had before. And most people recognized just one man as the central figure in the story: Thomas Rosser.

It is possible to excuse Rosser's rashness on Coffman's Hill, where his fighting spirit was set aboil by the opportunity to take on Custer. Less easy to condone is the egotism that drove him to evade responsibility for his own decisions. His postwar campaigns to discredit other men offer little to admire. Supporting evidence would have helped Rosser make a credible case for his claims. A reputation for consistency in public statements would have further aided his cause. But Rosser had neither. Jubal Early described Rosser's statements about Tom's Brook as "monstrous misrepresentations." Surviving evidence suggests Early was correct.

Perhaps Gen. William Payne came closest to the truth when he suggested Rosser possessed a superabundance of a warrior's version of *gaudium certaminis*—the intoxicating sensation Homer and Anglo-Saxons

58 James Henry Edward Secretan, *Canada's Great Highway: From the First Stake to the Last Spike* (Ottawa, 1924), 88; D. C. Gallaher, *Diary*, 31; *The Times Dispatch* (VA), March 30, 1910; *The Daily Progress* (VA), March 30, 1910.

called "battle joy," the joy of the fight. Rosser never gave any indication he regretted making the fight that day, for to express regret would be a defeat in itself. He loathed the result at Tom's Brook and the embarrassment that came with it, but because Tom Rosser lived life as a series of contests in which he was determined to fight for everything he valued and because to him, always, his willingness to fight was more important than any result, even the derisive laughter of his enemies could not make him regret his decision at Tom's Brook.

Organization of the Cavalry Forces
Present at the Engagement at Tom's Brook,
Shenandoah County, Virginia, October 9, 1864[1]

The basic organizational unit in the armies of the Civil War was the company, which usually consisted of 100 men and officers. Customarily, 12 companies were banded together to form a cavalry regiment. The regiment was given a number that indicated the sequence in which it was formed within its home state. Thus, the 5th Michigan Cavalry, for example, was the fifth mounted regiment formed in the state. Each company within the regiment received a letter designation, running from Company A to Company M, with no Company J. Ordinarily, regiments were commanded by a colonel, and companies by captains. Generally, four or five regiments were placed together to form a brigade, which would be commanded by a brigadier general. Most frequently, between four and five brigades were placed together to form a division, which, theoretically, was to be commanded by a major general. A brigade at full strength could number as many as 5,000 men, and a division as many as 25,000. These numbers represent abstract scenarios, however, and after three years of war, casualties, disease, desertion, and other causes had, in practical terms, reduced regiments and brigades to perhaps a third of their "paper" strength.

Nowhere in the *Official Records of the Union and Confederate Armies* are the commanders of all the Confederate brigades, regiments, battalions, and batteries engaged at Tom's Brook identified. The Confederate officers named here are those

---

1 General Sheridan's statements of the organization of his army on September 19 (*OR* 43, pt. 1, 110-11) and October 19 (*OR* 43, pt. 1, 130) serve as the basis for the Federal portion of this listing with adjustments according to reliable sources as noted.

identified in unit histories, rosters, or in reliable firsthand accounts as being in command on or about October 9, 1864. Sources valuable in identifying commanders of Confederate units include Robert K. Krick's *Lee's Colonels*, and the books published in the H. E. Howard Virginia regimental series listed in the Rosters section in the bibliography.[2]

Cavalry, Army of the Shenandoah
Bvt. Maj. Gen. Alfred T. A. Torbert[3], Chief of Cavalry

Escort: 1st Rhode Island, Maj. William H. Turner, Jr.

FIRST DIVISION
Brig. Gen. Wesley Merritt

FIRST BRIGADE
Col. James H. Kidd
1st Michigan, Capt. Andrew W. Duggan
5th Michigan, Maj. Smith H. Hastings
6th Michigan, Maj. Charles W. Deane
7th Michigan, Maj. Daniel H. Darling
25th New York, Lt. Col. Aaron Seeley
New York Light Artillery, 6th Battery, Capt. Joseph W. Martin

SECOND BRIGADE
Bvt. Brig. Gen. Thomas C. Devin[4]
6th New York, Capt. George E. Farmer
9th New York, Col. George S. Nichols
19th New York (1st New York Dragoons), Col. Alfred Gibbs
1st U. S. Artillery, Batteries K and L, Lt. Frank E. Taylor

RESERVE BRIGADE
Col. Charles R. Lowell, Jr.
2d Massachusetts, Lt. Col. Casper Crowninshield

---

2   Robert K. Krick, *Lee's Colonels: a Biographical Register of the Field Officers of the Army of Northern Virginia* (Dayton, OH, 1979).

3   Torbert's second division, under Col. William H. Powell, was on detached duty in the Luray Valley and was not present at Tom's Brook.

4   The 4th New York Cavalry and the 17th Pennsylvania Cavalry belonged to Devin's brigade, but evidence suggests neither was at Tom's Brook. The 4th New York was detailed for duty at Sheridan's headquarters. The 17th Pennsylvania was detailed to detached duty in Winchester in October 1864 with another detachment detailed for duty as escort for Gen. Horatio G. Wright and was not present at Tom's Brook. *OR* 43, pt.1, 125, 130; pt. 2, 515.

1st United States, Capt. Eugene M. Baker
2d United States, Capt. Robert S. Smith
5th United States, Lt. Gustavus Urban
2d U. S. Artillery, Battery D, Lt. Edward B. Williston

THIRD DIVISION
Brig. Gen. George A. Custer

FIRST BRIGADE
Col. Alexander C. M. Pennington[5]
3d New Jersey, Maj. William P. Robeson
2d New York, Maj. Walter C. Hull
5th New York, Maj. Abram H. Krom
2d Ohio, Lt. Col. George A. Purington
18th Pennsylvania, Maj. John W. Phillips

SECOND BRIGADE
Col. William Wells
3d Indiana (two companies), Lt. Benjamin F. Gilbert
1st New Hampshire (battalion), Col. John L. Thompson
8th New York, Lt. Col. William H. Benjamin
22d New York, Maj. Caleb Moore[6]
1st Vermont, Lt. Col. John W. Bennett

HORSE ARTILLERY
2d U. S. Batteries B and L, Capt. Charles H. Peirce
3d U. S. Batteries C, F, and K, Capt. Dunbar R. Ransom

5 The 1st Connecticut Cavalry Battalion belonged to Pennington's brigade, but most, and perhaps all, of the unit was detached to escort a wagon train to Martinsburg, Virginia, and was not at Tom's Brook. See New York *Herald* of October 14, 1864, and *OR* 43, pt. 1, 535 for references to Robeson, Hull, and Krom.

6 Moore, of the 8th New York Cavalry, was detached to command the 22nd regiment, which was short of officers. New York *Herald* of October 14, 1864.

Cavalry, Army of the Valley
Lt. Gen. Jubal A. Early

LOMAX'S DIVISION
Maj. Gen. Lunsford L. Lomax[7]

JOHNSON'S BRIGADE
Col. Bradley T. Johnson[8]
8th Virginia
21st Virginia
22d Virginia
25th Virginia
36th Virginia Battalion
37th Virginia Battalion

JACKSON'S BRIGADE
Lt. Col. William P. Thompson
2d Maryland, Capt. Warner G. Welsh[9]
19th Virginia
20th Virginia
46th Virginia Battalion, Lt. Col. Joseph R. Kessler
47th Virginia Battalion

HORSE ARTILLERY
Baltimore Battery, Lt. John McNulty (six guns)

---

7   *OR* 43, pt.1, 567. Lomax's division consisted of four brigades, but two of those, John Imboden's and John McCausland's, were on detached duty and not present at Tom's Brook.

8   The 25th Virginia Cavalry transferred to McCausland's brigade after Tom's Brook. *OR* 43, pt. 2, 914; Dobbie E. Lambert, *25th Virginia Cavalry* (Lynchburg, 1994), 75-78. The 34th Virginia Battalion was officially attached to this brigade in late August 1864, but operated independently in West Virginia and was not present at Tom's Brook. Cole, *34th Virginia Battalion*, 87-94.

9   The 1st and 2nd Maryland Cavalry Battalions were both much reduced in strength and had been operating together, unofficially, as a single unit. In August, only 175 men were present in both battalions combined. Ruffner notes that the 2nd Battalion was in disarray with many officers absent in the autumn of 1864 and fewer than 100 men present for duty. Driver describes the surviving records as "scant." Welsh belonged to the 1st Maryland Cavalry Battalion, and appears to have commanded the joint organization after the battle of Winchester. The assertion that he led the battalion at Tom's Brook is speculative. Captain Gustavus W. Dorsey may have exercised some practical control. Kevin Conley Ruffner, *Maryland's Blue & Gray: A Border State's Union and Confederate Junior Officer Corps* (Baton Rouge, LA, 1997) 207, 306; Robert J. Driver, *First & Second Maryland Cavalry, CSA* (Charlottesville, VA, 1999), 185, 187; Harry Gilmor, *Four Years in the Saddle* (Baltimore, MD, 1986), 240.

FITZHUGH LEE'S DIVISION
Brig. Gen. Thomas L. Rosser

WICKHAM'S BRIGADE
Col. Thomas T. Munford
1st Virginia, Col. Richard W. Carter
2d Virginia
3d Virginia, Maj. Henry Carrington
4th Virginia

ROSSER'S "LAUREL" BRIGADE
Lt. Col. Richard H. Dulany, Col. Oliver R. Funsten, Sr.
7th Virginia, Capt. Daniel C. Hatcher, Lt. Col. Mottram D. Ball[10]
11th Virginia, Col. Oliver R. Funsten, Sr., Lt. Col. Mottram D. Ball,
Maj. Edward H. McDonald
12th Virginia. Lt. Col. Thomas B. Massie
35th Virginia Battalion, Lt. Nicholas Dorsey, Capt. William Dowdell

PAYNE'S BRIGADE
Col. William H. F. Payne
5th Virginia, Col. Reuben Boston
6th Virginia, Maj. Daniel A. Grimsley[11]
15th Virginia, Capt. Cyrus W. Harding, Jr.[12]

HORSE ARTILLERY
Maj. James Breathed[13]
Thomson's Virginia battery, Capt. James W. Thomson (two guns)
Johnston's Virginia battery, Capt. Philip P. Johnston (four guns)
Lynchburg Artillery, Capt. John J. Shoemaker (six guns)

10 Because Lieutenant Colonel Dulany was commanding the brigade and no other field officers of the regiment were present, Hatcher, as the senior captain, would have been in command at Tom's Brook. Lieutenant Colonel Ball of the 11th Virginia Cavalry stated that he exercised command of the 7th during the fight. See "Annals of the War: Rosser and His Critics."

11 After the wounding of Lt. Col. Daniel Richards on September 24, 1864, Grimsley apparently was the senior officer present. Musick, *6th Virginia Cavalry*, 67, 69, 120, 149.

12 Harding was the senior captain. No field officers are known to be present. See Fortier, *15th Virginia Cavalry*, 89, 140.

13 Wallace, Lee A., Jr. *A Guide to Virginia Military Organizations 1861-1865* (Lynchburg, VA, 1986), 15, 31.

APPENDIX B

Strengths and Losses

The absence of complete records means that the numerical strengths of the forces engaged at Tom's Brook can only be estimated. Furthermore, when discussing the size of their forces, officers in both armies often failed to distinguish between the aggregate strength (or "paper strength") and the present-for-duty strength (or actual strength). Best estimates of the relative sizes of the troops on the field at Tom's Brook on October 9, 1864, suggest that 2,300 Confederates opposed 6,000 Federals.

Confederate records regarding the number of men present in the fight are especially few and incomplete. Maj. Gen. Fitzhugh Lee reported that the strength of his division in June 1864 was about 1,500 men in two brigades. Wickham's brigade, which would later be led by Thomas Munford, numbered about 1,100 men in Lee's summertime estimate, and the brigade that would be led by William H. F. Payne numbered about 400 at that time. By the beginning of October, after three months of active campaigning, the combined present-for-duty strength of the two brigades did not exceed 1,000. Given the attrition in the limited pool of horses available to the Confederate cavalry at that time of the war, and that the loss of a horse due to decrepitude also meant that the rider of that horse could not participate in mounted operations, the present-for-duty strength of Lee's two brigades was likely closer to 800 around October 1.[1] When Rosser's Laurel Brigade arrived in the Valley on the evening of October 5, it numbered roughly 600 men, and it combined with the other two brigades to raise the strength of the division, now commanded by Rosser, to at most 1,500 men. Casualties and straggling in the three-day, 50-mile march to Tom's Brook would have reduced Rosser's force. Col. Thomas Munford believed

---

1   Theodore C. Mahr, *The Battle of Cedar Creek: Showdown in the Shenandoah, October 1-30, 1864* (Lynchburg, VA, 1992), 370-71; Patchan, *Winchester*, 484.

unauthorized absences also weakened Rosser's force at this time because many of the men in the ranks were marching through their home territory and, Munford suggested, slipped away to learn of the safety of their homes and families during The Burning.[2] Rosser commanded about 1,400 men at Coffman's Hill on the morning of October 9. Lomax commanded more men, but they were dispersed over a larger area. The entire division composed about 2,000 men present for duty, but some of them were on duty at various points in western Virginia and even West Virginia and therefore were not with Lomax during The Burning. In any case, Lomax specified that he had but 800 men with him when he began his march to Tom's Brook on October 6.[3] The entire Confederate force at Tom's Brook did not exceed 2,300 men, including the artillerymen serving the 12 field pieces.

U.S. government records make it easier to estimate the strengths of Federal units. In a return dated September 10, 1864, about a month before the engagement at Tom's Brook, Custer's and Merritt's two divisions, combined, numbered 6,465 officers and men present for duty. Casualties in the Third Battle of Winchester and in other actions, as well as the discharge of soldiers whose terms of service had expired, reduced the combined strength of the two divisions to between 5,700 and 6,000 men by the time they reached Tom's Brook.[4]

In terms of relative advantage, the Federal superiority was even greater than the five to two odds that the total strengths suggest because the Confederates did not work together as the Federals did. Custer enjoyed an advantage over Rosser of about 2 to 1, but those odds tipped further in Custer's favor when he received assistance from one of Merritt's brigades (Kidd's Michigan men and New Yorkers). Even after sending Kidd to work with Custer, Merritt held an edge of almost three to one over Lomax and his broken-down force.

Accurate casualty figures are likewise difficult to ascertain. By late 1864, officers did not always submit reports after engagements, and such was the case after the fight at Tom's Brook. The published *Official Records* include only a cursory statement of Federal losses and no statement at all of Confederate losses. Although official information regarding casualties at Tom's Brook and in the days of The Burning is available as raw data in the thousands of personnel files of the soldiers who were involved, the dispersal of that information into thousands of files in

2   Munford, "Reminiscences . . . No. 3," 135.

3   Patchan, *Winchester*, 484; *OR* 43, pt. 1, 612.

4   Sheridan reported that his cavalry sustained 441 casualties on September 19 at Third Winchester. William Averell, commander of the Second Cavalry Division, stated his command lost 250 men in the battle. Given that Sheridan and Averill were engaged in a feud after the engagement and that Averill accused Sheridan of not giving credit where credit was due, it is difficult to determine whether Sheridan's statement of 441 casualties in his cavalry that day includes the 250 claimed by Averill. *OR* 43, pt. 1, 61, 498.

various archives remains a principal reason for the difficulty in enumerating casualties. Fortunately, many researchers have worked at mining the unpublished official records of the armies—specifically the compiled service records of individual soldiers and records kept by the states the soldiers served. Much of the labor of those researchers and compilers appears in the books listed in the Rosters section in the bibliography of this work. The admirable thoroughness of historians Robert O'Neill, whose database of casualties in cavalry regiments served as starting point for the compilation below, and Richard Armstrong, who published his roster research in the H. E. Howard regimental series, makes their work especially useful.

While the volumes of the *Official Records* do not include casualty lists, journalists for the New York *Herald* obtained official lists of Federal losses from the provost marshals of Merritt's and Custer's divisions, and these lists appear in the newspaper's issues of October 14 and October 17, 1864. On November 4, 1864, the Burlington *Free Press* printed an unofficial list of Vermont casualties. Any name appearing in the compilation below was cross checked in multiple sources, including service records, to ensure the correct regiment or battery and the presence of the soldier with unit in October 1864. In the newspapers used as sources, some casualties are identified as having occurred on one of two days. Some casualties in Merritt's division, for example, were given as occurring on October 8 or 9. If multiple sources state that a soldier became a casualty on a specific day, his name appears on the appropriate daily list below. The names of soldiers who may have been wounded on either day are marked with an asterisk (*) and placed on the list of casualties for the day on which the regiment of the soldier in question was most actively engaged with the enemy. The following lists are in no way complete, but they offer a fragmentary picture of the human losses in the cavalry action that covered almost 80 miles between October 6 and October 9, 1864.

All units mentioned are cavalry except for artillery batteries. Names are arranged first by division (Rosser's men first followed by Lomax's for Confederates, and Custer's followed by Merritt's for Federals), next by state, unit number, and name of soldier. (See Appendix A for organization tables). Abbreviations: KIA: killed in action; WIA: wounded in action, MWIA: mortally wounded in action; MIA: missing in action; POW: prisoner of war; DIC: died in captivity; Bttn.: battalion; Btty.: battery.

An Itinerary Showing Casualties in Context
October 6-9, 1864

October 6, 1864

At dawn, the Federal cavalry left its camps north of the North River. Custer's division abandoned the town of Bridgewater and headed north on the Harrisonburg-Warm Springs Turnpike and then moved to the Mountain Road (also known as the

Back Road). Merritt's division moved northward from Mt. Crawford on the Valley Turnpike and along the Middle Road. Both divisions sent large burning details off the main roads to destroy crops, barns, storehouses and mills and to confiscate or kill livestock. Merritt's division covered some 20 miles during the day, pursued by Lomax's division, and went into camp around Timberville.[5] Rosser's division pursued Custer's command. The Confederates harassed the Federal columns and details throughout the day. Toward evening, after covering about 20 miles during the day's march, Custer's men were making camp north of Cootes's Store at Brock's Gap when Rosser's division, led by Munford's Brigade, fell upon the Federal rear guard.

Listed as Confederate casualties:

Chapman, James C., 4th VA, WIA
Cave, Benjamin F., 7th VA, POW
Feller, Mahlon G., 7th VA, POW

Listed as Federal casualties:

Kalaher, Cornelius D., 1st NH, POW
McGivern, Michael, 1st NH, POW
Smith, Augustus, 1st NH, KIA
Tehen, Norris, 1st NH, POW
McCollom, George, 5th NY, POW
Pletcher, John, 18th PA, WIA
Warner, John A., 18th PA, POW
Ralph, Thomas, 1st VT, MWIA
Burgess, James, 7th MI, MIA
Saunders, Franklin T., 6th NY, MWIA

October 7, 1864

Custer's division left its camps north of Cootes's Store and headed east and northeast toward Timberville and Forestville before turning northwestward toward the Back Road to cross Mill Creek west of Mt. Clifton. In the afternoon, Rosser launched regiments of his Laurel Brigade in a strong attack at the rear of Custer's column where the Back Road crossed the creek. This action accounted for most of the casualties of the day, as the Laurel Brigade led the attack at Mill Creek, and the

5   *OR* 43, pt. 1, 90.

1st Vermont, acting as Custer's rearguard, received the force of the Confederate attack and sustained great loss. Elements of the 5th New York supported the Vermonters. Custer's division ended the day's long march of almost 25 miles at Columbia Furnace on Stony Creek. Merritt's division covered some 18 miles during the day and went into camp around Edinburg.[6]

Listed as Confederate casualties:

Harrington, C.M., 1st VA, POW
Bass, Thomas, 2nd VA, WIA
Bolling, Richard M., 4th VA, WIA
Mountcastle, Robert E., 5th VA, WIA
Bull, Americus, 7th VA, MWIA
Bush, Erasmus, 7th VA, POW
Cockrell, Seth, 11th VA, WIA
Law, Benjamin, 11th VA, WIA
Painter, John, 12th VA, KIA
Goard, John, 35th VA Bttn., WIA
Myers, Franklin M., 35th VA Bttn., WIA
Goode, Anthony, Thomson's Btty., POW

Listed as Federal casualties:

Grant, William T., 1st NH, POW
Bixby, Daniel, 5th NY, POW
Campbell, Dennis, 5th NY, POW
Curkendall, Walter, 5th NY, WIA
Kennedy, John, 5th NY, POW
Rew, Milton D., 5th NY, POW
Whitney, Charles, 5th NY, KIA
Bacon, Lyman, 8th NY, KIA
Brown, Daniel, 8th NY, POW
Kellogg, Frederick, 2nd OH, POW
Abbott, Horace M., 1st VT, POW, DIC
Adams, Dan, 1st VT, POW
Bates, George, 1st VT, WIA, POW
Bixby, Russell, 1st VT, POW
Buckman, Henry, 1st VT, MIA

6 *OR* 43, pt. 1, 91.

Butts, Harvey, 1st VT, POW
Cameron, William, 1st VT, POW, DIC
Cassady, Thomas, 1st VT, POW
Champlain, Joseph, 1st VT, MIA
Clark, Thaddeus, 1st VT, POW, DIC
Cohaskey, Nelson, 1st VT, POW
Connelly, John C.- 1st VT, WIA
Conroe, Bertrand, 1st VT, WIA
Corse, Malcolm, 1st VT, POW
Domina, Derious, 1st VT, POW
Farnsworth, Henry, 1st VT, POW
Fassett, Dean, 1st VT, WIA, POW
Fitzgerald, William, 1st VT, POW
Fletcher, George, 1st VT, POW
Gay, Rufus, 1st VT, POW
Hall, Alexander, 1st VT, POW
Hamilton, Horace, 1st VT, WIA
Hammond, Orange, 1st VT, POW
Hartson, Abel, 1st VT, POW
Harvey, Charles, 1st VT, WIA, POW
Hatch, Clarence, 1st VT, POW
Hinds, Justin, 1st VT, POW, DIC
Hinkson, Edwin, 1st VT, POW
Jones, Edwin, 1st VT, MWIA, POW, DIC
Maredith, Mark, 1st VT, MIA
Martin, Joseph, 1st VT, POW
McCollom, Ira, 1st VT, POW, DIC
Parkhurst, Oscar, 1st VT, POW
Peck, Julius, 1st VT, WIA, POW
Quimby, Elijah, 1st VT, WIA
Reed, Lucius, 1st VT, WIA
Rogers, Harrison, 1st VT, POW
Rushford, Zimri, 1st VT, MIA
Sansouci, Francis, 1st VT, WIA
Scott, Marcus, 1st VT, WIA
Stearns, Samuel, 1st VT, POW
Stewart, Alvin, 1st VT, POW
Stuart, William, 1st VT, MIA
Thompson, William, 1st VT, POW
Varnum, Charles P., 1st VT, POW, DIC
Washburn, Andre, 1st VT, MIA, POW, DIC
Wheaton, William, 1st VT, POW

Wheeler, Henry, 1st VT, POW
Williams, Albert, 1st VT, POW
Wright, Joseph, 1st VT, WIA, POW, DIC
McAllister, Ziba, 1st VT, WIA
Morse, John W, 1st VT, POW
Connolly, John, 1st VT, WIA
Robinson, Joseph, 1st VT, WIA, POW
Depuy, Charles, 1st MI, POW
Bemus, George, 9th NY, WIA

October 8, 1864

After Custer's division broke camp at Columbia Furnace, men of the 18th Pennsylvania, acting as the rear guard, fired the iron-making shops. Payne's brigade of Rosser's division vigorously harassed the Pennsylvanians at the rear of the Federal column. Rosser accompanied Payne's and Munford's brigades beyond Tom's Brook and Mt. Olive to near Tumbling Run before turning back to engage elements of Col. Charles Lowell's 2nd Massachusetts and other regiments of Merritt's division. The ensuing skirmish ended with the Confederates holding the high ground of Coffman's Hill south of Tom's Brook.

On the Valley Pike, after Michigan troops burned a barn on the southern end of Woodstock, the flames spread to dwellings in the village and the Michigan troopers halted their northward progress to fight the fires. Lomax's men charged into the town and forced the Northerners to continue northward. Lomax's men skirmished with the Federals north of Woodstock. Merritt's division covered some 15 miles during the day and went into camp near Round Hill.[7] Custer's division encamped near Fisher's Hill, having ridden some 13 miles during the day.[8]

Listed as Confederate casualties:

Arnall, John, 1st VA, MWIA
Bayne, Frank, 1st VA, WIA
Cottrell, Henry, 1st VA, WIA
Grove, Francis T., 1st VA, POW
Anderson, Meriweather, 2nd VA, KIA
Cobb, James, 2nd VA, KIA
Dabney, Robert, 4th VA, POW, DIC (typhoid fever)

---

7   *OR* 43, pt. 1, 91.

8   *OR* 43, pt. 1, 100.

Yates, Booten, 4th VA, POW,
Wilson, Straughan, 5th VA, MWIA
Flournoy, Henry, 6th VA, WIA
Brown, Edward, 7th VA, MWIA
Koontz, Hugh R., 7th VA, KIA
Brittner, Thaddeus, 11th VA, KIA
Frye, Joseph, 11th VA, KIA
Kirby, Francis, 11th VA, WIA
Silvers, Joseph, 11th VA, MWIA
Smith, L.J., Johnston's Btty., MWIA
Murphy, Thomas, 19th VA, WIA
Johnson, B.H., 21st VA, POW
Kessler, Joseph R., 46th VA Bttn., POW
Nichols, Richard, 46th VA Bttn., POW
Smith Samuel S., 46th VA Bttn., POW, DIC
Apperson, James R., 47th VA Bttn., POW

Listed as Federal casualties:

Jones, Joseph, 2nd OH, POW
Follansbee, Benjamin, 18th PA, POW
Fry, Alvin, 18th PA, KIA
Hendershot, Thomas, 18th PA, POW
Jack, Peter, 18th PA, WIA
Kies, John, 18th PA, WIA
Lohr, Henry, 18th PA, WIA
Ralph, Patrick, 18th PA, KIA
Root, Peter, 18th PA, POW
Street, Frank, 18th PA, KIA
Thomas, John, 18th PA, KIA
Harvey, Charles, 1st VT, WIA, POW, DIC
Lowell, James, 1st VT, KIA
Boston, John, 2nd MA, KIA
Collins, James, 2nd MA, WIA
Hardy, John Q., 2nd MA, WIA
Lynch, Michael M., 2nd MA, WIA
Gudith, John D., 5th MI, KIA
Perry, Augustus G., 5th MI, WIA*
Hale, Elvin, 5th MI, POW
Bass, Nathan, 6th MI, MIA
Lang, James, 2nd NY, POW
O'Donnell, Patrick, 2nd NY, MWIA

Woolf, Augustus, 2nd NY, POW
McGill, John F, 25th NY, WIA

October 9, 1864

At dawn, the Federal cavalry altered the pattern of the previous few days and, turned southward to meet the Confederate pursuers. In two separate engagements south of Tom's Brook, one on the Valley Pike and the other on the Back Road, the two Confederate forces, under Lomax and Rosser respectively, assumed generally defensive postures, and the Federals, under Merritt and Custer respectively, turned the flanks of the defenders' and routed them.

In the engagement on the Valley Pike, Lomax withdrew his command in time to avoid the substantial losses sustained by Rosser on Coffman's Hill and the Back Road. Munford's brigade suffered heavily, losing about 50% of all Confederate casualties in the Back Road fighting. The two artillery units operating with Rosser were essentially destroyed, losing all their guns and most of their personnel. A majority of the documented casualties in Custer's division occurred in William Wells's brigade, which executed both the flanking movement around the Confederate left and the coordinated frontal assault against Munford's men.

The Federals declared that on October 9, 1864, they lost 9 men killed and 48 wounded for a total of 57. The fragmentary records below show 8 killed or mortally wounded, 2 presumed taken prisoner and 59 wounded for a total of 69.[9]

Listed as Confederate casualties:

Bryarly, Robert, 1st VA, WIA
Deppish, Edward, 1st VA, POW
Gold, Samuel, 1st VA, WIA
Jordan, Charles, 1st VA, WIA
Kilmer, Barney S., 1st VA, POW*
McCue, Samuel, 1st VA, WIA
Moore, John Wilson, 1st VA, WIA
Myers, John, 1st VA, MWIA
Payne, Orrick F., 1st VA, POW*
Ruff, James, 1st VA, KIA
Stewart, Robert H., 1st VA, WIA
Akers, Joseph H., 2nd VA, WIA
Bishop, Marshall, 2nd VA, WIA

9   *OR* 43, pt. 1, 60.

Blankenship, Edward, 2nd VA, POW*
Callaham, James, 2nd VA, POW
Cobbs, Thomas A. 2nd VA, MWIA
Coleman, John, 2nd VA, POW
Davis, Thomas B., 2nd VA, WIA, POW, DIC
Elliot, Thomas, 2nd VA, WIA
Fuqua, Benjamin, 2nd VA, KIA
Harvey, Simeon, 2nd VA, WIA
Hatcher, Abner, 2nd VA, MWIA[10]
Hayth, Edward, 2nd VA, WIA
Holtzman, B. S., 2nd VA, POW
Kale, Edward, 2nd VA, WIA
Kinney, Bryant, 2nd VA, POW*
Lakes, John, 2nd VA, WIA
Lay, John, 2nd VA, WIA
Lee, James, 2nd VA, KIA
Major, James, 2nd VA, MWIA
Morgan, William, 2nd VA, WIA
Noland, Lloyd, 2nd VA, POW
Oliver, Yelverton, 2nd VA, KIA
Singleton, Henry, 2nd VA, KIA
Singleton, John, 2nd VA, WIA
Taylor, Thomas P., 2nd VA, POW
Thomas, Reuben, 2nd VA, POW*
Wade, William, 2nd VA, WIA
Walker, C. C., 2nd VA, POW*
Ware, S. J., 2nd VA, WIA
Whittle, Beverly, 2nd VA, WIA
Williams, James, 2nd VA, WIA
Williams, S. T., 2nd VA, WIA
Beardley, George, 3rd VA, POW
Brown, Richard, 3rd VA, WIA
Davis, Philip, 3rd VA, POW
DuPuy, William, 3rd VA, WIA
Flippen, Hartwell, 3rd VA, WIA
Marston, Oliver, 3rd VA, POW
Minor, Edward, 3rd VA, WIA
Orgain, Albert, 3rd VA, WIA

---

10 Killed near Pugh's Run according to Munford, *SHSP*, 13:138.

Overton, William, 3rd VA, KIA
Watkins, Richard, 3rd VA, WIA
West, Arthur, 3rd VA, POW
Witt, Edward, 3rd VA, POW
Womack, Eugene, 3rd VA, KIA
Adams, William, 4th VA, POW
Anderson, John W. 4th VA, POW
Ball, John W., 4th VA, WIA
Bridwell, Haywood, 4th VA, POW
Ellett, James, 4th VA, POW
Fisher, William F., 4th VA, POW
Fones, John R., 4th VA, POW
Foster, James, 4th VA, POW
Glenn, N.C., 4th VA, POW
Gregory, Obadiah, 4th VA, POW, DIC
Hill, William P. 4th VA, WIA
James, Marshall K., 4th VA, POW
Jeffries, Hill, 4th VA, POW
Jeffries, Marion, 4th VA, POW
Jordan, W. H., 4th VA, POW
Keys, Charles, 4th VA, POW
Luttrell, Burrell, 4th VA, POW
Lynn, Benjamin, 4th VA, POW
Morris, R. J., 4th VA, POW
Norman, Andrew, 4th VA, POW
Nuckols, Jacob, 4th VA, POW
Riley, Patrick, 4th VA, POW
Scott, Charles, 4th VA, POW
Selectman, Redman, 4th VA, POW
Selectman, Thomas, 4th VA, POW
Smith, A.W., 4th VA, POW
Smith, Christopher, 4th VA, POW
Smith, William E, 4th VA, WIA
Spicer, M. H., 4th VA, POW
Stallard, Albert, 4th VA, POW
Stallard, James, 4th VA, POW
Timberlake, David A., 4th VA, WIA
Webster, Charles, 4th VA, POW
Werth, James, 4th VA, WIA, POW
Whit, John A., 4th VA, POW
White, Thomas, 4th VA, POW
Williams, Gellie, 4th VA, POW

Yager, Benjamin, 4th VA, WIA
Yates, A.B., 4th VA, POW
Yates, Benjamin, 4th VA, POW
Baytop, James, 5th VA, WIA
Browne, Junius, 5th VA, WIA, POW
Campbell, B.B., 5th VA, WIA*
Dix, William, 5th VA, POW
Nunn, James, 5th VA, KIA
Overby, James, 5th VA, POW
Perkins, John, 5th VA, POW
Barbee, George, 6th VA, WIA
Bready, Daniel, 6th VA, WIA
Burruss, John, 6th VA, WIA
Carson, Thomas, 6th VA, POW
Carter, Robert, 6th VA, WIA
Childress, Henry, 6th VA, WIA
Coleman, Johnston, 6th VA, WIA
Duncan, Robert, 6th VA, WIA, POW
Eastham, George, 6th VA, KIA
Galt, Robert, 6th VA, POW
Hughes, George, 6th VA, POW
LaRue, Christopher C., 6th VA, WIA
Martz, Samuel, 6th VA, POW
Meade, Francis, 6th VA, POW*
Morton, William, 6th VA, KIA
Plaster, George, 6th VA, WIA
Renoe, Henry, 6th VA, KIA
Simpson, William, 6th VA, POW*
Smith, James, 6th VA, WIA
Watson, James, 6th VA, WIA
Watson, Thomas S., 6th VA, WIA
Dulany, Richard H., 7th VA, WIA
Herndon, John, 7th VA, WIA[11]
Manly, George, 7th VA, WIA
Payne, Lafayette, 7th VA, WIA
Shoup, John C., 7th VA, KIA
Ball, Mottrom, 11th VA, WIA
Eastham, George, 11th VA, KIA

11 Obituary *Confederate Veteran*, 34:6 (June 1928), 225.

Funsten, Oliver R., Jr., 11th VA, WIA
Pownell, Jasper, 11th VA, WIA
Sonner, John, 11th VA, POW
Swisher, Joseph, 11th VA, POW
Thompson, Joseph, 11th VA, POW
Wilson, Theo, 11th VA, POW
Adkins, Henry, 12th VA, POW
Anderson, Isaac, 12th VA, WIA
Atkins, John, 12th VA, POW
Atkins, M. Jefferson, 12th VA, POW
Conner, O., 12th VA, POW
Doran, William, 12th VA, POW
Long, Isaac, 12th VA, WIA
Moler, Rollin, 12th VA, KIA*
Osbourn, Alexander, 12th VA, POW
Osbourn, Robert, 12th VA, POW
Ranson, Thomas, 12th VA, POW
Reinhart, William, 12th VA, POW
Watson, George, 12th VA, POW
Amonette, J. R., 15th VA, POW
Munt, John, 15th VA, POW
Beans, Elwood H., 35th VA Bttn., WIA
Grubb, Thomas S., 35th VA Bttn., MWIA
Sellman, Alonzo, 35th VA Bttn., WIA
Simpson, E.B., 35th VA Bttn., WIA
Sinclair, Charles W., 35th VA Bttn., MWIA
Terry, Robert, 35th VA Bttn., WIA
Thomas, William, 35th VA Bttn., WIA
Titus, William, 35th VA Bttn., WIA
Beall, Lloyd, Johnston's Btty., POW
Bennett, William V., Johnston's Btty., POW
Coit, N., Johnston's Btty., POW
Crabb, Robert, Johnston's Btty., POW
Elam, William, Johnston's Btty., POW
Glenn, N.C., Johnston's Btty., POW
Grubbs, W.A., Johnston's Btty., POW
Harris, Alex, Johnston's Btty., POW
Harrison, William, Johnston's Btty., POW
Haynes, Hayden, Johnston's Btty., POW, DIC
Haynes, Virgil, Johnston's Btty., POW, DIC
Higgins, James, Johnston's Btty., POW
Lewis, William, Johnston's Btty., POW

Lindsey, Elijah, Johnston's Btty., POW
Lindsey, James S., Johnston's Btty., POW
Mangum, W.W., Johnston's Btty., POW
Miller, Benjamin F., Johnston's Btty., POW
Morton, Nicholas, Johnston's Btty., POW
Roach, R.J., Johnston's Btty., POW
Ryan, James, Johnston's Btty., POW
Smith, William G., Johnston's Btty., POW
Supinger, J., Johnston's Btty., POW
Watkins, W.C., Johnston's Btty., POW
Emmett, John W., Rosser's Staff, WIA
Walke, Isaac T., Jr., Rosser's Staff, KIA
Frazier, William S., Thomson's Btty., POW
Kagey, Joseph, Thomson's Btty., POW
Longerbeam, Charles, Thomson's Btty., POW
McGuire, William P., Thomson's Btty., POW
McWilliams, George, Thomson's Btty., POW
Neese, George M., Thomson's Btty., POW
Pierce, John F., Thomson's Btty., POW
Roberts, Stephen, Thomson's Btty., POW
Shaffer, Jacob, Thomson's Btty., POW
Williams, J., Thomson's Btty., POW
Williams, J.C., Thomson's Btty., POW
Wright, James K., Thomson's Btty., POW
Bailey, C., 8th VA, MWIA
Harman, Thomas B, 8th VA, KIA
McNutt, J., 8th VA, WIA
Penton, Hyram, 8th VA, POW
Sesler, Mark, 8th VA, POW
Whiteley, Charles, 8th VA, KIA
Arthur, Joseph D., 19th VA, POW
Given, Robert E., 19th VA, WIA
McLaughlin, John M., 19th VA, WIA
Smith, Jasper N., 19th VA, POW
Smith, S. P., 19th VA, POW
Halsey, Stephen Peters, 21st VA, WIA
Hepinstall, T.J., 21st VA, POW
Roop, Martin W., 21st VA, POW
Shelburne, James, 21st VA, KIA
Sullins, J.L, 21st VA, POW, DIC
Woolwine, Charles, 21st VA, POW
Mahaney, John T., 46th VA Bttn., POW

Henderson, George W., 25th VA, MWIA
Ingles, William, 25th VA, POW
Reid, Wilbur L., 25th VA, WIA
Wilhelm, Joseph H., 25th VA, WIA

Listed as Federal casualties:

Bemis, Arvin C., 1st NH, WIA
Crystal, John M., 1st NH, WIA
Eaton, Alvin S., 1st NH, WIA
Goodwin, Henry, 1st NH, WIA
Palmer, Robert M., 1st NH, POW
Steele, George H., 1st NH, WIA
Wilder, Lyman F., 1st NH, WIA
Cadmus, Abraham, 3rd NJ, WIA
Davis, John G., 3rd NJ, WIA
Montson, Thomas, 3rd NJ, WIA
Ulrich, John, 3rd NJ, WIA
Church, Edwin, 2nd NY, WIA
McDonald, William, 2nd NY, WIA
Montgomery, Francis, 2nd NY, WIA
Clooney, John J., 5th NY, WIA
Hall, Archibald, 5th NY, WIA
Howe, Ralph, 5th NY, WIA
Peterson, Mahlon J., 5th NY, WIA
Smith, George, 5th NY, WIA
Dailey, Francis, 8th NY, WIA
Ellwood, Solomon, 8th NY, WIA
Wells, Omer, 8th NY, KIA
Wimple, John J., 8th NY, WIA
Leavitt, Enoch, 2nd OH, WIA
Thompson, William, 2nd OH, WIA
Wolfer, John, 2nd OH, WIA
Zediker, Absolom, 2nd OH, WIA
Hughes, William P., 18th PA, WIA
Sayers, William, 18th PA, WIA
Allen, Smith, 18th PA, WIA
Winters, John, 18th PA, KIA
Daniels, Charles, 1st VT, WIA
Hodgdon, Carlos, 1st VT, KIA
Lyman, Wyllys, 1st VT, WIA
Ranney, Edson, 1st VT, WIA

Ray, Frank, 1st VT, KIA
Smith, Clark, 1st VT, WIA
Wright, James, 1st VT, WIA
Ball, George A., Peirce's Btty., WIA
Davis, George, Peirce's Btty., WIA
Kimbro, Robert, Peirce's Btty., WIA
Lent, August, Peirce's Btty., WIA
Meeks, David J., Peirce's Btty., WIA
Garman, Henry G., Peirce's Btty., WIA
Ayer, Osborn, 2nd MA, WIA
Conners, Cornelius, 2nd MA, WIA
Hogue, Thomas R., 2nd MA, WIA*
Lawrence, Lawson J., 2nd MA, WIA
Morris, William, 2nd MA, WIA
Tucker, Samuel F., 2nd MA, WIA
Wakefield, Elhanan W., 2nd MA, WIA
Bronner, Solomon, 1st MI, WIA*
Swarthout, Charles, 1st MI, WIA*
Dudley, Jerry, 6th MI, WIA*
Finch, Edward, 6th MI, WIA*
Moulthrop, Albert, 6th MI, POW
Bennett, Nelson, 7th MI, WIA
McGregor, Alexander, 7th MI, WIA*
Robinson, James B., 7th MI, KIA
Pomeroy, David H., 7th MI, KIA
Richards, Joseph, 6th NY, MWIA
Barrs, Joseph, 25th NY, KIA
Beischon, Joseph, 25th NY, WIA*
Burns, John T., 25th NY, WIA*
LaForge, Charles, 25th NY, WIA*
Lorentz, William, 25th NY, WIA
Seeley, Aaron, 25th NY, WIA*
Cavins, James D., 5th US, WIA
Rufrecht, Buglar L., Taylor's Btty., WIA

Documented Casualties of October 9, 1864,
by Brigade and Division

CONFEDERATE

Rosser's Command

Laurel Brigade: 34 casualties (13 POW, or 38% of the brigade's total loss)
Munford's Brigade: 96 casualties (51 POW, or 53% of the brigade's total loss)
Payne's Brigade: 30 casualties (11 POW, or 36% of the brigade's total loss)
Breathed's artillery: 35 casualties (35 POW, 100% of the battalion's total loss)
Rosser's Staff: 2 casualties (0 POW)
Total: 197 casualties (110 POW, or 55% of the division's total loss)[12]

Lomax's Command

Thompson's Brigade: 6 casualties (4 POW, or 66% of the brigade's total loss)
Johnson's Brigade: 16 casualties (7 POW, or 44% of the brigade's total loss)
Total: 22 casualties (11 POW, or 50% of the division's total loss)

FEDERAL

Merritt's Division

Devin's brigade: 1 casualty (0 POW)
Kidd's brigade: 15 casualties (1 POW)
Lowell's brigade: 8 casualties (0 POW)
Taylor's battery: 1 casualty (0 POW)
Total: 25 casualties (1 POW)

Custer's Division

Pennington's brigade: 20 casualties (0 POW)
Wells's brigade: 18 casualties (1 POW)
Peirce's battery:, 6 casualties (0 POW)
Total: 44 casualties (1 POW)

12 Custer's provost marshal reported 106 prisoners, which approximates the 110 enumerated above.

APPENDIX C

Notes on Maps and Topography

The Name of the Hill

While the battlefield of First Manassas has Henry House Hill, and Antietam has the Miller Cornfield, and Fredericksburg Marye's Heights, the best name for the dominant terrain feature on the field of Tom's Brook has proved elusive.

The "best" name would be that in common use at the time of the battle. What did residents call that high ground? None of the official reports of the engagement suggests a name for the hill, nor do period maps. Garland Hudgins, a resident of the area with significant knowledge of the battlefield, influenced research in the late 1990s. Hudgins wrote on history and hunted relics. He used the locations of the relics he found to analyze the reports and other primary documents to add to his understanding of the battle. According to Hudgins, the hill on which Rosser made his stand was known as "Spiker's Hill." Hudgins served as a consultant for the *Study of Civil War Sites in the Shenandoah Valley of Virginia* produced in 1992 by the National Park Service, which likewise referred to the eminence as "Spiker's Hill." However, another local resident, respected historian Richard B. Kleese, author of the valuable history *Shenandoah County in the Civil War*, referred to the elevation as "Coffman's Hill." Historian Jeffry D. Wert, in his biography of George Custer, labeled the high ground "Wisman's Hill." Although Hudgins's preferred name for the hill prevailed at the turn of the 21st century, recent research supports Kleese's use of "Coffman's Hill" as the best name for ground from which Custer drove Rosser.

The U.S. Censuses from 1830 through 1870, war-era maps, and local churchyards all reveal that Spikers, Wismans, and Coffmans resided in the area, including along or near the Back Road in the vicinity of Tom's Brook. The 1885 *Historical Atlas of Shenandoah and Page Counties* identifies two homes on the hill as being occupied by William L. Wisman.[1] At that time, Spikers lived south of the hill near the village of Saumsville. Wartime maps show no Spikers, Wismans, or Coffmans as residents of the hill proper. Shenandoah County deeds reveal that both the Wismans and the Spikers came to the hill after 1864, so while their names might have been attached to the hill after the war, it seems unlikely that the hill would bear their names before they had lived there.

A wealth of evidence, however, connects the hill with Coffmans. The 1830 and 1840 Censuses suggest two George Coffmans lived on or near the hill. At least four George Coffmans bought or sold land around Tom's Brook in the years before the war. The elder George Coffman owned land near Tom's Brook, and his son, Jacob, lived on the property before and after the war.[2] Obed, another son of George Coffman, owned property along the brook at the base of the hill, and sold the parcel to his sister Elizabeth and her husband, James Wright, who owned a house that stood directly between Rosser's and Custer's lines in 1864. Maps by Confederate topographers identify this structure as the "Write" house. According to the *Historical Atlas of Shenandoah and Page Counties of 1885*, Elizabeth Wright, by then a widow, still lived on the property. Elizabeth's mother Mary—George Coffman's widow—still lived on the property after the war.

Such evidence tying the Coffmans to the property supports two contemporary sources that reveal the name used by area residents to refer to the hill in 1864. Levi Pitman, a cabinet maker in Mt. Olive, just a mile from Tom's Brook, wrote in his diary that on October 8 and 9, 1864, "The rebels formed a line of battle on G. Coffman's hill."[3]

That reference alone would be strong justification for referring to the ground as Coffman's Hill, but another contemporary source independently confirms the local usage. The regimental history of the 18th Pennsylvania Cavalry includes lists of names of the men in the regiment who were killed, wounded, captured, died of disease, or otherwise lost. This roster relates that Lt. John A. Winters was "Killed at Kauffman's Hill, Va., October 9, 1864." In 1864, the absence of readily available maps and highway signs made local residents the best source of information about

1   *Historical Atlas of Shenandoah and Page Counties Virginia, Featuring Reprints from Lake's Atlas 1885 with Added Maps from Gray's Atlas 1878* (Edinburg: Shenandoah County Historical Society, 2009).

2   1850 U.S. Census NARA microfilm publication M432, roll 976, images 15, 117 and 95; 1840 U.S. Census M704, roll 578, p. 374, 352, 342; 1830 U.S. Census M19, roll 200, page 54. Shenandoah County Land Books, 1854-55, 1856-57, 1858-59, 1866-67. See Shenandoah County Deed Books beginning with DB 7, page 435.

3   Pitman diary, University of Virginia.

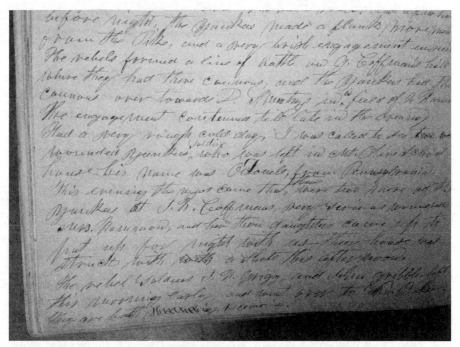

A portion of Levi Pittman's diary mentioning Coffman's Hill. *University of Virginia*

the name of hills in rural Virginia. It seems likely that some resident provided the name of the place for an inquiring Pennsylvanian wishing to know the name of the place where Lieutenant Winters died. The Pennsylvanian, whoever he was, apparently did not ask for the correct spelling.[4]

The names Spiker's Hill and Wisman's Hill may have in common usage at different points in the neighborhood's history, but solid evidence confirms that in 1864 "Coffman's Hill" prevailed as the proper noun used to refer to the high ground on the south side of Tom's Brook.

Cartographic Sources

Most of the cartographic sources used in preparing the text and maps for this book rest in the geography and map collections of the Library of Congress in Washington, DC, particularly in the Jedediah Hotchkiss Map Collection. Hotchkiss, a self-taught surveyor and cartographer, lived in the Shenandoah Valley and surveyed much of the region before and during the war. His sketchbooks contain

4 Rodenbough, *18th Regiment,* 217.

detailed drawings and notes. Hotchkiss served as topographical engineer for Gen. Thomas J. Jackson and later Gen. Jubal A. Early during their operations in the Valley. While most records relating to the Confederate government and its war effort were destroyed before the end of the war, Hotchkiss preserved scores of Confederate maps, which make up the bulk of the Hotchkiss Map Collection.

Hotchkiss's *Map of the Shenandoah Valley*, based largely on 1862 surveys, is the most famous of his maps and retains much of its usefulness.[5] This is the map produced in response to Jackson's famous directive, "I want you to make me a map of the valley." More than eight feet long and almost four feet wide, the map shows the Shenandoah Valley from Winchester to Staunton, and from the Blue Ridge to the Alleghany mountains, as well as the names of many residents. Hotchkiss marked the sites of most points of value to a military commander, including major roads, byroads, bridges, fords, elevations, and hundreds of houses and mills labeled with the name of the resident or owner. The map, drawn in ink and colored pencil on tracing linen and mounted on cloth for durability, included a ¾-inch grid that would assist draftsmen making copies, enlargements, or reductions for special use. The *Map of the Valley* served as a seminal source for Confederate mapmakers. Its influence is especially strong in the 1865 *Map of the Vicinity of Strasburg and Fisher's Hill* by P.W. Oscar Koerner for the Confederate Engineers Office.[6]

James Innes Randolph put his considerable talents to work for the Confederate engineers during the war and as a poet afterward. His 1864 *Map of Vicinity of Fisher's Hill* is both handsome and useful.[7] *Sketches of Roads in the Shenandoah Valley Between Winchester and Woodstock, Virginia* by an anonymous surveyor consists of field sketches made in 1863 and is invaluable for its annotations on the nature of structures or roads. For example, the surveyor judged the Back Road on Coffman's Hill a "very steep bad road."[8] Another anonymous map, *Five Sketches Along the Valley Pike in the Vicinity of Fishers Hill, Strasburg, Cottontown, Mount Hope, Toms Brook, etc.* conveys detailed information about the roads, residences, and especially the terrain and wood lines in the vicinity of Tom's Brook.[9]

Two other charts—*Map of Shenandoah Valley from Winchester to New Market, Virginia and from Millwood to Waverly P.O., including parts of Frederick, Clarke, Warren, Shenandoah, and Page counties, Virginia*[10] and *Map of the Shenandoah*

5 Library of Congress Digital Id: g3882s.cwh00089. The map bears no formal title.

6 Library of Congress Digital Id: g3884s cwh00189.

7 Library of Congress Digital Id g3882f cwh00187.

8 Library of Congress Digital Id g3882s cwh00151.

9 Library of Congress Digital Id g3882f cwh00188.

10 Library of Congress Digital Id g3882s cwh00147.

Valley from Mt. Jackson to Midway, Including Parts of Shenandoah, Page, Rockingham, and Augusta Counties, Virginia—offer valuable information.[11] Although neither map can be positively identified as having been created by Hotchkiss, they were produced under Hotchkiss's direction in the topographical office of General Early's Second Corps. The latter map, showing Mt. Jackson to Midway, holds special interest because Hotchkiss supplied copies to Confederate cavalry commanders during the 1864 Valley Campaign.

Hotchkiss's 1875 *Map of Shenandoah and Page Counties and Part of Warren County, Virginia* is a handsome and polished work that incorporates much of the information shown on the wartime maps of the areas around Tom's Brook.[12] Hotchkiss created a series of maps of Virginia counties after the war and this one, published in conjunction with the U.S. Army Office of the Chief Engineer, is a fine representative of that series.

An eighth source, Hotchkiss's *Sketch Book showing Positions of Second Corps, A. N. Va. in Engagements of 1864-5* is a hardbound book used by Hotchkiss in the field and during interviews with officers about the roles of their troops in various engagements in the final year of the war. Page after page of sketches and commentary by Hotchkiss on the activities of General Early's Second Corps in eastern Virginia and in the Shenandoah Valley make this an invaluable source for researchers.[13]

The Names of Roads

The modern Back Road, sometimes referred to in the nineteenth century as "the North Mountain Road" still largely follows the nineteenth century route. The modern Valley Turnpike likewise generally follows the historic route, but because it has served continuously as a major traffic route, the pike's course has been altered in many places to adapt to the needs of a growing population. Most changes in the course of the Pike have been small, as is the case with the alteration between Maurertown and Tom's Brook. In the 1930s, the Virginia Department of Transportation constructed a new road bed for the Pike just a few yards to the east of the original Pike. The original section is still in use as of this writing and is referred to as "Toll House Road." This alteration is of significance for our understanding of the engagement between Lomax and Merritt on the morning of October 9, 1864, for the Pike served as a principal topographical feature and the central axis of the fighting.

11 Library of Congress Digital Id g3882s cwh00145.

12 Library of Congress Digital Id g3883s la001345.

13 Library of Congress Digital Id g3881sm gcwh0002.

While modern roads closely follow the nineteenth-century routes of the Back Road and the Valley Turnpike, the third main path used by the armies in October 1864 is not so easily traced. The term "the Middle Road" is deceptive because it does refer not to one road but to a few different roads. No single continuous "Middle Road" ran from the North River in Rockingham County to Tumbling Run 70 miles to the north. A few local byways combined to compose a route that runs generally parallel to both the Valley Pike and the Back Road, but this "middle route" could not in the nineteenth century, and cannot today, be followed over a single road. So a soldier's account that refers to "the middle road" in the vicinity of Harrisonburg and another account that refers to "the middle road" near Woodstock, do not refer to a single road but to different roads that both occupy a "middle" position between the Back Road and the pike.

The varying references to "middle roads" can cause confusion when interpreting primary documents. For example, some maps and accounts seem to refer to the road that connected Woodstock and Mt. Olive, as "the middle road"— modern Swartz Road (Rte. 642)—and other accounts use "the middle road" to refer to the road ¾ of a mile to the east of Swartz Road— modern Country Brook Road (also numbered Rte. 642). Such inconsistencies impair the interpretation of primary sources, with Jed Hotchkiss's *Sketch Book Showing Positions of Second Corps, A.N.Va. in Engagements of 1864-5* being a notable example of ambiguous information.

The Two Ridges: Lomax's Positions on the Valley Pike, October 9, 1864

In the absence of abundant primary sources, Lomax's position or positions during the engagement on the morning of October 9 must remain speculative. As is the case with all but a few engagements in human history, the men who fought at Tom's Brook did not return after the war and erect monuments and markers, and no historian undertook a comprehensive effort to gather firsthand testimony.

In 1927, The Commonwealth of Virginia erected a marker near the village of Tom's Brook. Whether the marker stands where originally placed in 1927 is not known, but the marker now stands on a ridge between Tom's Brook and Jordan's Run. The text reads: "Action of Tom's Brook. Here Early's cavalry under Rosser and Lomax was driven back by Sheridan's cavalry under Torbert, October 9, 1864."

The 1990s saw the placement of a second marker, this one erected about 700 yards southwest of the 1927 marker. The second marker stands on the ridge immediately south of Jordan's Run in a county park and not far from where the county Alms House stood in 1864. This marker purports to mark the position of Lomax's troops during the engagement of October 9, 1864, but if any evidence exists to support that claim, it has not been discovered or made public.

Given the nature of cavalry battles, which typically sprawled over large areas, it is reasonable to speculate that fighting likely occurred on both of these ridges. Each ridge would have offered Lomax advantages as a defensive position, with the northernmost (Toll House Ridge) offering the best position for artillery.

The 1885 *Historical Atlas of Shenandoah and Page Counties* shows a toll house standing west of the Valley Pike just north of Jordan's Run. Though no known evidence confirms that a toll house stood on that same spot in 1864, Confederate maps and sketches (Hotchkiss's and Randolph's) show an isolated and unlabeled structure standing in precisely the same place as the labeled tollbooth on the 1885 atlas map. A structure similar in design to known Toll Houses at other points along the Valley Pike, still stands in the position indicated by the atlas and the Confederate maps.

Two Churches on the Battlefield

St. Matthew's Evangelical Lutheran Church is today a prominent structure on the battlefield. The congregation erected the church building after the war in 1875, and war-era maps show no structures on the hill now occupied by St. Matthew's. In 1864, many of those who would eventually found St. Matthew's attended a "Union Church," which stood on the Back Road north and west of the current site of St. Matthew's. Union churches were structures shared by two or more congregations, usually of different denominations. Congregations of German descent often referred to such buildings as "frieden" churches, "frieden" being the German word for "peace." Friedens Church, as it was called, was built about 1824 to serve Lutheran and German Reformed congregations. Period maps place it on the Back Road north of the hill on which St. Matthew's stands and thus it would have been within Custer's lines during the fight on October 9, 1864. A marker commemorating Friedens Church stands on the west side of the Back Road about three-quarters of a mile from the crossing of Tom's Brook.[14]

Rosser's Advance Toward Tumbling Run

On the afternoon of October 8, 1864, Rosser led elements of Payne's and Munford's brigades beyond Tom's Brook to some point north of Mt. Olive. Precisely where Rosser stopped his advance toward Winchester and received word from a local man that Federals were in his rear, is not known, but sources suggest that Rosser reversed course near Tumbling Run. The Back Road crosses Tumbling Run proper near St. Stephens Church, some four and a half miles north of Tom's

---

14 Wayland, *History of Shenandoah County, Virginia*, 418-19.

Brook. However, the Back Road crosses the South Fork of Tumbling Run only two miles north of the ford on Tom's Brook. The Back Road also crosses a small stream between the South Fork and Tumbling Run proper in the vicinity of the Barb House (on modern Route 601). Soldiers writing about military activity in this area, whether during the Tom's Brook operations or the Fisher's Hill operations a few weeks earlier, favored brevity and referred to this apparently unnamed rivulet as "Tumbling Run." More regrettably, mapmakers sometimes adopted the same careless habit. What is gained in brevity is lost in clarity, however, and after later writers adopted the imprecision, the result has been confusion. This unnamed tributary, which runs behind the Barb house, is a fork of the South Fork of Tumbling Run. To judge by its renderings on war-era maps, this little branch was more robust in the 1860s than it is in the early 21st century. For an excellent example of the imprecision in distinguishing among these three watercourses, see the field maps (referenced above) labeled *Sketches of Roads in the Shenandoah Valley Between Winchester and Woodstock, Virginia*, in which all three of the streams that cross the Back Road are labeled "Tumbling Run."

Bibliography

Archival Materials

Chicago History Museum, Chicago, IL
   Goggin, E. B. Letter to Gen. Lomax, "Last Days of the Confederacy," 1867.

Cincinnati Historical Society Library, Cincinnati Museum Center, Cincinnati, OH
   Hannaford, Roger, Memoir, Civil War Papers.

Rubenstein Library, Duke University, Durham, NC
   Munford-Ellis Family Papers, 1777-1942, Thomas T. Munford Division.

Handley Regional Library Archives, Winchester, VA
   McVicar, Charles William, Diary.

Library of Congress Manuscript Division, Washington, DC
   Hotchkiss, Jedediah, Papers.

Library of Congress Geography and Map Division, Washington, DC
   Campbell, Albert H. and P. W. Oscar Koerner. *Map of the Vicinity of Strasburg and Fisher's Hill. 1865.*
   Hotchkiss, Jedediah. *Map of Shenandoah & Page counties and part of Warren County, Virginia.*
   ——. *[Map of the Shenandoah Valley].*
   ——. *Sketch Book Showing Positions of Second Corps, A.N.Va. in Engagements of 1864-5.*

[*Map of the Shenandoah Valley from Mt. Jackson to Midway, including parts of Shenandoah, Page, Rockingham, and Augusta counties, Virginia*].

Randolph, J. Innes. *Map of Vicinity of Fisher's Hill.*

[*Sketches of Roads in the Shenandoah Valley Between Winchester and Woodstock, Virginia*].

Meigs, John R. *Map of the Shenandoah & Upper Potomac Including Portions of Virginia and Maryland. 1864.*

Library of Virginia, Richmond, VA

Borden Family Papers, 1845-1999.
Dulany Family Papers, 1821-1906.
Early, Jubal Anderson, Letter, 24 April 1884.
French, Samuel Bassett Papers.
Imboden, George W., Letter, 12 October 1864.
McVicar, Charles William, Diary 1862-1865.
Neese, George M., Papers.
Payne, William H. F., Papers.
Tynes, Achilles James, Letters, 1864-1951.

Museum of the Confederacy, Richmond, VA

Steele, Milton B., Diary.

National Archives and Records Administration (NARA), Washington, D.C

Compiled Service Records of Confederate Generals and Staff Officers, and Nonregimental Enlisted Men. War Department Collection of Confederate Records (Record Group 109). NARA Microfilm Publications M331A and M331B.

Inspection Reports and Related Records Received by the Inspection Branch in the Confederate Adjutant and Inspector General's Office, 9/3-J-39, and 8-J-39. War Department Collection of Confederate Records (Record Group 109). NARA Microfilm Publication M935.

Field Records of Hospitals, 1821-1912. Entry 544, New York, U.S. Military Academy. Records of the Adjutant General's Office, 1762–1984 (Record Group 94).

Records relating to the U.S. Military Academy, Monthly Class Reports and Conduct Rolls, 1831-1866. Records of the Adjutant General's Office, 1762-1984 (Record Group 94).

Engineer Department Records Relating to the US Military Academy, 1812-1867. Records of the Adjutant General's Office, 1762-1984 (Record Group 94). NARA Microfilm Publication M91.

Index to the Letters Received by the Confederate Adjutant and Inspector General and by the Confederate Quartermaster General, 1861-1865. War Department Collection of Confederate Records (Record Group 109). NARA Microfilm Publication M410.

Letters Received by the Confederate Adjutant and Inspector General, 1861-1865. War Department Collection of Confederate Records (Record Group 109). NARA Microfilm Publication M474.

Letters and Telegrams Sent by the Confederate Adjutant and Inspector General, 1861-1865. War Department Collection of Confederate Records (Record Group 109). NARA Microfilm Publication M627.

Bentley Library, University of Michigan, Ann Arbor, MI

Barbour, George W., Diary, 1863-1865.
Kidd, James, Letters, September 9, 1864, and October 15, 1864.

Archives and Historical Collections, Michigan State University, East Lansing, MI

Havens, Edwin, Letters.

Southern Historical Collection, University of North Carolina, Chapel Hill, NC

McDonald, Edward H., Papers.

Special Collections Library, University of Notre Dame, South Bend IN

Moore, Alfred, Diary.

Small Special Collections Library, University of Virginia, Charlottesville, VA

Brand, William Francis, Civil War Letters, 1856-1959.
Daniel, John W. and the Daniel Family, Papers.
Early, Jubal A., "Soldiers of the Army of the Valley." Broadside. n.p. 1864.
Hubard, Robert Thruston, Papers, 1860-1866.
Pitman, Levi, Papers, 1831-1892.
Pratt, George Julian, Civil War Letters.
Rosser, Thomas Lafayette, Papers.
Rosser, General Thomas L. and Rosser Family, Papers, 1774-1983.
Rosser, Thomas L. and the Rosser, Gordon and Winston Families Papers.
Stuart, Alexander Hugh Holmes, Papers.
Whittle, Beverley, Papers, 1863-79.

U.S. Army History and Education Center (USAHEC), Carlisle, PA

Farr, Charles R., Diary.
Peters, Lewis Leigh, Collection.
Second Virginia Cavalry Morning Reports.

Virginia Historical Society, Richmond, VA

Ball, William Selwyn, Reminiscences.

Ellis, James Tucker, Papers.

Hunton Family, Papers.

McClellan, H. B., Papers, 1862-1866.

Gilmer, Jeremy Francis, Map Collection. LOC, [Map of the lower Shenandoah Valley of Virginia].Digital Id gvhs01 vhs00381

Meade Family, Papers, 1837-1981.

Stuart, Jeb, Letterbook, 1862 October 24-1864 May 2.

Stuart, Jeb, Papers, 1851-1968.

Wellford, Beverley Randolph, Papers, 1773-1907.

Virginia Military Institute, Lexington, VA

Black, William J., Civil War Diary, Shoemaker's Artillery Battery Manuscript #1.

Langhorne, J. Kent, Civil War Papers, Manuscript #00361.

Private Collections

Brown, John J., Memoir, 8th New York Cavalry, Marshall Krolik.

Brent, William A., Memoir, 7th Virginia Cavalry, Fredericksburg, VA.

Books and Articles

A Missionary in the East. "Gaudium Certaminis." *The Christian Church: A Journal in Defense of Christian Truth*, vol. 3. London: S. W. Partridge and Co., 1883. 161-64.

Ackinclose, Timothy R. *Sabres & Pistols: The Civil War Career of Colonel Harry Gilmor, C.S.A.* Gettysburg: Stan Clark Books, 1997.

Adeleye, Gabriel and Kofi Acquah-Dadzie. *World Dictionary of Foreign Expressions: A Resource for Readers and Writers*. Mundelein, IL: Bolchazy-Carducci Publishers, 1999.

Agassiz, George R. *Meade's Headquarters, 1863-1865. Letters of Colonel Theodore Lyman from the Wilderness to Appomattox*. Boston: Atlantic Monthly Press, 1922.

Akers, Anne Trice Thompson. *Colonel Thomas T. Munford and the Last Cavalry Operations of the Civil War in Virginia*. Master's Thesis, Virginia Polytechnic Institute and State University, 1981.

Alvord, Henry E. "A New England Boy in the Civil War." Edited by Caroline B. Sherman. *The New England Quarterly*, vol. 5, no. 2 (April 1932), 310-344.

American Civil War Research Database, Duxbury, MA: Historical Data Systems, Inc. http://www.civilwardata.com/index.html.

Angelovich, Robert B. *Riding for Uncle Samuel*. Grand Rapids, MI: InnerWorkings, Inc. 2014.

Arnold, Thomas J. "A Battle Fought in the Streets (Rosser's Beverly Raid of 1865)." Historic Beverly Preservation, Inc. Accessed September 29, 2014. http://www.historic beverly.org/rossraid.htm.

Association of Graduates, USMA. *Register of Graduates and Former Cadets of the United States Military Academy*. West Point, NY: Association of Graduates, 1990.

Avery, James Henry. *Under Custer's Command: The Civil War Journal of James Henry Avery*. Compiled by Karla Jean Husby, Edited by Eric J. Wittenberg. Washington, D.C.: Brassey's, 2000.

Baylor, George. *Bull Run to Bull Run: Four Years in the Army of Northern Virginia*, 1900. Reprint, Washington, DC: Zenger, 1983.

Beane, Thomas O., "Thomas Lafayette Rosser." *The Magazine of Albemarle County History*. XVI (1957-1958): 25-46.

Beaudry, Louis N. *War Journal of Louis N. Beaudry, Fifth New York Cavalry*. Edited by Richard E. Beaudry. Jefferson, NC: McFarland & Co., Inc., 1996.

Bliss, George N. *Cavalry Service with General Sheridan and Life in Libby Prison*. Providence, RI: Soldiers and Sailors Historical Society, 1884.

Booth, George Wilson. *Personal Reminiscences of a Maryland Soldier in the War Between the States, 1861-1865*. Privately printed, 1898. Reprint, Baltimore, MD: Butternut Press, 1986.

Borden, Duane Lyle. *Tombstone Inscriptions, Tom's Brook and Vicinity, Shenandoah County, Virginia*. Ozark, MO: Yates Publishing Company, 1981.

Bridges, David P. *Fighting with Jeb Stuart: Major James Breathed and the Confederate Horse Artillery*. Alexandria, VA: Breathed-Bridges-Best LLC, 2006.

Bushong, Millard Kessler, and Dean McKoin Bushong. *Fightin' Tom Rosser, C.S.A.* Shippensburg, PA: Beidel Printing House, 1983.

Carter, Thomas H. *Gunner in Lee's Army: The Civil War Letters of Thomas Henry Carter*. Edited by Graham T. Dozier. Chapel Hill: University of North Carolina Press, 2014.

Calkins, Chris M. *The Battles of Appomattox and Appomattox Court House, April 8-9, 1865*. Lynchburg, VA: H. E. Howard, 1987.

Collea, Joseph D. *The First Vermont Cavalry in the Civil War: A History*. Jefferson, NC: McFarland & Co., 2010.

Cooke, Philip St. George. *Cavalry Tactics or Regulations for the Instruction, Formations, and Movements of the Cavalry of the Army and Volunteers of the United States*. vol. 2. Washington, DC: Government Printing Office, 1861.

Cooney, Mark. "Honor Cultures and Violence." In *Oxford Bibliographies*. Accessed January 8, 2015. doi: 10.1093/obo/9780195396607-0160.

Cootes, Carolyn, "Samuel Cootes of Rockingham, Co., VA." RootsWeb, COUTS-L Archives, 2 June, 2002. Accessed December 19, 2014. http://archiver.rootsweb.ancestry. com/th/read/COUTS/2002-06/1023038391.

Corson, William C. *My Dear Jennie: A Collection of Love Letters from a Confederate Soldier to his Fiancée During the Period 1861-1865*. Richmond, VA: Dietz Press, 1982.

Cullum, George W. *Biographical Register of the Officers and Graduates of the U.S. Military Academy at West Point, N.Y., from its Establishment, in 1802, to 1890.* 3 vols. Boston: Houghton, Mifflin and Co., 1891.

Cummings, W. G. "Six Months in the Third Cavalry Division Under Custer." *War Sketches and Incidents as Related by Companions of the Iowa Commandery Military Order of the Loyal Legion of the United States*, vol. 1. Des Moines, IA: P. C. Kenyon, 1893.

Custer, Elizabeth Bacon. *Boots and Saddles; or, Life in Dakota with General Custer.* New York: Harper & Brothers, 1885.

——, Elizabeth Bacon and Marguerite Merington. *The Custer Story: The Life and Intimate Letters of General George A. Custer and his Wife Elizabeth.* New York: Devin-Adair, 1950.

——, Elizabeth Bacon. *The Civil War Memories of Elizabeth Bacon Custer.* Edited by Arlene Reynolds. Austin: University of Texas Press, 1994.

Custer, George A. "War Memoirs." *The Galaxy*, vol. 21, no. 4 (April 1876), 448-460.

Danby, John. "Torbert in the Valley." In King, W. C. and W. P. Darcy, *Camp-fire Sketches and Battle-field Echoes of the Rebellion*, 361-68. Springfield, MA: W. C. King & Co., 1887.

Davis, William C., ed. *The Confederate General*, 6 vols. National Historical Society, 1991.

Dawson, John Harper. *Wildcat Cavalry.* Dayton, OH: Morningside House, Inc., 1982.

Denison, Frederic. *Sabres and Spurs: The First Regiment Rhode Island Cavalry in the Civil War, 1861-1865.* Regimental Association, 1876.

Douglas, Henry Kyd. *I Rode with Stonewall.* Chapel Hill: University of North Carolina Press, 1940.

Downs, Janet B. and Earl J. Downs. *Mills of Rockingham County.* vol. 4. Dayton, VA: Harrisonburg-Rockingham Historical Society, 2003.

Drury, Albert. *The Better Part of Valor: Albert Drury and His 1st Vermont Cavalry in the Civil War's Eastern Campaign.* Privately printed, 1995.

Early, Jubal A. *A Memoir of the Last Year of the War for Independence.* Lynchburg, VA: Charles W. Button, 1867.

——. "Winchester, Fisher's Hill, and Cedar Creek." In *Battles and Leaders of the Civil War*, 4:522-530. New York: The Century Co., 1887-88.

——. *Lieutenant General Jubal Anderson Early, C.S.A.: Autobiographical Sketch and Narrative of the War Between the States.* Philadelphia: J. B. Lippincott Co., 1912.

Emerson, Edward W. *Life and Letters of Charles Russell Lowell.* Port Washington, NY: Kennikat Press, 1971.

Flinn, Frank M. *Campaigning With Banks in Louisiana, '63 and '64, and With Sheridan in the Shenandoah Valley in '64 and '65.* Boston: W. B. Clarke & Co., 1889.

Foraker, Joseph Benson. *Notes of a Busy Life*, 2 vols. Cincinnati, OH: Stewart & Kidd, 1916.

Foster, Alonzo. *Reminiscences and Record of the 6th New York V. V. Cavalry.* Brooklyn, NY: n.p., 1892.

Fuller, Lena French. *Original Land Survey Atlas of Shenandoah County, VA 1739-1850s.* Edinburg, VA: n.p., 2010.

Gallagher, Gary W. *Jubal A. Early, The Lost Cause, and Civil War History: A Persistent Legacy.* Milwaukee, WI: Marquette University Press, 1995.

———, ed. *The Shenandoah Valley Campaign of 1864.* Chapel Hill: University of North Carolina Press, 2006.

Gallaher, Dewitt Clinton. *A Diary Depicting the Experiences of DeWitt Clinton Gallaher in the War Between the States while Serving in the Confederate Army.* Edited by DeWitt C. Gallaher, Jr. n.p., 1961.

"General Wesley Merritt." *Journal of the Illinois State Historical Society*, vol. 3, no. 4 (1911). 130-33.

Gilmor, Harry. *Four Years in the Saddle.* New York, Harper & Brothers, 1866. Reprint, Baltimore: Butternut and Blue, 1986.

Giunta, Mary A., ed. *A Civil War Soldier of Christ and Country.* Urbana, IL: University of Illinois Press, 2006.

Grant, Ulysses S. *Personal Memoirs of U. S. Grant.* 2 vols. New York: Charles L. Webster, 1885-86.

Grimes, Bryan, and Pulaski Cowper. *Extracts of Letters of Major-General Bryan Grimes, to his Wife: Written While in Active Service in the Army of Northern Virginia, Together with Some Personal Recollections of the War.* Edited by Gary W. Gallagher. Wilmington, N.C.: Broadfoot Publishing Co., 1986.

Guerrant, Edward O. *Bluegrass Confederate: The Headquarters Diary of Edward O. Guerrant.* Edited by William C. Davis and Meredith L. Swentor. Baton Rouge: Louisiana State University Press, 1999.

Gwathmey, John Hastings. *Legends of Virginia Courthouses.* Richmond, VA: Dietz Printing Company, 1933.

Haden, B. J. "Reminiscences of J. E. B. Stuart's Cavalry." Edited by Timothy Parrish. Palmyra, VA: Fluvanna County Historical Society, 1993.

Hall, Hillman. *History of the Sixth New York Cavalry (Second Ira Harris Guard), Second Brigade, First Division, Cavalry Corps, Army of the Potomac, 1861-1865.* Worcester, MA: The Blanchard Press, 1908.

Harding, Joseph French. *French Harding: Civil War Memoirs.* Elkins, WV: McClain Publishing, 2000.

Harris, Moses. "With the Reserve Brigade." *Journal of the United States Cavalry Association.* 3 (1890): 9-20; 235-247; 363-370.

———. "The Union Cavalry." *Journal of the United Stated Cavalry Association* 5 (1892).

Heatwole, John L. *The Burning: Sheridan's Devastation of the Shenandoah Valley.* Charlottesville, Va.: Rockbridge Publishing, 1998.

Helm, Lewis Marshall. *Black Horse Cavalry.* Falls Church, Va.: Higher Education Publications, 2004.

Henry, Guy Vernor. *Military Record of Civilian Appointments in the United States Army.* New York: Carleton Publisher, 1869.

Hewett, Janet B, Noah Andre Trudeau, Bryce A. Suderow, eds. *Supplement to the Official Records of the Union and Confederate Armies.* Part I, vol. 7, Serial No. 7. Wilmington, NC: Broadfoot Publishing Company, 1997.

Hinrichs, Oscar. *Stonewall's Prussian Mapmaker: The Journals of Captain Oscar Hinrichs.* Edited by Richard Brady Williams. Chapel Hill, University of North Carolina Press, 2014.

Hoge, John Milton. *A Journal by John Milton Hoge, 1862-5.* Cincinnati, OH: M. H. Bruce, 1961.

Holbrook, Thomas. "Men of Action: The Unsung Heroes of East Cavalry Field." *Gettysburg Seminar Papers: Unsung Heroes of Gettysburg.* Accessed May 2, 2015. http://npshistory.com/series/symposia/gettysburg_seminars/5/essay5.htm.

Hotchkiss, Jedediah. *Confederate Military History*, vol. 3, *Virginia.* Edited by Clement Evans. Atlanta: Confederate Publishing Company, 1899.

——. *Make Me a Map of the Valley: The Civil War Journal of Stonewall Jackson's Topographer.* Edited by Archie P. McDonald. Dallas, TX: Southern Methodist University Press, 1973.

Huddle, B. Paul. *A Self Guided Tour of Hottel-Keller Historical Sites in Shenandoah County.* Shenandoah Germanic Heritage Museum. Hottel-Keller Memorial, Inc. Accessed April 23, 2015. http://www.hottelkeller.org/tour.php.

Hubard, Robert Thruston. *The Civil War Memoirs of a Virginia Cavalryman.* Edited by Thomas P. Nanzig. Tuscaloosa: University of Alabama Press, 2007.

Humphreys, Charles A. *Field, Camp, Hospital and Prison in the Civil War, 1863-1865.* Boston: Geo. H. Ellis Co., 1918. Reprint, Freeport, NY: Books for Libraries, 1971.

Hunter, Alexander. *Johnny Reb and Billy Yank.* New York: The Neale Publishing Co, 1905.

Johnson, E. M. *A Cavalryman Under Custer '64-'65, Reminiscences of the Civil War.* Edited by Janet Carson. n.p., 2005.

Kennedy, Joseph C. G. *Agriculture of the United States in 1860; Compiled from the Original Returns of the Eighth Census.* Washington, DC: Government Printing Office, 1864.

Kidd, James H. *Personal Recollections of a Cavalryman.* Ionia, MI: Sentinel Printing Co., 1908.

Kinsley, D. A. *Favor the Bold*, 2 vols. New York: Promontory Press, 1957.

Kleese, Richard B. *Shenandoah County in the Civil War.* Lynchburg, VA: H. E. Howard, 1992.

Krick, Robert E. L. *Staff Officers in Gray: a Biographical Register of the Staff Officers in the Army of Northern Virginia.* Chapel Hill: University of North Carolina Press, 2003.

Krick, Robert K. *Lee's Colonels: A Biographical Register of the Field Officers of the Army of Northern Virginia.* Dayton, OH: Press of Morningside Bookshop, 1979.

——. "The Coward Who Rode With J. E. B. Stuart." In *The Smoothbore Volley that Doomed the Confederacy: The Death of Stonewall Jackson and Other Chapters on the Army of Northern Virginia*, 172-184. Baton Rouge: Louisiana State University Press, 2002.

——. "'The Cause of all My Disasters': Jubal A. Early and the Undisciplined Valley Cavalry." In *The Smoothbore Volley that Doomed the Confederacy: The Death of Stonewall Jackson and Other Chapters on the Army of Northern Virginia*, 184-213. Baton Rouge: Louisiana State University Press, 2002.

Kauffman, Charles Fahs. *A Genealogy and History of the Kauffman-Coffman families of North America, 1584 to 1937*. York, PA: published by the author, 1940.

Lambert, Dobbie E. *25th Virginia Cavalry*. Lynchburg, VA: H. E. Howard, 1994.

Lathrop, J. M. *Historic Atlas of Shenandoah and Page Counties, Virginia: Featuring Reprints from Lake's Atlas–1885, with Added Maps from Gray's Atlas–1878*. Edinburg, VA: Shenandoah County Historical Society, 2009.

Leslie, Frank. *The Soldier in our Civil War: A Pictorial History of the Conflict, 1861-1865*. New York, Atlanta: Stanley Bradley Publishing Co., 1893.

Library of Congress. *Chronicling America: Historic American Newspapers. U. S. Newspaper Directory, 1690-Present*. Accessed November 1, 2014. http://chronicling america.loc.gov/.

Mahr, Theodore C. *The Battle of Cedar Creek: Showdown in the Shenandoah, October 1-30, 1864*. Lynchburg, VA: H. E. Howard, 1992.

Malone, Dumas, ed. *Dictionary of American Biography*. 20 vols. New York: Charles Scribner's Sons. 1928-1936.

Mathes, J. Harvey. *The Old Guard in Gray*. Memphis: TN: Toof & Co., 1897.

McAulay, John D. *Carbines of the U. S. Cavalry*. Lincoln, RI: Andrew Mowbray, 1996.

McCrae, Tully. *Dear Belle: Letters From a Cadet & Officer to his Sweetheart, 1858-1865*. Edited by Catherine Crary. Middletown, CT: Wesleyan University Press, 1965.

McDonald, Edward H. and William N. McDonald. "Editorial." *Southern Bivouac*, vol. 11, no. 11 (July 1884), 525-26.

McDonald, Edward H. "Generals Early and Rosser at Cedar Creek." *Southern Bivouac*, vol. 11, no. 12 (August 1884), 534-36.

McDonald, William N. and Bushrod C. Washington. *A History of the Laurel Brigade, Originally the Ashby Cavalry of the Army of Northern Virginia and Chew's Battery*. Baltimore: Sun Job Printing Office, 1907.

McGuire, Hunter H. "Gun-shot Wounds of Joints." *Richmond Medical Journal*. February 1866, 147-150.

Melton, Herman E. "Pittsylvania's Missing Confederate Cannons." Mitchell's Publications, 2004. Accessed September 29, 2014. http://www.victorianvilla.com/sims-mitchell/local/articles/phsp/021/.

Merritt, Wesley. "Sheridan in the Shenandoah Valley." In *Battles and Leaders of the Civil War*, 4:500-521. New York: The Century Co., 1887-88.

Michie, Peter S. "Reminiscences of Cadet and Army Service." In *Personal Recollections of the War of the Rebellion, Addresses Delivered Before the Commandery of the State of New York, Military Order of the Loyal Legion of the United States*, second series, 183-197. Edited by A. Noel Blakeman. New York: G. P. Putnam's Sons, 1897.

Miller, Edward A., Jr. *Lincoln's Abolitionist General*. Columbia: University of South Carolina Press, 1997.

Miller, Francis, T. *The Photographic History of the Civil War*. 10 vols. New York: The Review of Reviews Co., 1911.

Miller, William J. "Demons That Day." *Civil War Magazine*. Issue 59 (December 1996), 46-55.

——. "Never Has There Been a More Complete Victory: The Cavalry Engagement at Tom's Brook, October 9, 1864." In *The Shenandoah Valley Campaign of 1864*, 134-160. Edited by Gary W. Gallagher. Chapel Hill: University of North Carolina Press, 2006.

Monaghan, Jay. *Custer: The Life of General George Armstrong Custer*. Boston: Little Brown, 1959.

Morris, Jr., Roy. *Sheridan: The Life and Wars of General Phil Sheridan*. New York: Crown Publishers, Inc., 1992.

Morrison, James L. *"The Best School in the World," West Point, the Pre-Civil War Years, 1833-1866*. Kent, OH: The Kent State University Press, 1986.

Mosby, John S. *Take Sides with the Truth*. Edited by Peter A. Brown. Lexington: University of Kentucky Press, 2007.

Munford, Thomas T. "Reminiscences of Cavalry Operations, Paper No. 1." *Southern Historical Society Papers*, 12 (1884):342-350.

——. "Reminiscences of Cavalry Operations, Paper No. 2." *Southern Historical Society Papers*, 12 (1884):447-459.

——. "Reminiscences of Cavalry Operations, Paper No. 3." *Southern Historical Society Papers*, 13 (1885):133-144.

Myers, Frank M. *The Comanches: A History of White's Battalion, Virginia Cavalry*. Baltimore: Kelly, Piet & Co., Publishers, 1871. Reprint, Marietta, Ga.: Continental Book Co., 1956.

——. *The Comanches: A History of White's Battalion, Virginia Cavalry*, Introduction by Lee A. Wallace. Alexandria, VA: Stonewall House, 1985.

National Park Service. "Tom's Brook." *Study of Civil War Sites in the Shenandoah Valley of Virginia*. Washington, DC: U.S. Department of the Interior, 1992. Accessed September 24, 2012. http://www.nps.gov/abpp/shenandoah/svs3-14.html.

Neese, George M. Three Years in the Confederate Horse Artillery. New York: The Neale Publishing Co., 1911.

Nettleton, A. B. "How the Day Was Saved at the Battle of Cedar Creek." In *Glimpses of the Nation's Struggle: A Series of Papers Read Before the Minnesota Commandery of the Military Order of the Loyal Legion of the United States*, vol. 1. St. Paul: St. Paul Book and Stationery Co., 1887.

New Horizons Genealogy. My Free Census Records, Virginia Census Records. Accessed September 2, 2014. http://www.myfreecensus.com/virginia-census-records.htm.

Newcomer, Elsie Renalds and Janet Renalds Ramsey. *1864 Life in the Shenandoah Valley*. Mechanicsville, VA: Battlefield Press, 2014.

Nolan, L. E. *Cavalry: Its History and Tactics*. Columbia, SC: Evans and Cogswell, 1864.

Northern Illinois University Libraries. "Whittaker, Frederick." The Beadle and Adams Dime Novel Digitization Project. Accessed August 5, 2013. http://www.ulib.niu.edu/badndp/whittaker_frederick.html.

Norton, Henry. *Deeds of Daring, or History of the Eighth New York Volunteer Cavalry*. Norwich, NY: Chenango Telegraph Printing House, 1889.

Paine, Sarah Cushing. *Paine Ancestry. The Family of Robert Treat Paine, Signer of the Declaration of Independence, Including Maternal Lines*. Boston: privately printed, 1912.

Painter, Fred P. *A Brief History of the Alms House of Shenandoah County*. Stephens City: Commercial Press, 1979.

Patchan, Scott C. *The Last Battle of Winchester*. El Dorado Hills, CA: Savas Beatie, 2013.

Pate, Henry Clay. *Proceedings of the General Court Martial, in the Case of Lieut. Col. H. Clay Pate, 5th Va. Cavalry*. [Richmond [?] 1863].

Perkins, George. *Three Years a Soldier: The Diary and Newspaper Correspondence of Private George Perkins, Sixth New York Independent Battery, 1861-1864*. Edited by Richard N. Griffin. Knoxville: University of Tennessee Press, 2006.

Phillips, John W. "The Civil War Diary of John Wilson Phillips." Edited by Robert G. Athearn. *The Virginia Magazine of History and Biography*, 62 (1954): 94-123.

Pickerill, William N. *History of the Third Indiana Cavalry*. Indianapolis, IN: Aetna Printing Co., 1906.

Pond, George E. *The Shenandoah Valley in 1864*. New York: Charles Scribner's Sons, 1883.

Rhea, Gordon C. "Union Cavalry in the Wilderness." In *The Wilderness Campaign*, 106-135. Edited by Gary W. Gallagher. Chapel Hill: University of North Carolina Press, 1997.

Rodenbough, Theophilus F. "Cavalry War Lessons." *Journal of the United States Cavalry Association*, 2 (1889): 103-123.

——. *History of the Eighteenth Regiment of Cavalry, Pennsylvania Volunteers (163d Regiment of the Line) 1862-1865*. New York: Wynkoop, Hallenbeck, Crawford Co., 1909.

Rosser, Elizabeth Winston. Scrapbook 1861-1865. Unpublished, Albert and Shirley Small Special Collections Library, University of Virginia, Accession #1171-a, Box 2.

——. *Scrapbook 1877-1902*. Unpublished, Albert and Shirley Small Special Collections Library, University of Virginia, Accession #1171-a, Box 2.

Rosser, Thomas L. *Riding with Rosser*. Edited by S. Roger Keller. Shippensburg, PA: Burd Street Press, 1997.

———. *Addresses of General T.L. Rosser at the Seventh Annual Reunion of the Association of the Maryland Line, Academy of Music, Baltimore, MD. February 22, 1889 and on Memorial Day, Staunton, VA., June 8, 1889*. NY: The L. A. Williams Printing Co, 1889.

———. *"The Cavalry, A.N.V." Address by Gen'l T.L. Rosser at the Seventh Annual Reunion of the Association of the Maryland Line, Academy of Music, Baltimore, Md. February 22, 1889*. Baltimore: The Sun Book and Job Printing Office, 1889.

Ruffner, Kevin Conley. *Maryland's Blue & Gray: A Border State's Union and Confederate Junior Officer Corps*. Baton Rouge: Louisiana State University Press, 1997.

Sanford, George B. *Fighting Rebels and Redskins; Experiences in Army Life of Colonel George B. Sanford, 1861-1892*. Edited by E. R. Hagemann. Norman: University of Oklahoma Press, 1969.

Schaff, Morris. *The Spirit of Old West Point 1858-1862*. Boston: Houghton Mifflin Co., 1908.

Schmitt, Martin F. "An Interview with General Jubal A. Early in 1889." *The Journal of Southern History*, 11, no. 4 (November 1945): 547-563.

Sedinger, James D. "War-Time Reminiscences of James D. Sedinger: Company E, 8th Virginia Cavalry (Border Rangers)." *West Virginia History*, 51 (1992): 55-78.

Secretan, James Henry Edward. *Canada's Great Highway: From the First Stake to the Last Spike*. Ottawa, ON: Thorburn & Abbott, 1924.

Sheehan-Dean, A. "Desertion (Confederate) During the Civil War." In *Encyclopedia Virginia*. Accessed September 25, 2012. http://perma.cc/M78S-5LW8.

Sheridan, Philip H. *Personal Memoirs of P. H. Sheridan*, 2 vols. New York: Charles L. Webster & Co., 1888.

Shoemaker, John J. and Edmund H. Moorman. *Shoemaker's Battery: Stuart Horse Artillery, Pelham's Battalion, Afterwards Commanded by Col. R. P. Chew, Army of Northern Virginia*. Reprint, Gaithersburg, MD: Butternut Press, 1983.

Slade, A. D. *A. T. A. Torbert: Southern Gentleman in Union Blue*. Dayton, OH: Morningside, 1992.

Smith, Christine, M. "Biographies of Homan Correspondents." *Rockingham County, Virginia VAGenWeb Project*. Accessed October 24, 2014. http://perma.cc/9PDZ-DJ38.

Sprague, Homer B. *Lights and Shadows in Confederate Prisons, A Personal Experience, 1864-5*. New York: G. P. Putnam's Sons, 1915.

Starr, Stephen Z. *The Union Cavalry in the Civil War*. vol. 2. Baton Rouge: The Louisiana State University Press, 1981.

Stoneburner, Paul D. *Children of the Shenandoah*. Accessed October 28, 2015. http://gean.wwco.com/query/.

Storie, Ken. *General Rosser's Legacy. Manitoba History*, Manitoba Historical Society, No. 56 (October 2007). Accessed December 16, 2014. http://www.mhs.mb.ca/docs/mb_history/56/rosserlegacy.shtml.

Stuart, James E. B. *The Letters of Major General James E. B. Stuart*. Edited by Adele H. Mitchell. Stuart-Mosby Historical Society, 1990.

Swift, Eben. "General Wesley Merritt." *Journal of the United States Cavalry Association*, 21 (March 1911):829-37.

Taylor, James E. *With Sheridan up the Shenandoah Valley in 1864: Leaves from a Special Artist's Sketch Book and Diary*. Dayton, OH: Morningside House, Inc. 1989.

Tenney, Luman Harris. *War Diary of Luman Harris Tenney, 1861-1865*. Cleveland, OH: Evangelical Publishing House, 1914.

"The Confederate Dead in Stonewall Cemetery, Winchester, VA. Memorial Services, June 6, 1894." *Southern Historical Society Papers,* 22 (1894): 41-48.

Thomas, Emory M. *Bold Dragoon: The Life of J.E.B. Stuart*. New York: Harper and Row, 1986.

Thomas, William G. III. "'Under Indictment': Thomas Lafayette Rosser and the New South." *The Virginia Magazine of History and Biography*, 100, no. 2 (April 1992): 207-232.

Towle, George W. "Some Personal Recollections of George W. Towle." *The Second Mass and Its Fighting Californians*. Accessed March 12, 2015. http://perma.cc/DFU3-PR9T.

Townsend, George Alfred. *Major General Alfred Thomas Archimedes Torbert: Delaware's most Famous Civil War Hero*. Bowie, MD: Heritage Books, 1993.

Trout, Robert J. *Galloping Thunder: The Stuart Horse Artillery*. Mechanicsburg, PA: Stackpole Books, 2002.

——. *Memoirs of the Stuart Horse Artillery Battalion*. Knoxville: University of Tennessee Press, 2008.

Tucker, Spencer C. *Brigadier General John D. Imboden, Confederate Commander in the Shenandoah*. Lexington, University Press of Kentucky, 2003.

Urwin, Gregory J. W. *Custer Victorious*. Rutherford, NJ: Fairleigh Dickinson University Press; London: Associated University Presses, 1983.

United States Congress. *Report of the Joint Committee on the Conduct of the War at the Second Session, Thirty-eighth Congress*. Washington, DC: Government Printing Office, 1865.

U.S. War Department. *Cavalry Tactics, First Part, School of the Trooper, of the Platoon, and of the Squadron, Dismounted*. Philadelphia: J. B. Lippincott & Co., 1862.

——. *Cavalry Tactics in Three Parts*. Washington, DC: Government Printing Office, 1864.

——. *The War of the Rebellion: A Compilation of the Official Records of the Union and Confederate Armies*, 128 vols. Washington, D.C.: Government Printing Office, 1880-1901.

——. *Atlas to Accompany the Official Records of the Union and Confederate Armies*. Washington, DC: Government Printing Office, 1891-95.

Vann, Marvin J. *Shenandoah County, Virginia: A Study of the 1860 Census*, 9 vols. Berwyn Heights, MD: Heritage Books, Inc., 1993-2010.

Virginia Department of Transportation. VDOT CTB Meeting Archives. "Minutes of the Meeting of the State Highway Commission of Virginia, Held in Richmond, March 14, 1934." Accessed August 25, 2014. http://www.ctb.virginia.gov/meetings/minutes_pdf/CTB-03-1934-01.pdf

Vogtsberger, Margaret Ann. *The Dulanys of Welbourne: A Family in Mosby's Confederacy*. Charlottesville, VA: Howell Press, 1997.

Walters, Everett. *Joseph Benson Foraker: An Uncompromising Republican*. Columbus: The Ohio State Archaeological and Historical Society, 1948.

Watson, George W. *The Last Survivor; The Memoirs of George William Watson*. Edited by Brian S. Kesterson. Parsons, WV: McClain Printing House, 1993.

Waugh, John "The New England Cavalier: Charles Russell Lowell and the Shenandoah Valley Campaign of 1864." In *The Shenandoah Valley Campaign of 1864*, 299-340. Edited by Gary W. Gallagher. Chapel Hill: University of North Carolina Press, 2006.

Wayland, John W. *A History of Rockingham County, Virginia*. Dayton, VA: Ruebush-Elkins Co., 1912.

——. *Scenic and Historical Guide to the Shenandoah Valley*. Dayton, VA: Joseph K. Ruebush Co., 1923.

——. *Stonewall Jackson's Way; Route, Method, Achievement*. Staunton, VA.: The McClure Company, Inc. 1940.

——. *The Valley Turnpike, Winchester to Staunton and Other Roads*. Typescript. Winchester-Frederick County Historical Society, vol. VI, 1948.

——. *A History of Shenandoah County, Virginia*. Baltimore: Regional Publishing Co., 1980.

Wells, William. *A Vermont Cavalryman in War and Love: The Civil War Letters of Brevet Major General William Wells and Anna Richardson*. Lynchburg, VA: Schroeder Publications, 2007.

Welsh, Jack D. *Medical Histories of Confederate Generals*. Kent, OH: Kent State University Press, 1995.

Wert, Jeffry D. *Cavalryman of the Lost Cause: A Biography of J. E. B. Stuart*. New York: Simon & Schuster, 2008.

——. *Custer: The Controversial Life of George Armstrong Custer*. New York: Simon & Schuster, 1996.

——. *From Winchester to Cedar Creek: The Shenandoah Campaign of 1864*. Carlisle, PA: South Mountain Press, 1987.

Whittaker, Frederick. *A Complete Life of Gen. George A. Custer*. New York: Sheldon, 1876.

Wilson, James Harrison. *Under the Old Flag*. New York: D. Appleton and Co., 1912.

Wise, Jennings C. *The Long Arm of Lee or the History of the Artillery of the Army of Northern Virginia*. 2 vols. Lynchburg, VA: J. P. Bell Company, Inc., 1915.

Wittenberg, Eric J. *Glory Enough for All: Sheridan's Second Raid and the Battle of Trevilian Station*. Washington, DC: Brassey's, 2001.

Woodward, Harold R., Jr. *Defender of the Valley: Brigadier General John Daniel Imboden, CSA*. Berryville, VA: Rockbridge Publishing Co., 1996.

Rosters, Registers and Associated Works

Armstrong, Richard L. *7th Virginia Cavalry*. Lynchburg, VA: H. E. Howard, 1992.

——. *11th Virginia Cavalry*. Lynchburg, VA: H. E. Howard, 1989.

——. *19th and 20th Virginia Cavalry*. Lynchburg, VA: H. E. Howard, 1994.

——. *26th Virginia Cavalry*. Lynchburg, VA: H. E. Howard, 1994.

Bates, Samuel P. *History of Pennsylvania Volunteers, 1861-5*. 5 vols. Harrisburg, PA: B. Singerly, state printer, 1869-71.

Benedict, G. G. *Vermont in the Civil War: A History of the Part Taken by the Vermont Soldiers and Sailors in the War for the Union, 1861-5*, 2 vols. Burlington, VT: Free Press Association, 1886-1888.

Bohannon, Keith S. *The Giles, Alleghany and Jackson Artillery*. Lynchburg, VA: H. E. Howard, 1990.

Beaudry, Louis N. *Historic Records of the Fifth New York Cavalry, First Ira Harris Guard*. Albany, NY: S. R. Gray, 1865.

Bowen, James R. *Regimental History of the First New York Dragoons, with Lists of Names, Post-Office Addresses, Casualties of Officers and Men, and Number of Prisoners, Trophies &c. Captured, From Organization to Muster Out*. Washington, DC: Gibson Brothers, 1865.

——. *Regimental History of the First New York Dragoons During Three Years of Active Service in the Great Civil War*. Published by the author, 1900.

Cole, Scott C. *34th Battalion Virginia Cavalry*. Lynchburg, VA: H. E. Howard, 1993.

Dickinson, Jack L. *8th Virginia Cavalry*. Lynchburg, VA: H. E. Howard, 1986.

Divine, John E. *35th Battalion Virginia Cavalry*. Lynchburg, VA: H. E. Howard, 1985.

Driver, Robert J. *1st Virginia Cavalry*. Lynchburg, VA: H. E. Howard, 1991.

——. *2nd Virginia Cavalry*. Lynchburg, VA: H. E. Howard, 1995.

——. *5th Virginia Cavalry*. Lynchburg, VA: H. E. Howard, 1997.

——. *First & Second Maryland Cavalry, CSA*. Charlottesville, VA: Howell Press, Inc., 1999.

Fortier, John. *15th Virginia Cavalry*. Lynchburg, VA: H. E. Howard, 1993.

Frye, Dennis E. *12th Virginia Cavalry*. Lynchburg, VA: H. E. Howard, 1988.

Goldsborough. W. W. *The Maryland Line in the Confederate Army, 1861-1865*. Baltimore, MD: Press of Guggenheim, Weil & Co., 1900.

Heitman, Francis B. *Historical Register and Dictionary of the United States Army: From its Organization, September 29, 1789, to March 2, 1903*, 2 vols. Washington, DC: Government Printing Office, 1903.

Holland, Darryl. *24th Virginia Cavalry*. Lynchburg: H. E. Howard, 1997.

Ledoux, Tom. *Vermont Civil War Database*. Accessed September 25, 2015. VermontCivil War.org.

Lewis, Louise Quarles. *Index to The Maryland Line in the Confederate Army, 1861-1865*. Annapolis, MD: Hall of Records Commission, 1944.

McMurry, Richard M. *Virginia Military Institute Alumni in the Civil War*. Lynchburg, VA: H. E. Howard, 1999.

Moore, Robert H., II. *1st and 2nd Stuart Horse Artillery*. Lynchburg, VA: H. E. Howard, 1985.

——. Chew's Ashby, *Shoemaker's Lynchburg, and the Newtown Artillery*. Lynchburg, VA.: H. E. Howard, 1995.

Musick, Michael P. *6th Virginia Cavalry*. Lynchburg, VA: H. E. Howard, 1997.

Nanzig, Thomas P. *3rd Virginia Cavalry*. Lynchburg, VA: H. E. Howard, 1989.

New York Adjutant General's Office. *Annual Report . . . for the Year 1895*. No. 7. Albany, NY: Wynkoop, 1896.

Official Register of the Officers and Cadets of the U.S. Military Academy June 1853. New York: W. L. Burroughs, 1853.

Olson, John E. *21st Virginia Cavalry*. Lynchburg, VA: H. E. Howard, 1989.

Phisterer, Frederick, comp. *New York in the War of the Rebellion, 1861-1865*. 6 vols. Albany, NY: J. B. Lyon Company, state printers, 1912.

Reid, Whitelaw. *Ohio in the War: Her Statesmen, Her Generals and Soldiers*, 2 vols. Cincinnati, OH: Moore, Wilstach & Baldwin, 1868.

Roster Commission. *Official Roster of the Soldiers of the State of Ohio in the War of the Rebellion, 1861-1866*. 12 vols. Published by authority of the General Assembly. Akron, OH: Werner co., 1886-95.

Scott, J. L. *36th and 37th Battalions Virginia Cavalry*. Lynchburg, VA: H. E. Howard, 1986.

Stiles, Kenneth L. *4th Virginia Cavalry*. Lynchburg, VA: H. E. Howard, 1985.

Trout, Robert J. *"The Hoss": Officer Biographies and Rosters of the Stuart Horse Artillery Battalion*. United States: JebFlo, 2003.

United States Military Academy. *Official Register of the Officers and Cadets of the United States Military Academy, West Point, New York*. New York: United States Military Academy Printing Office (editions 1857-1862).

Wallace, Lee A., Jr. *A Guide to Virginia Military Organizations 1861-1865*. Lynchburg, VA: H. E. Howard, Inc. 1986.

Weaver, Jeffrey C. *22nd Virginia Cavalry*. Lynchburg, VA: H. E. Howard, 1991.

Sources Printed in Newspapers

"A Shenandoah County Fair." Shenandoah *Herald* (VA), October 21, 1887.

A Bugler. "The 5th Michigan Cavalry." Detroit *Advertiser and Tribune*, October 8, 1864, p. 3.

A Soldier. "The Cavalry—Letter from 'A Soldier.'" Richmond *Sentinel*, November 10, 1864.

"Another Rebel Yell." *National Tribune*, February 28, 1889.

Alexander, Peter W. "Our Army Correspondence: Letter From Gen. Lee's Army." Mobile *Advertiser & Register* (AL), October 4, 1864.

Anderson, Finley. "Shenandoah. Details of the Battle and Victory of Sunday Last." New York *Herald*, October 12, 1864.

——. "Shenandoah. The Successful Operations of the Union Cavalry." New York *Herald*, October 14, 1864.

"As Seen Abroad." St. Paul *Globe* (MN). February 24, 1889.

Ball, M. D. "Annals of the War: Rosser and his Critics." Philadelphia *Weekly Times*, July 12, 1884.

Bean, Theodore W. "Sheridan in the Shenandoah." *Grand Army Scout and Soldiers' Mail* (Philadelphia, PA), March 10, 1883.

——. "Sheridan in the Shenandoah." *Grand Army Scout and Soldiers' Mail* (Philadelphia, PA), March 17, 1883.

——. "Sheridan in the Shenandoah." *Grand Army Scout and Soldiers' Mail* (Philadelphia, PA), March 24, 1883.

——. "Sheridan in the Shenandoah." *Grand Army Scout and Soldiers' Mail* (Philadelphia, PA), March 31, 1883.

——. "Sheridan in the Shenandoah." *Grand Army Scout and Soldiers' Mail* (Philadelphia, PA), April 7, 1883.

Benjamin, W. H. Letter to "Friend C." October 18, 1864. Rochester *Daily Union and Advertiser* (NY). October 28, 1864.

Burkholder, Newton. "The Barn Burners." Richmond *Dispatch* (VA), July 22, 1900.

"Col. William P. Thompson." New York *Times*, February 4, 1896. *New York Times* Obituary Record. Accessed August 28, 2014. http://perma.cc/C7PJ-3F87.

Crosby, H. O. "On the Move: Cavalry Doings in Virginia During the Last Days of the Rebellion." *National Tribune* (Washington, DC), July 5, 1894.

"Custer and Rosser." *Daily State Journal* (Alexandria, VA), October 31, 1873, p. 3, col. 1.

Danby, John. "Scouting for Sheridan." Philadelphia *Weekly Times*, October 11, 1884.

"Daniel on Early." Unidentified newspaper clipping, Jedediah Hotchkiss Papers, Reel 58, frame 443.

"Death of Gen. T. L. Rosser." *National Tribune* (Washington, DC), April 14, 1910. p. 4.

"Differs With Rosser." *Daily Progress* (Charlottesville, VA), March 4, 1901.

"Dr. Huffman Not There." *The Times* (Richmond, VA), October 7, 1902.

Early, Jubal A. "Relating to the Annals." Philadelphia *Weekly Times*, May 17, 1884.

"Early Jumps on Rosser." Shenandoah *Herald* (VA), July 1, 1887.

"Early on Rosser" *The State* (VA), June 22, 1887.

"Early Replies to Rosser." Alexandria *Gazette* (VA), June 23, 1887.

"Early's Compliments to Rosser." Omaha *Daily Bee* (NB), June 24, 1887.

Field, James G. "Defense of General Hill." *Daily Progress* (Charlottesville, VA), March 7, 1901.

"From Washington." Alexandria *Gazette*, evening edition (VA), June 24, 1887.

"Gen. T. L. Rosser." Little Falls *Transcript* (MN), June 17, 1887.

"Gen. Rosser and Gen. Early." Staunton *Spectator* (VA), June 29, 1887.

"Gen. Rosser Again." *Virginian*, circa July 2, 1887. See Jedediah Hotchkiss Papers, Reel 58, frame 439.

"Gen. Rosser Denounces Gen. Sheridan." New Ulm *Review* (MN), May 11, 1887.

"Gen. Rosser Explains." Alexandria *Gazette* (VA), June 15, 1887.

"General Rosser's Deadly Peril." unidentified newspaper cites the *Washington Post* as the source, page 92 in Elizabeth Winston Rosser's Scrapbook 1877-1902. Special Collections Library, University of Virginia, Accession #1171-a, Box 2.

"General Rosser's Flop." *The Times* (Richmond, VA), October 26, 1893.

"General Rosser's Position." Roanoke *Times* (VA), October 5, 1883.

"Going After Hazen." *New-Northwest* (Deer Lodge, MT), March 14, 1878.

"Grant's Orders to Sheridan." Staunton *Spectator* (VA), May 8, 1887.

Gray Jacket. "The Cavalry Fights in the Valley–The Fight of Sunday Last." Richmond *Sentinel* (VA), October 15, 1864.

——. "Yankee Atrocities in the Valley—The Effect on the People." Richmond *Sentinel* (VA), October 19, 1864.

——. "The Cavalry." Richmond *Sentinel* (VA), November 1, 1864.

Greeley, S. S. N. "From the Sixth Cavalry" Grand Rapids *Daily Eagle* (MI), December 1, 1864, p. 3.

"His Name is Dennis–How a Rebel General is 'Scorched' by Patriots." Salt Lake *Daily Herald* (UT), May 7, 1887.

Hott, J. E. "Through the Valley: Events Recalled by a Trip Through Shenandoah." *National Tribune* (Washington, DC), September 15, 1898. 10-11.

Long, Francis. "Sheridan." New York *Herald*, October 9, 1864.

"Major General Custer,' Detroit *Advertiser and Tribune*, November 12, 1864, p. 4.

Munford, Thomas T. "Annals of the War: Munford on Rosser." Philadelphia *Weekly Times*, May 17, 1884.

"Musn't Breathe The Air." Salt Lake *Democrat* (UT), May 27, 1887.

Now and Then. "Career of a Regiment." Detroit *Advertiser and Tribune* (MI), November 12, 1864, p.4.

"Old 'Jube's' Reply." Unidentified newspaper, Jedediah Hotchkiss Papers, Reel 58, frame 438.

"Pistols and Coffee for Two." St. Paul *Daily Globe* (MN), June 24, 1887.

"Politicians in a Fight." *The Times* (Washington, DC), November 29, 1900.

Prussian. "The Cavalry.' Richmond *Sentinel* (VA), November 1, 1864.

"The Vermont Cavalry. Battle of Cedar Creek." Rutland *Herald* (VT), November 1, 1864.

"Rampant Rebel." Belmont *Chronicle* (St. Clairsville, OH), June 13, 1889.

Rosser, Thomas L. "Annals of the War: Rosser and His Men." Philadelphia *Weekly Times*, March 22, 1884.

——. "Annals of the War: Rosser and His Men." Philadelphia *Weekly Times*, April 5, 1884.

——. "Annals of the War: Rosser and His Men." Philadelphia *Weekly Times*, April 19, 1884.

——. Letter to *The State* (Richmond), Unidentified clipping [January 1885] in Elizabeth Rosser Scrapbook 1877-1902, p. 40.

——. "A Brave Soldier." Anderson *Intelligencer* (SC), October 19, 1898.

——. "Criticizes General Lee." *Daily Progress* (Charlottesville, VA), February 28, 1901.

——. "Battle of Gettysburg." *Daily Progress* (Charlottesville, VA), March 1, 1901.

——. "Lee's Mistakes Tactical." *Daily Progress* (Charlottesville, VA), March 5, 1901.

——. "Criticism of Gen. Robert E. Lee." *The Times* (Richmond, VA), March 10, 1901.

"Rosser and Massey." Staunton *Spectator and Vindicator* (VA), September 7, 1900.

"Rosser, Early, Sheridan." Shenandoah *Herald* (VA), July 1, 1887.

"Rosser Grows Wrathy." St. Paul *Globe* (MN), February 23, 1889.

"Rosser on Sheridan." Arizona *Weekly Journal-Miner* (Prescott), June 22, 1887.

"Rosser Puts Humbert Out." *Times Dispatch* (Richmond, VA), August 12, 1908.

"Rosser's Attack on Sheridan." *National Republican* (Washington, DC), June 15, 1887.

"Rosser's Rant." *Holt County Sentinel* (OR), June 15, 1894.

"Senile Gen. Rosser." Staunton *Spectator and Vindicator* (VA), July 3, 1903.

Seymour, Charles J. "Sheridan Defended from Charge of Cruelty." Burlington *Weekly Press* (VT), May 27, 1887.

"Sheridan on Rosser." New Ulm *Review* (MN), May 11, 1887.

"Sheridan's Army." *Evening Telegraph* (Philadelphia, PA), October 17, 1864, third edition, p. 1, col. 4.

"Sheridan's Scouts." *Western Appeal* (St. Paul, MN), July 23, 1887.

"St. Paul to Puget." St. Paul *Globe* (MN), August 19, 1892.

"The Hooker Statue." *National Tribune* (Washington, DC), July 2, 1903.

"The Inevitable Rosser." *National Tribune* (Washington, DC), June 7, 1894.

"The Late Operations in the Valley." Richmond *Dispatch* (VA), October 15, 1864, p. 1, col. 4

"The Reason Why." clipping from Richmond *Dispatch* (VA), [unknown month] 1892. Elizabeth Winston Rosser, comp. Scrapbook 1877-1902. Small Special Collections Library, University of Virginia, Accession #1171-a, Box 2.

"The Veterans at Staunton." *The Times* (Richmond, VA), October 12, 1900.

"Thomas L. Rosser." *National Tribune* (Washington, DC), June 30, 1898. p. 5

Untitled. *National Tribune* (Washington, DC), July 21, 1898, p.4.

Untitled. *Pioneer Press* (MN), July 23, 1884, p. 31 in Elizabeth W. Rosser's Scrapbook 1877-1902.

"Virginia Veterans." Richmond *Dispatch* (VA). October 12, 1900.

Watkins, S. V. "Rosser vs. Rosser." *Times Dispatch* (Richmond, VA), July 5, 1903.

"Whipped Him Again." New Ulm *Review* (MN), July 13, 1887.

White, P. J. "'The Bloody Fifth' Cavalry." *Times Dispatch* (Richmond, VA), November 8, 1908.

"William P. Thompson: Financier, connected with Standard Oil." Wheeling *Intelligencer*, February 4, 1896. Ohio County Public Library. Accessed August 28, 2014. http://perma.cc/3663-HJUS.

Index

Gilbert, Benjamin F., 215
Gordon, John B., 180-181
Grandstaff Mill, 88
Grant, Ulysses S., xv, 1; strategy in Virginia, 1-3,
 8-9, 10, 13, 15, 56, 58, 180; *image*, 2
Gray Jacket, 143, 151, 174
Grimsley, Daniel A., 217
Guerillas, 58, 61-62, 63, 66, 74
Haden, Jerry, 101, 106
Hagerstown, Maryland, 93
Hampton, Wade, 48, 52, 166
Hanford, Edward, 166
Hannaford, Roger, 65, 69, 71-72, 74
Harding, Cyrus W., Jr., 217
Harpers Ferry, West Virginia, 3, 10, 16
Harris, Moses, 151
Harrisonburg, Virginia, 57, 59, 63, 66, 68-69
Hastings, Smith H., 103, 214
Hatcher, Daniel, 84, 217
Hawkinstown, Virginia, 156, 160
Heaton, Edward, 108, 125
Helsey, Joseph, 153
Higgins, Onnie, 137
Historical markers, 240
Hoge, Moses, 89, 91, 145, 149, 156
Hood, John B., 182
Horses, condition of, 29, 156, 159,
Hotchkiss, Jedediah 8, 32, 237-239, 241; sketch-
 book of, 239
Hubris, xiii, 26, 54-55, 112
Hudgins, Garland, 142, 235
Hull, Walter C., 215
Hunter, Alexander, 32
Hunter, David, 73-74
Imboden, John and his brigade, 57, 216
Jackson, Thomas, J. "Stonewall," 4, 6, 23, 57-58
Jackson, William L., 57, 216
Johnson, Bradley T. and his brigade, xviii, 13,
 30-31, 54, 57, 58, 142, 145, 147-149, 216;
 image, 142
Johnston, Joseph E., 182
Johnston, Philip P., 110, 119, 217
Jordan's Run, 144-145, 148, 154, 240
Joy of the fight, xii-xiii, 50-51, 93, 211-212
Kearny, Philip, 21
Keezletown Road, 69
Kessler, Joseph R., 216
Kidd, James H. and his brigade, xvii, 19, 65-66,
 90-91, 102-103, 129-131, 135-136, 146, 214
Kleese, Richard, 235
Krom, Abram H., 215
Kyle, Chris, xii
Laurel Brigade, 46, 53-55, 77, 84, 86, 91, 101-102,
 104, 107, 110, 115-118, 127, 135-138, 177,

194, 198, 201, 202, 217; armament of, 126;
 and The Burning, 69-71
Lee, Fitzhugh and his division, 28, 29, 52, 57, 81,
 110, 175, 181, 217
Lee, Robert E., xvii, 1-4, 6-8, 10, 13, 15, 16, 28,
 30-32, 43-46, 48, 51-53, 56-58, 62, 74, 77,
 108, strategy in Virginia, 1, 8-9, 10, 13, 15, 56,
 81, 143, 168, 170, 173, 179, 180, 191, 194,
 197, 199; *image*, 4
Lent, August, 125
Letcher, John, 74
Lexington, Virginia, 3
Lincoln, Abraham, 1, 4, 6, 26, 60, 70, 74, 157
Linville Creek, Virginia, 75
Livestock, 71, 73, 82, 86-87, 90, 166
Lomax, Lunsford L. and his division, xviii, 29-33,
 56-58, 69, 80, 107, 110, 112, 116, 129,
 141-142, 144-147, 149-151, 154-161, 165-
 166, 168-171, 182, 187, 190, 193-194, 207,
 216, 240; escape, 160; image, 32
Lowell, Charles R., Jr. and his brigade, xvii, 101-
 103, 106, 130, 146-151, 154, 159, 168, 214;
 and equine casualties, 148; *image*, 146
Luray Valley, Virginia, 57, 64, 69, 80, 98, 187
Luray, Virginia, 17
Lynchburg Artillery. *See Shoemaker, John J. and
 his battery*
Lynchburg, Virginia, 3, 6, 43
Maps, war-era, 237-239, 241, 243
Luttrell, Marcus, xiii
Marshall, Thomas, 77, 93
Martin, Joseph W. and his battery (*New York Light
 Artillery, 6th Battery*), 130, 135, 214
Martinsburg, West Virginia, 215
Massanutten Mountains, 156
Massie, Thomas B., 217
Maurertown, Virginia, 103, 142, 145, 154, 239
McCleary, John W., 47
McCausland, John and his brigade, 57, 216
McClellan, George B., 3, 16, 21, 23, 182
McDonald, Edward, 110, 139, 185, 217
McDonald, William N., 107, 116
McIntire, Samuel B., 107, 125
McKinley, William, 207
McNulty, John R. and his battery, xx, 57-58, 145,
 151, 154, 159-161, 165, 170, 216
McVicar, Charles, 51, 119
Medal of Honor, 166
Meeks, David, 125
Meem's Bottom, Virginia, 159, 161, 170
Meigs, John R., 60, 62, 74
Meigs, Montgomery C., 60, 62
Mennonites, 89

About the Author

William J. Miller is a writer, teacher, and preservationist. A former editor of *Civil War Magazine*, his books include the 1993 *Mapping for Stonewall: The Civil War Service of Jed Hotchkiss* (recipient of the Fletcher Pratt Award for best work of Civil War nonfiction of the year), and the top-selling *Great Maps of the Civil War: Pivotal Battles and Campaigns* (2004). *Decision at Tom's Brook* is his ninth book of Civil War history. He lives in the Shenandoah Valley.

Read more about continuing research into the people and events in the story of Tom's Brook at decisionattomsbrook.com.